Daughters and Mothers

DAUGHTERS
AND MOTHERS

Margaret Thomson Davis

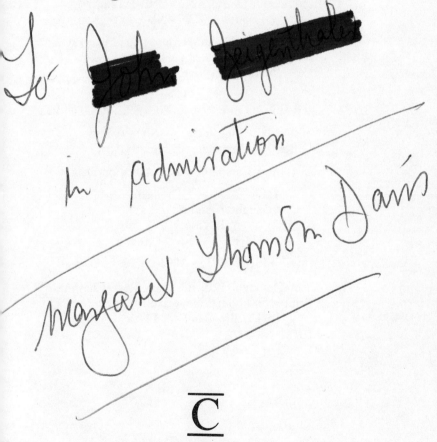

To ~~John Seigenthaler~~

in admiration

Margaret Thomson Davis

C
CENTURY
LONDON MELBOURNE AUCKLAND JOHANNESBURG

First published in Great Britain in 1988 by
Century Hutchinson Ltd
Brookmount House, 62–65 Chandos Place
London WC2N 4NW

Century Hutchinson Publishing Group (Australia) Pty Ltd
16–22 Church Street, Hawthorn
Melbourne, Victoria 3122

Century Hutchinson Group (NZ) Ltd
32–34 View Road, PO Box 40–086, Glenfield, Auckland 10

Century Hutchinson Group (SA) Pty Ltd
PO Box 337, Bergvlei, 2012 South Africa

British Library Cataloguing in Publication Data

Davis, Margaret Thomson
Daughters and mothers.
I. Title
823′.914[F]   PR6054.A8926

ISBN 0–7126–1804–X

Photoset by Deltatype Ltd, Ellesmere Port, Cheshire
Printed and bound in Great Britain by
Anchor Brendan Ltd, Essex

*To my dear friends Flora and Peter Maxwell Stuart
of Traquair House, Peebleshire
and to Russia with love.*

Acknowledgements

I would like to thank all the kind friends who helped with the research for this book and especially the following who gave so generously of their time:

Valerie Freebairn (ex-secretary to MP for East Kilbride)
Andy Freebairn (MP's agent)
Mrs Jean Richmond (ex-wardress of Duke Street Prison)
George McAlister and Alan Henderson (of the Soviet-Scottish Friendly Society)
Tom Fraser (MP for Hamilton 1943–67, Under-Secretary of State in the Scottish Office 1945–51, and Minister of Transport 1964–5)
Richard Buchanan (MP for Springburn 1964–79)
Kathleen Dayell (secretary to MP husband, Tam)
Solicitors Joseph Beltrami and Laurence Dowdall
and last, but certainly not least, Jim Jones, who acted as my interpreter in the Soviet Union and in the process caused some hilarious confusion.

Sometimes I'll believe,
That time heals the pain,
Sometimes I believe, I'll forget.
Sometimes I'll believe,
Then I see her again.
Sometimes I'll believe,
But not yet.

(From 'Sometimes?'
by Richard Thomson.)

1

Sometimes sixteen-year-old Amelia was tied to a tree while a faceless man made love to her. That way, pinioned and helpless, she was unable to struggle. At other times she put up a furious fight. The man was always stronger, however, and his strength and virility never failed to win in the end. Sometimes, in the middle of a desperate panting battle, when she could feel the man's hot hairy skin rubbing against hers like electric sandpaper, her mother would order her to go and peel the potatoes for her daddy's dinner. That was if her daddy were at home. When he did come home they hardly ever saw him. Everybody in Glasgow, it seemed, had urgent business with the tall mysterious Member of Parliament for Springburn. At least, she thought he was mysterious and it was not just because his dark eyes made such a startling contrast to his pale skin. Despite being old (he was forty-seven) he still had the gangling body of a much younger man. His shock of black hair was speckled with grey and there were delicate creases at the edges of his eyes, but these signs of ageing only served to clothe him with a distinguished air. There was also a dark brooding look about him that people found disturbing. Amelia's emotions were tightly tied up in a *bouquet garni* of love, fear and distress. Every week-end she prayed that he would come home, yet dreaded his arrival. For one thing, loving Matthew Drummond was like drifting near a mine. At any moment of meeting there could be an explosion. For another, his presence was a reminder that he had betrayed her.

Now, today, he was due home to stay for three weeks to fight the 1945 General Election. The last time she'd seen him had been just over a month ago; on 8 May to be exact. She remembered the date because it was VE day. It had been a confused but joyous occasion. Her mother had

1

joined Matthew in a celebration dram. This in itself was an event. Nothing short of the cessation of world-wide hostilities would have persuaded Victoria to indulge in what she so often referred to as 'the demon drink'.

Normally Victoria and Matthew fought like tigers. Her mother's illogicality obviously drove her father to distraction. They could be arguing about anything, from where she had put his collar studs to the concept of papal infallibility, when she would suddenly say things like, 'Aye, but the publican's wife will have a fur coat all right!'

'What the hell's that got to do with anything?' he would roar at her in exasperation. No matter what he said, however, it always ended in another bitter catalogue of his faults and failings.

'What gives you the right to waste so much money on the demon drink?' was one of Victoria's most often and most bitterly repeated questions.

On VE day, however, Victoria had accepted his celebratory dram without one reference to its demonic dangers. Instead she said, 'Thank God it's all over, and I'm not being blasphemous.' Sadly she shook her head, 'All those poor mother's sons. On both sides.'

'Yes,' Matthew agreed. 'What a waste. Remember the last time?'

'Yes, the war that was supposed to end all wars. How could anyone forget it? All those poor boys with limbs missing, propped in doorways begging, or trying to sell matches or shoe-laces. What their mothers must have suffered, Matthew, and no jobs even for the able-bodied. Surely it won't be the same as that again? Surely people wouldn't stand for it.'

'No, I don't believe they will.' He lifted his glass to hers. 'Here's to the General Election!'

Now the election date of Thursday 5 July was known and everything at home would be thrown into turmoil and confusion. She would have to force herself to move soon. There could be no curling up like this in her father's big chair for long today. Most days she retreated into a dream-world, her head resting on the chair's leather arm,

2

eyes wide but unseeing, or closed to the world. But no retreating into a masochistic make-believe world today, no feverish encounters that left passion exhausted but all other emotions unfulfilled. Her time and energies were needed to trail the streets to deliver Labour Party pamphlets from which her father's brooding face stared out. She wished she felt better. She wanted to help make Matthew's election campaign a success. The idea of him suffering defeat was unendurable. Not that her mother believed there was any danger of that happening.

'Springburn's such a strong Labour place,' Victoria said. 'They'll have to weigh the votes for your daddy rather than count them.'

Still, all elections entailed hard work and she would need to feel well enough to do her share. She had always been thin and pale-faced and 'a bit of a queer one, just like her daddy,' as her mother often accused. 'If only you'd be more like your brother, you'd get on a lot better,' was another of her mother's favourite remarks.

Jamie at twenty-three was seven years older than her and worked on the railway as her daddy had once done. Jamie was different from her all right. Swaggering from his work, with shoulders on him the width of two men and a grin that could flash from his sooty face like white lightning. He was a natural with the Glasgow patter and often left a trail of chuckling women and giggling girls as he passed along Hilltop Road.

Her mother adored him and had never been able to deny him anything. Amelia remembered when they had been children. Jamie was twelve and she was five and Jamie had wanted a meccano set for Christmas. Meccano sets were expensive and, she realized now, her mother had performed a small miracle in scraping enough money together to buy him one. Unfortunately this meant she could not buy one other thing that Christmas, not even an orange for a stocking, and certainly not a present for her daughter.

Amelia could still recall her feelings when her mother had drawn her aside before Christmas and asked, 'Would you like half a meccano set for Christmas, Amelia?'

Knowing how Jamie longed for one and sensing that it would please her mother if she said yes, she said yes. . . .

She loved her big brother and accepted, without any conscious thought, that her mother loved him better than her. She never believed, in fact, that her mother loved her at all. She just accepted this as the normal order of things. She tried to please her mother though, on the off-chance that it might help. And it did please her mother when she said she wanted half a meccano set for Christmas. However, at the back of her mind she still believed that Santa would bring her a doll as well. But Christmas morning came and there on the rug in front of the living room fire sat one solitary box of meccano. Instinctively she knew that it was vitally important for her and her need for her mother's approval to hide her true feelings. This she managed to do.

Later that day, when a neighbour asked what she had got from Santa, she had told her in detailed and dramatic terms how she had received a chocolate handbag, and when she had opened it there was a chocolate purse and when she opened that, inside she found lots and lots of chocolate money.

Now Jamie went more or less his own way and lived his own life, but when he'd been younger she'd taken him everywhere with her. Memories of her mother vanishing with Jamie and leaving Amelia went back as far as her mind could reach. As a very small child these disappearances were totally incomprehensible, but now Amelia guessed they must have been the result of the many battles between her parents. One of her mother's ways of punishing Matthew and getting the better of him in those early days was unexpectedly to dump his daughter on him.

'Let him worry about his family and take some responsibility for a change, instead of spending so much time looking after the interests of strangers,' would be her mother's attitude.

This must have caused terrible problems for her father, who had worked long shifts on the railway and spent most of his free time with union, Labour Party and local council work. She could not remember how he had resolved the problem of being left with her.

4

It was an area of her life that had paralysed and continued to paralyse her thinking processes. She dare not remember what happened before primary school. All she knew was that from the infants class onwards lessons, playtime, teachers were almost a complete blank. What she *could* recall was kissing her mother goodbye in the morning. The door of their top flat shutting behind her. The stiffening in mindless apprehension. The compulsion to knock at the door and kiss her mother again. She knew it spoiled Victoria's previously quite affectionate parting. She sensed the impatience and the intense irritation at having been brought to the door for no reason at all. The reluctant walk down the long flight of stairs, then the suspension in an agony of slowly passing time until she returned after school to discover if her mother was still there. Or had gone.

On the way home she was not aware of any of the other children laughing and chattering and skipping along. A tense figure, with stiff pleated hair, she had no interest in anything but what might await her at 23 Hilltop Road. Up the few steps of the entrance into the close. The main stairs now, never-ending mountainous height. Heart hiccuping. Holding her breath as she peeked through the letter-box. If the pungent odour of pine disinfectant hit her nostrils, if her anxious eyes caught the sight of the newspapers spread over the linoleum of the lobby floor, her mother had gone. Normally Victoria never bothered much with housework. Certainly Amelia had no memory of her mother scrubbing floors. Except when she left and seemed to wash her hands of the whole place. It was typical of her mother to act with grand and impulsive gestures.

She would stand helplessly on the jaggy orange and brown doormat in a state of shock. Time had no meaning. There were no concepts of days, or weeks, or months or years. Her mother had gone. Guided only by instinct and intuition she descended the stairs. Through the close and down the few steps outside it, to sit on the last one.

She would eventually see her father coming along the road in his navy-blue dungarees, greasy jacket and railway cap. She went to meet him with a mixture of love, trepidation and apology for herself. She was the sign that indicated to him that the house would be icy-cold and unwelcoming. (Victoria always left all the windows wide open to dry the floors.) She was the sign that told him there would be no hot meal waiting for him. Worst of all, the sight of her meant he would have to worry about asking a neighbour, or make some sort of arrangement to have her looked after while he was at work. To a man who found it an ordeal to raise his eyes and say good morning or good evening to any of the neighbours this was torment indeed. It never failed to cause an explosion of rage that was terrifying to witness. At least for a small child.

'Are you going to sit there in your pyjamas all day?' Her mother's voice came as a surprise, a jet of cold water drowning her dreams.

'My stomach's sore again.'

Victoria's regal face stiffened, tipped up as if determined to defend herself against embarrassment. 'You heard what the doctor said. Take an Askit powder.'

The doctor had actually said, 'At sixteen she's certainly late, but it'll come!'

'What will come?' Amelia had ventured to ask on the return journey home.

'Just do as you're told,' her mother's steps quickened as if to escape the dilemma of her. 'That doctor cost money we could ill afford.'

The Askit powders helped, but the relief they gave never lasted. The pain kept increasing in strength and frequency. She prayed the powders would see her through the day. Her mother was wrapping a floral 'pinny' around her voluptuous curves. 'I'll rake out the fire while you're getting dressed,' she said. 'I've had my porridge. Yours is in the pot, but give yourself a shake and get your clothes on first. As God's my witness, Amelia, I don't know what to make of you. You're worse than your daddy.'

Amelia walked cautiously through to the kitchenette. Her face twisted as growing discomfort changed to razor-sharp knives ripping downwards. She poured herself a cup of hot tea and gulped at it, oblivious of scalding her mouth

6

and throat. Heat, either in the form of drinks or hot water bottles, usually brought comfort. She opened an Askit and spilled the powder into her mouth. The taste made her shudder and take another swig of tea. Her legs had gone weak and she eased herself down onto the only seat in the narrow strip of kitchenette. It was a wooden sparred chair and the cold of it entered her like an icicle. Resting her elbows on the clothes boiler, she supported her head and pressed her lips determinedly together. The Askits would soon work, she assured herself. She would be all right. She shifted her position, trying to concentrate on other things. The kitchenette of the two-bedroomed council house, as flats were called in Glasgow, (their mother slept on a bed-settee in the living room) was not broad enough for two people to pass shoulder to shoulder. It had two sinks at the window; a shallow one in which to wash dishes, the other deep to accommodate the rinsing of clothes from the gas boiler. Above her head dangled a wooden clothes pulley. On the wall opposite within easy touching distance was the gas cooker and a slatted shelf cluttered with pots. The floor was covered with orange and brown linoleum. It was while Amelia's eyes were feverishly counting the orange and brown squares that she noticed the stain on her pyjamas. The stain paralysed her with horror. Now she knew the reason for all the pain. She must have cancer. She'd heard conversations between her mother and her mother's friend, Mrs McDade, about someone who'd suffered this terrible disease.

'She died in agony, poor soul,' her mother said. Then added, brown eyes dark with drama, 'She bled to death and there wasn't a thing anyone could do to help her.'

Amelia struggled up and somehow managed the return journey through the windowless lobby to the living room where her mother was down on her knees in front of the fire, her wavy hair protected by a scarf. She was attacking the bars of the fire basket with a poker, shaking and clattering it about to dislodge the fine ash into the ashpan and leave the cinders. The cinders would be used to pile on top of screwed-up papers and pieces of stick, and help get a good blaze going. The fire was needed to heat the water.

7

'Mummy!'

'Are you not dressed yet?' Victoria responded irritably. 'You're worse than your daddy. He used to sit for hours in that chair staring into space like a dead man. There was no getting through to him when he was in one of his moods.'

Standing behind her mother, Amelia clutched at the table for support. 'Mummy, there's something seriously wrong with me. There's blood all over my pyjamas.'

Victoria stopped raking and, still on her knees, twisted head and shoulders round. Her handsome face was ugly. It was screwing up, shrinking back as if from a putrid smell. 'Get away from me!' she said.

Amelia managed to find her way back to the lobby. There she stood in the darkness wondering what to do. She was neither surprised at her mother's lack of help, nor unsurprised. Shocks of this magnitude had long since found an escape route into the deep, dark pool of her unconscious. She had never cried since she was a baby. Eventually she managed to wash herself but, because she was still bleeding, she was forced to secure a piece of folded linen rag between her legs by pinning it to either side of her suspender belt. It felt hard and bulky and dangerously insecure. She knew the fear of it falling out and shaming her would plague her all day.

Victoria came through to the kitchenette to empty the ashes into the rubbish pail. 'The ration books and the Store book are on the sideboard,' Victoria said. 'Go to the fruit shop as well and try to get some parsnips. I've got a recipe for making bananas.'

Amelia had not been able to eat any porridge, but was seeking help from another cup of tea. Her mind had fogged up, making her feel stupid.

'If you don't go soon,' Victoria insisted, 'your daddy'll be here, and his secretary and his agent and dear knows who all.'

Amelia collected the buff-coloured ration books and the darker 'Store book' as the Co-operative book was known and put on her coat. It had been made out of a khaki army blanket by Mrs McDade. Army or air force blankets were warm and didn't need coupons, and many girls and women were now wearing them as coats, jackets and even skirts. Their dark blue, grey and khaki colours added to the general drabness of the streets.

'You don't need that on today,' Victoria said.

'I'm cold.' This was only half a lie. She was indeed shivering, but what really concerned her was the fact that a stain might show through her dress.

'On a lovely summer morning like this, feeling cold is just being perverse. You get more like your daddy every day.'

Amelia eased the door shut behind her and set off carefully down the stairs. When it wasn't the week for their neighbour across the landing to do the stairs, sometimes Amelia washed them, sometimes her mother took a turn. Her mother was too impatient however to bother with the pipe clay scrolls and decoration down the sides of each step. Amelia always drew the intricate patterns with great concentration. It was a clean and respectable 'close', as the entrance to Glasgow tenements were called. Everyone took their turn on the stairs and even gave the maroon-painted walls a quick wipe down while they were at it. The walls were only painted up to shoulder height, the top half being whitewashed, and it was this white part that found cause for complaint. It had become more grey and streaky than white, and damp patches darkened the ceiling and walls of the top landing causing plaster to flake off.

Hilltop Road sloped up from Broomknowes Road where the line of shops was situated. Amelia walked gingerly towards them to avoid the steep descent jarring her body. Then she waited for a bus to pass before crossing. The Co-op was round the corner and already there was a queue of drably clothed women like a trail of mud past the post office, the chemist, the fruit shop and nearly reaching the butcher's at the other end. The usual air of anxiety hung over the queue, plus a fatigue that had grown over the war years and now in the first weeks of peace had become almost unbearable. Every last soul was thoroughly sick of shortages and unpalatable food. The war in Europe was over, but smiles had worn thin. Rationing seemed to be

9

getting worse not better and people were having to accept whalemeat and often, without knowing it, horsemeat. All that could be said about whalemeat was that there was a lot of it and it was horribly smelly. It didn't taste of anything, neither meat nor fish, but it smelled the whole house for a week after it was cooked.

'How's yur mammy, hen?' Amelia took her place behind a small round-shouldered woman with a squashed face like a Pekinese under an equally crushed-looking bottle-green hat.

'She's fine, thanks.'

'An awful nice woman, yur mammy.'

Smiling, Amelia lowered her eyes. 'Yes.'

'Yur daddy'll be coming home for the election.'

'Yes.'

'A real gentleman, yur daddy.'

Still with eyes lowered, still smiling, Amelia nodded.

It was then Kate Milligan joined the queue. Kate lived on the top flat in Mrs McDade's close and, as Victoria said, was 'the talk of the place'. Kate's father had been killed at Arnheim, her mother worked in munitions and, in Victoria's view, was 'a disgrace to the name of mother'. Everyone knew she turned a blind eye to Kate's carry-on with Yanks. A never-ending stream of men of all shapes and sizes dressed in American uniforms kept disappearing up the stairs of Mrs McDade's close.

'Hallo, hen,' Kate greeted Amelia, making the woman in the bottle-green hat sniff and turn away. 'Here, you're looking as pale as a sheet. Are you coming down with anything, hen?'

Amelia's eyes widened tragically. She longed for help and advice about the terrible state she was in but her condition seemed too awful to put into words.

'It can't be that bad,' Kate said. 'Unless there's been an outbreak of bubonic plague I haven't heard about.'

Amelia began visibly to tremble as she struggled to gain enough courage to speak. Kate put an arm around her shoulders and gave her a comforting squeeze. 'Och, you poor wee thing, spit it out, hen. Tell me what's wrong.'

Amelia leaned closer to Kate's ear and whispered, 'I think I've got cancer.'

'Eh?' Kate's voice was shatteringly loud. 'What the hell makes you think that?'

Amelia continued to whisper. 'There's blood. It came this morning from between my legs.'

Suddenly Kate gave a screech of laughter. 'Silly wee midden! Every woman gets that. It comes every month. You just get sanny towels from the chemist and Bob's your uncle!'

Amelia's relief was so great she forgot to be embarrassed at the loudness of Kate's voice revealing the content of their conversation to all and sundry. 'You mean there's nothing wrong with me?'

'Not a thing, hen.'

Amelia began to laugh weakly. Kate enthusiastically joined in. 'Silly wee midden,' she repeated.

2

'It was bad enough when dad arrived home for the occasional week-end,' Helena Victoria Donovan complained, in between energetically chewing the spearmint gum given to her by an American seaman. 'But honestly, it will be sheer hell now that he is going to be demobbed.'

Her friend Veronica spat on her cake of mascara, then scrubbed a miniature brush over it. 'It will maybe take ages.'

'No such luck.' Helena walked her fingers up through her long auburn hair as she admired her slim body this way and that in the cloakroom mirror. Everyone said she looked like Rita Hayworth and she was careful to accentuate this image. 'If your civilian boss asks for you back and says a job's waiting for you, then you get out right away.'

'What's your dad like? A right old bastard, is he?' Veronica applied the brush to her eyelashes, her mouth contorting as she did so.

'He's old-fashioned. It's "Where are you going?" ' she mimicked, ' "When will you be home?" "Who are you going with?" "What's that muck on your face?" I mean, honestly, he's dead boring!'

'Why can't parents realize that, at seventeen nearly eighteen, we're grown women?'

'I know,' Helena groaned.

The cloakroom of Greens Playhouse was beginning to fill up with girls and not a few of them were eyeing with envy Helena and Veronica's nylon-stockinged legs. It was always assumed that stockings had come from an American serviceman and had been earned by allowing him to have a grope or, depending on how many pairs, to go the whole hog. There just wasn't any other way that they knew of to acquire nylons. As it happened, the stockings that graced

12

Helena and Veronica's legs had come from Helena's mother who owned one of the biggest shops in Glasgow called 'Rory's'. It was mainly famous for its ladies and gents dress hire departments, but had grown over the years to be stockists of every kind of garment and accessory, for sale as well as for hire. How 'Rory's' managed to get nylons when no other shop could, was a question better not asked and certainly one that did not interest either Helena or Veronica. Much to the girls' chagrin, Rory did not always manage to keep them supplied and they had to resort, like most other females, to painting or dyeing their legs. They had tried suntan lotion, and drawn a seam up the back with eyebrow pencil. Sometimes they were unable to find any suntan lotion. So many girls were using it as a stocking substitute, it was becoming scarce. They had, as a result, experimented with a variety of things including staining their legs yellow with onion skins and even gravy browning. Such expedients were not always successful and at more than one dance their 'stockings' had disintegrated half-way through the evening and rubbed off on their partner's trousers.

'Just ignore him,' Veronica mouthed, at the same time as smoothing her lipstick over her lips with an expert pinkie.

'Don't worry, I intend to.'

The band was belting out 'Don't sit under the apple tree with anyone else but me. . . .' Helena's feet began to tap and her shoulders jerk in time to the bouncy tune and she sang in a nasal voice, still chewing her gum, ' "Anyone else but me . . . anyone else but me. . . ." '

The cloakroom had fast become a riot of sounds, sights and smells. Girls were crushing in wearing utility skirts and home-made blouses, or dresses cleverly fashioned out of velvet curtains or brocade originally intended for covering chairs. Betty Grable girls were jostling for spaces at the mirror, bouncing up and down on heavy shoes. Brassy tarts were defiantly there, making good out of bad times with American combat jackets and pilfered army medical blue trousers. Cigarette smoke hazed the air along with puffs of face powder, their smells becoming more pungent when mixed with carnation and Goya perfume.

Helena gave her hair a shake to make it hang in careless curls à la Hayworth, and Veronica tugged her straight locks down over one eye and pouted at herself.

'You look real sultry and smashing,' Helena assured her. 'The dead spit of Lizbeth Scott. Come on!'

It was early enough in the evening to be able to see some wide patches of floor between couples. These patches would soon disappear. The crowd would become a choppy sea of movement filling to overflowing every inch of space. At the side of the hall, fat American servicemen with steel-rimmed glasses and melon-sized jowls mooched and sprawled and scratched their private parts, while Polish servicemen stood stiffly to attention as if ready to salute anybody that happened to pass. British servicemen and British civilian men gathered in self-defensive groups, trying to look nonchalant and unresentful. All the girls went for the Americans or the Poles because of their strange and romantic-sounding accents. The Poles looked very different too in their leather jackets and coats, but they could be a bit of a nuisance. Some of them were insanely jealous. All of them, despite their fine manners and clicking of heels, were as persistent as dogs after bitches in heat. The Americans were more of an attractive proposition with the nylons, chocolate bars and other priceless luxuries that they could provide. Although taxi-drivers, waiters and other menials, dependent on tips, were in the habit of complaining bitterly, 'They're maybe big spenders with girls, but with us they're mean bastards!'

Helena nudged Veronica. 'He's not bad, over there. The tall one leaning against the pillar chewing gum. I like the shape of him.'

'What part?'

Both girls erupted into high-pitched giggles that had to be suppressed with hands over mouths. Helena felt so stimulated and excited, she could hardly contain her energy. She was about to suggest, in her impatience to be on the move, that she and Veronica should take the floor together when the sailor, who had a muscular build and a

14

close-cropped mushroom-coloured head, left his pillar and came strolling towards her.

'You were quick giving him the come on.' Veronica started to giggle again.

The sailor, still chewing his gum, gave a jerk of his head in the direction of the dance floor and Helena followed him on to it. She was wearing a flared skirt that looked, as Veronica said, 'as if clothing coupons had never been invented.' Her blouse was daringly see-through, although she had decided to wear a bra underneath. Not because she lacked the courage or the inclination not to. She had no wish, however, to be classed as a tart or a prostitute. Quite a few of them could be seen on the floor, tits bobbing and hypnotizing their partners. It was all right, though, when Helena's partner twirled her round and her skirt umbrella-ed up to show her peach satin knickers. They were another special acquisition from her mother and well worth showing off. Helena knew that she was most fortunate in having such a parent. She had always been the envy of all her friends in this respect.

'What's your name, honey?' the sailor asked.

'Helena Victoria Donovan. But everybody just calls me Helena.'

'Helena.' The sailor chewed it around with his gum before adding, 'Yeah, I like that.'

'What's yours?'

'Eddie Warner.'

Introductions over, Eddie pulled Helena towards him and they continued the dance cheek to cheek. Helena felt as if she was glued against an electric fire. She could feel every contour of the man's body through the thin material of his navy suit. British seamen's uniforms were made of much thicker, coarser material. Eddie, by the feel of him, was especially well-endowed with the requisites of manhood. Helena sighed with pleasure and clung round his neck as they shuffled provocatively about. Helena thought nature was great. She thought men were great. Not all men, of course. But the right one, with the right shape and the right chemistry, could be sheer bliss. She felt blissful now and

15

could hardly wait to get Eddie in the back porch of her home in Pollokshields. Her mother never went in or out the back way and so there was no chance of being caught.

She blessed the day back in September of the previous year when she had graduated from her private girls-only school into the astonishingly different world of the Glasgow School of Art. It was there she first learned about men. Her lessons had come not only from the male models. At least one of them was a bit effeminate. He came in of a morning all eager for a gossip. Alaister, his name was, and he would chatter for ages about how he had henna-ed his hair the night before and wrapped his head in brown paper like a parcel to keep it warm. Apparently that made the henna work properly. He was too skinny to be interesting to look at naked, but some of the other models caused her to give Veronica knowing looks or nudges. Not that the male models were completely naked. The men always wore G-strings, something that Helena had said was not fair. After all, the female models had to strip off everything. It was explained to her, however, that men could get an erection which would be embarrassing. Helena thought it would be hilarious. Most of the fun and games and the lessons on life and the male species had come from the parties in private studios in students' digs, in the dark assembly hall corridor, and in the cloakroom near the refectory. Or at dances in the assembly hall and common room.

First of course everyone would go to the State Bar and buy a carry-out of beer or wine or whatever they could get. If it was a dance they were going to, the bottles would either be hidden in somebody's locker or in the cloakroom, and everyone would keep going back and forth all night for a tipple until thoroughly pissed. There would be plenty of necking and heavy petting all along the shadowy corridor. From events like that no one set off for home until morning. Quite often she arrived at her door at the same time as the milkman. She would fall into bed at the same time as her mother was getting up for work. Dances were always held on a Friday night and 'Rory's' busiest day was Saturday.

'You've got in with a right wild crowd,' her mother accused.

16

'I know.' Helena winked mischievously. 'I'm having a wonderful time!'

Her mother could never resist laughing but reminded her, 'As long as you look after yourself. Take good care of number one, that's the main thing. Don't allow a man to touch you in an intimate way before marriage. If you do, he'll treat you like dirt.' At other times she would say, 'Remember, never let a man put his hand up your skirt.'

Her mother was a good sport and meant well, but of course she didn't know what she was talking about. Helena was fond of her, however, and played along with her. 'Of course not, mother! What do you take me for? I mean, honestly! I just dance with them and have a laugh with them.'

Then she would make Rory laugh again by telling her how she and her friends had a noisy singsong. She would give a display for her mother's benefit, dancing about, kicking up her heels and yelling, ' "If you're ever in a jam, I'm your man. . . . If you're ever up a tree, send for me . . . friendship, friendship. . . ." '

Coming home with the tough-looking Eddie, round sailor hat squashed well down over his brow, fists jammed in the pockets of his navy jacket, Helena had no worries about her mother. Her father was a different kettle of fish altogether. However, her father was not at home yet, so she and Eddie would be quite safe. They managed to get a bus from George Square. It was beginning to get light, which was a nuisance. Not that she personally had any objections to making love in daylight or electric light or any kind of light. Indeed it gave her an extra thrill to see and be seen. It would not do, however, to be seen by her mother.

The big villa in Pollokshields towered at the top of a winding driveway. It looked black against the grey- and pink-streaked sky. The glass conservatory attached to one side of it had a ghostly glitter, but all the many windows of the house looked black and still, giving the place a formidable, almost menacing appearance.

'Gee! Is this really where you live?' Eddie was obviously impressed.

'Ssh! You don't want to waken my mother or my brother, do you?' She took his arm and hustled him round the side of the house to the shadows at the back. 'In here.'

The porch had glass windows, but also a long bench with cushions on it to make comfortable beds for the dog and the cat. Fluffy the cat objected to being catapulted out of bed. She glared venomously at Helena, spat and arched her back while angrily swinging her tail. Rover, on the other hand, being old and resigned to Helena's inexplicable behaviour (often she hugged him until he nearly choked), just curled up on the floor without a murmur.

'Are you sure this is all right?' Eddie whispered.

'I don't know till I try it,' she giggled back at him.

He relaxed and pulled her down on to the bench. He was a good kisser, quickly arousing her passions, and they were at the red-hot stage, fumbling with each other's clothes, when the sound of a car motor and then a car door banging impinged on their feverish brains. At first neither of them mentioned this intrusion or allowed the sounds to have any effect on what they were so intent on doing. Until a man's voice was heard to say something like, 'Right, Jimmy.' or 'Goodnight, Jimmy.'

Helena immediately struggled to her feet. 'My God, it's my father!'

'Christ! What'll we do?' Eddie was buttoning himself up with trembling hands.

'You stay here until the coast's clear,' Helena said. 'I'll go round and spin him some story about forgetting my key.'

Heavy steps were crunching on the gravel towards them. Helena flew from the porch, round the corner, and into the arms of the heavily built man in army officer's uniform who was approaching.

'Dad, am I glad to see you! I forgot my key and I didn't want to waken anybody. I've been here for absolutely ages!'

Donovan's eyes narrowed down at her through the shadows. 'Oh yeah?'

3

From behind the shield of his *Daily Herald* Matthew Drummond could see the railway carriage filling up with servicemen in khaki, air force and navy blue. They were a noisy lot, riotous with relief, and who could blame them. As he turned the page of the newspaper and his face become visible for a few seconds, he gave them a brief smile and a nod before widening the pages up in front of him again. Even as a young man, indeed *especially* as a young man he had never been any use at jolly *bonhomie* or social chit-chat. He used to pray for the social talent of Victoria.

If Victoria had been at his side at this moment, she would be laughing and talking to these servicemen as if she had known them all her life. His prayers were never answered. Instead his embarrassment had grown worse. Firstly because of Victoria's insistence in trying to force him to behave in the same easy way as her, a mode of behaviour he had long since come to realize was totally alien to him, something that Victoria should have long since come to realize too. Secondly he was embarrassed just because of Victoria being so typically Victoria. He felt guilty about that. He loved and admired his wife, but the intensity of his love and admiration had been somewhat tempered by the years he had spent in London. He had been three years on the National Executive of the National Union of Railwaymen before the war and since the start of the war he had been five years as a Member of Parliament.

To persuade Victoria to come to London with him had been a hopeless task. Springburn and Balornock were her world, Glasgow her universe. Their council house in Balornock, up the hill from Springburn, was her nest, the pivot of her life. There she baked scones without sugar and fairy cakes with dried egg for her endless stream of visitors. From there she sailed forth dressed in her utility coat, and hat rummaged from the last church jumble sale, to preside over the Women's Guild meeting or a meeting of the YWCA. She and the children had enjoyed listening to him tell of the wonders of London and the grandeur of the Palace of Westminster, but they regarded his stories simply as stories and showed no desire to experience the reality. Victoria made him tolerably welcome on his week-ends home. He was, after all, the source of her pride and special status as wife of the local MP. She always searched the shops for something special for his meal and made him aware in no uncertain manner of the trouble to which she had gone.

'Now you'd better eat that up and enjoy it,' she would say. 'I spent hours trailing from one end of Springburn to the other to get it for you.'

The way she treated him was more like a mother struggling to be conscientious with a difficult child than his wife. At the same time there was always an anxiety lurking behind her strong matriarchal manner. Victoria was neurotic about sex. She had an absolute abhorrence of it. Looking back he could see that even the first night of their honeymoon had been a disaster. He had meant it to be so different. Granted he had never been a success with women; after one or two meetings they had invariably stood him up. He had been forced to find release with prostitutes. He had studied numerous books on the subject of women, and also on sex and married love, to try to get things right before his marriage. He had struggled to obey all the rules once he had been successful in capturing Victoria as his bride. He had done everything in his power to be patient and gentle, all to no avail. Victoria had only got worse. Not that he had been a perfect marriage partner in other respects. He was only too aware of his anti-social behaviour, his black moods, his demonic temper. There could be no denying the fact that he was a difficult man to live with and especially to someone of Victoria's gregarious and happy-go-lucky nature.

'Smoke, mate?' a ruddy-faced soldier nudged him.

Matthew lowered his paper just enough to give a polite

smile and a shake of the head. He prayed that the soldier was not intent on starting a conversation.

'What takes you to Glasgow?' the soldier asked.

'I'm a Glaswegian,' Matthew said.

'You're not!'

Matthew made no comment.

'Bloody hell, you could have fooled me. You look and sound exactly like a London man.'

Matthew thought this an exaggeration but said nothing. He made to lift his paper again. The soldier, however, was not to be put off. The other servicemen, with the exception of the army lieutenant sitting opposite, were now caught up in a game of pontoon which the soldier apparently had no wish to join.

'You work in London then?'

Matthew resigned himself to the ordeal. After all, the man might be a voter in his constituency. Even if he did not belong to Springburn he could still be a potential Labour voter. 'I'm the Labour Member of Parliament for Springburn.'

'You're not! Bloody hell!' There was a pause while the soldier viewed him with delight. 'Let me shake you by the hand, mate. Did you hear that?' he shouted to the other occupants of the carriage. 'A bloody Labour MP.'

Accepting defeat with as much grace as he could muster, Matthew folded his paper and laid it aside. 'Do I take it by your enthusiasm that you are a Labour supporter?'

'You're right there and not only me. I've yet to meet a man in the army that isn't. Maybe he wasn't before but he is now.'

At this point the officer decided to join in the conversation. 'That includes all ranks. And not only young officers but quite a lot of older officers. I remember my major in a landing I did in southern Italy. He was very sympathetic to Labour.'

'Yes,' Matthew agreed, warming to the conversation now that it had taken a political turn rather than a personal or social one. 'The radicalization of the forces gives a clear demonstration of the war-time fusion between the ideals of patriotism and equality.'

21

'I belong to Clydebank,' the first soldier said. 'I lost my home in the bombing, but thank God my wife and wean were all right. They're staying with my mother and it's nearly driving my wife up the wall. Where are we going to stay now, that's what I want to know.'

'Whatever government gets in after this election is obviously going to have to face an acute housing shortage because of war damage,' Matthew told him. 'It's estimated that about half a million dwellings have been either destroyed or made completely uninhabitable, and a further quarter of a million severely damaged. House-building is something that must be given priority. Families need a home of their own. In my view it is absolutely essential.'

'Quite right, mate,' the soldier agreed. 'I'm with you all the way.'

'And, of course,' Matthew added, 'to exacerbate the shortage, a war-time boom in the birth-rate has increased the population by a million. . . .'

'I'm not surprised,' the soldier guffawed. 'The way some of my mates have been at it. Not me, though, I swear I'm only responsible for one.'

Matthew gave him a thin smile. Somebody had to take the responsibility not only for the babies born within marriage but also for the doubling of illegitimate births during the war years. He was all too often faced with trying to help young mothers in their grim ordeal. They were usually penniless and homeless, and having to cope with prejudice and rejection from all sides. Illegitimacy was paramount to prostitution in the eyes of people brought up by Victorian mothers. To his wife for instance it represented the depths of shame and moral impurity, and she spoke of local 'fallen women' in shocked whispers and with much shaking of her head. If one of these unfortunate girls came to his house instead of to the empty shop in Springburn where he held his week-end surgeries, Victoria would hustle Amelia out of the way into another room as if she was afraid her daughter would be contaminated by even a glimpse of the wretched girl.

Thinking of Amelia made his heart and mind keel over in

anguish. For the millionth time he flayed himself for the occasion – was it four years ago now? – when he had been home one week-end and got drunk after a particularly savage quarrel with Victoria. Victoria had packed a case and walked out. He had been left wondering why the hell he bothered travelling the long journey up from London. Why he was faithful to Victoria. Why he kept hoping against hope that some vestige of their love could still be salvaged and expressed in the normal loving way through sex. That was the day he had to admit to himself, at long last, that it was no use. Victoria had never allowed him to touch her since Amelia had been conceived and she would never allow him to touch her again. He had to face this irrefutable fact. But first there was the terrible upsurge of longing, of desperate desire. He had gone to the Boundary Bar and sat alone in his usual corner and downed one whisky after another. That night the alcohol only served to increase his sexual longings to an unbearable degree. He was drunk. He was crazy. He was incapable. He was not responsible for his actions. He had told himself all of these things and more over the years. Nothing helped. He still suffered the agony of hazy remembrance. Had Amelia called out? She had always been very anxious when her mother left unexpectedly and gave no clue to where she was off to, or how long she would be away. Had Amelia called for her mother? Or had the voice floating faintly from the bedroom said, 'Is that you, daddy?'

He had stumbled into the darkness and felt his way into bed beside her. She had not moved or made a sound. He had never known anyone so still and quiet. Her still silence reverberated down through the years in never-ending accusation. He had not gone the whole hog, but he might have done had Jamie not come home and, in his usual brash way, flung the door open, switched on the light and asked, 'Where's mum?' Then, seeing Matthew lying with Amelia in his arms, his face had contorted with shock and disgust and he had spat out, 'Aw shit!' before disappearing, banging the door behind him.

Amelia had seen the look of disgust too. Indeed the look

had been directed more at her than at Matthew. He would never forget, after Jamie had gone, the way she stared up at him in helpless bewilderment, her eyes brimming with the unspoken question, 'Why did you do this to me?'

He had staggered up then and out of the room. He had tried Jamie's door hoping somehow to explain or in some way put things right. Jamie's door was locked. Almost in tears he leaned up against it. 'I'm so bloody drunk,' he yelled, 'I don't know what I'm doing.' But Jamie too was silent.

He had returned to London first thing next morning, without seeing either of his children. He had not known how he would ever be able to face them again. Life had to go on, however, and after a few weeks he returned to Glasgow. On the surface all was exactly as usual. Victoria greeted him with the usual peck on the cheek and 'Hello, dear, had a good journey?' Jamie had swaggered through, dressed in his best suit with his hair carefully Brylcreemed.

'Hello, dad, sorry I've to rush off. I've a date for the pictures.'

'What's this one like?' he had asked, forcing a veneer of pleasant normality over his face and voice.

'A great wee dancer. I met her at the Locarno last week.'

'I told him,' Victoria said, 'that no good would come of going to one of those dens of iniquity.'

Matthew dug into his pocket and produced two half-crowns. It was a ridiculous gesture because he could not afford it. Paying for digs in London and continuing to keep a house in Glasgow was a constant financial worry. 'This will help you to give her a good time.'

He remembered how Jamie's face lit up.

'Thanks, dad!'

Yet Matthew sensed the undercurrent of embarrassment. It was only the merest hint and could have been his over-sensitive imagination. There was no imagining Amelia's furtive eyes, however, and the delicate shrinking when he went to put his arm around her and give her his usual hug. The shrinking hurt him deeply. It was no more than he deserved, of course. Fortunately no one other than

24

himself would be able to detect any change in anyone's behaviour. Victoria was blissful in her ignorance and bright-eyed with excitement.

'You'll never guess, Matthew,' she burst out, as soon as he had deposited his case beside his leather armchair by the empty fireplace. He accepted the cup of tea she presented him, ready milked and sugared and briskly stirred.

'The folk from the wireless have asked me to speak about what it's like being an MP's wife!'

He smiled. 'And what is it like?'

'Och!' she brushed him aside with a flick of her hand. 'I'll make up something.' Of that he had no doubt. He had long since overcome the urge to help her prepare notes or think any talk out in a constructive or logical manner. Victoria had no patience for notes or preparation or thinking things through. She had a happy knack of going to a meeting, standing up and spouting forth whatever happened to come into her head. Or she would tell a re-hash of some romantic story she had read or a film she had seen, adding, if she deemed it necessary, a Christian moral. Her women's meetings seemed to lap it up. Sometimes he thought she ought to have been an actress. She enjoyed giving a performance. Half the time she lived in a make-believe world and it was then she came to sparkling-eyed vivacious life. He could just imagine her with expressive gestures fantasizing to all and sundry about what a perfect partnership they had, how their love was only strengthened by their long periods of separation, how each meeting was like another honeymoon, et cetera, et cetera, on and on, ad nauseam.

Of course, it did not do his image or his standing in the community any harm. She was, so it seemed to the voters, behind him and giving him full support all the way. They liked and admired her. He could never be so certain of what they thought about him. He was a good MP, and he represented their interests and looked after their welfare most conscientiously. He believed no one could or would deny that. What they thought of him as a private person, though, was quite a different matter.

He thanked God for his agent and his secretary who, along with Victoria, acted as social buffers between him and the electorate. The three women were the best of friends although he suspected that, given the slightest encouragement, both Jessie McGregor and Bridget Dunbar would jump into bed with him. Several times he had picked up unmistakable signals, but chose to ignore them. Jessie was a tireless agent, Bridget a most dependable secretary, and both were devoted to the cause as well as to him. They worked on a part-time basis and for nothing, because he could not afford to pay them. They were vital to him in the furtherance of his career. Although he did not regard himself as a career man in the devious, cut-throat way of many of his colleagues in the house. Some accused him scathingly of being an idealist, something he resented and which never failed to irritate him. He was a realist. He knew what life was about. As a man he had experienced hard, physical labour. In his youth he had existed and nearly starved in a Glasgow rat-ridden hovel. He wanted to do his job to the best of his ability, to improve the conditions of working-class people, not just talk about it. He knew he had the power to impress others in the debating chamber with his oratory, but it was only what his oratory could achieve in terms of his constituency that interested him. Cynical members, 'old hands at the game' as they described themselves, told him that they had all wanted 'to set the heather on fire' when they had first been elected. 'But we mellowed in time and so will you.'

He had not mellowed in the sense they meant. He was still as full of fire and commitment as he had been on the day of his maiden speech. If he *had* been a career man he would have made sure he mellowed, compromised his beliefs, tempered his opinions, watered down the expression of them, become more careful and more diplomatic in order to ingratiate himself with the powers-that-be. Had he done this, he would have earned himself a place in the war-time coalition government. Or so he had been told. But the fire in him would not be doused. It burned and churned up from his soul to erupt like a volcano every time he began a speech in the House of Commons, although he could outwardly be cool in debate. Indeed the only person with whom he lost his temper in argument was Victoria. She was the only person who could rattle him into losing control.

Now he was on his way to spend three weeks with her during the build-up to the election. Already he was beset with worries and apprehensions, including financial troubles. Victoria had always been reckless with whatever little money she had. She blithely careered from one 'hunger to a burst' to another, one credit club card to another. It was a case of robbing Peter to pay Paul. It drove him to distraction at the best of times but, while Parliament was dissolved and an election being fought, MPs salaries stopped. How they were going to manage for the next three weeks, he had no idea. He had managed to save a few pounds during the last session of Parliament, but would he be able to persuade Victoria to spend it frugally? Nor did he know what was his greatest torment, his wife with her frigidity and her total disregard for thrift, or what he thought he saw behind his daughter's vaguely evasive eyes.

4

'I might have known,' Donovan, who was up on one of his week-end visits home, tossed his cigarette into the empty fireplace in disgust. 'You've always had a knack of turning everything to your advantage.'

Rory's pencilled eyebrows arched higher. 'So? I thought that was one of the things you admired about me.'

Donovan stared at her in contemplative silence for a minute and it occurred to her that his officer's khaki uniform added to his toughness and authority. If anything, his grey eyes had grown flintier since she had first met him – was it really twenty-three years ago? He had always been a hard-nosed cynical kind of man, of course. She had never expected much sympathetic understanding from him and she had no reason to expect any now.

'You also had a good supply of common sense. Enough, I thought, to keep you honest. Just shows how wrong a man can be.'

'Oh, come off it,' laughing, she leaned back in her chair, crossed her shapely nyloned legs, and made impudent little kicking motions with a high-heeled foot. 'Don't try to act the saint with me. You've done all right for yourself out of the war. You landed a cushy job in London making army films. You've eaten in posh restaurants and lacked for nothing for the past six years. You've not known what coupons and rationing are.'

'Most people have been involved in small fiddles from time to time and I admit I'm no exception.'

'So?'

'Rory, you've been making a fortune in everything from black market deals to fraud. Think yourself damned lucky to have got away with it this long. You should be behind bars and that's where you will be if you don't call a halt right now.'

Rory laughed again, fitted a cigarette into her holder and lit it with quick confident movements. 'Darling, why don't you get back to your newspaper job and let me get on with what I know best, and that's running a very successful business. The way I look at it is – my customers come first. I give them good service. That's what I've always done and that's what I mean to continue doing.'

'Pack it up. Right now!'

Smoke streamed upwards from Rory's cigarette. 'Nobody tells me what to do.'

'Oh yeah? And here was me thinking you'd been bending an ear to your dear old dad. After all, he's been at it for a lifetime.'

The mention of her father immediately nettled Rory. 'Leave my father out of this.'

'How can I? Like father like daughter, it seems. I can also remember a time when your brothers weren't quite the fine upstanding citizens they are now. . . . '

'Shut up!' She jerked from her chair and paced restlessly across the room. A glimpse of herself in the oval, gold-crested mirror was enough to reassure her, however. She had never looked smarter in her figure-hugging black frock, with Chinese elegance in its small straight collar and side buttoning.

'The terror of Springburn your brothers were. "The Burners" was the name of their illustrious gang, I believe.'

She patted her hair and gave an approving touch to her emerald ear-rings. 'That's all in the past and nothing whatsoever to do with me, or my brothers now, for that matter.'

'They certainly followed in the footsteps of the infamous "Scrap" for quite a spell. Even the prison authorities will have lost count of how many times he has been behind bars.'

'Shut up, I said.'

'Everyone's supposed to have a skeleton in the cupboard but you've got enough of them to fill a graveyard.'

She whirled round to glare at him. 'You enjoy trying to bait me and hurt me. You always have.'

He gave her one of his humourless smiles – a baring of the teeth that only served to accentuate his cleft chin. 'You're not the type to respond to soft words and pleadings, even if I was the type to use them. But as it happens I am concerned about you.'

'Gee, thanks.'

'Drop the sarcasm. This is serious.'

She crushed out her cigarette in the metal ashtray. 'Of course it's bloody serious; the last six years have been worse than serious. They've been absolute shit. If I could get my hands on Hugh Dalton, President of the bloody Board of Trade, I'd wring his neck.'

Her rage grew at the thought of all the difficulties with which she had had to cope, and not only the shortages. There were the mountains of paperwork, the endless regulations, most of them petty, stupid and completely unworkable. Not to mention highly unpopular with the public. One law that caused particularly bitter complaints from the customers stated that all mens' jackets were to be single-breasted only, with at most three pockets and only three buttons on the front. There were to be no buttons on the cuffs and no belts. The restriction to two pockets for waistcoats, the ration of no more than a nineteen-inch-wide trouser leg, and the prohibition of elastic waistbands, although keenly resented, might have been accepted. The total ban on turn-ups however, had let loose a storm of protest that had never died down. Dalton had still insisted that 'the prohibition of turn-ups to mens' trousers was saving millions of square feet of cloth a year.' This was nonsense. She knew it and the Board of Trade inspector knew it. He had prosecuted a tailor for making an illicit pair of turn-up trousers, but had admitted that 'utility trousers were very unpopular and . . . the general opinion of the trade was that they saved no cloth at all.' She had instructed her tailors to make customer's trousers several inches too long 'by mistake' so that they could then quite legally be made to fit by turning the legs up.

It wasn't this, though, that was angering Donovan, nor was it the buying up of dead people's coupons. (It must seem to the authorities that the final thing that a person did before he died these days was to go on a shopping spree. There were seldom any occasions where a deceased had any coupons left in his or her ration book when it was handed back.) Nor even her black market, under-the-counter dealings in scarce 'luxury' items like combs, hair grips, powder puffs and stockings. It was her plan to mis-appropriate, as he called it, some of the cloth supplied to her by the Ministry of Supply for making overcoats for demobilized ex-servicemen. The fact that she had been doing the same thing for years, with material which was supposed to go solely into the making of officers' uniforms, and never falling foul of the law, only served as another incendiary bomb to his anger. She had never been nearer to wishing he would stay in England and leave her to get on with her life in her own way. She certainly wished she had never confided in him about her business methods. Previously it had not occurred to her to do so. Only this time, with the war in Europe being over and his demob imminent, she had felt more relaxed and expansive. Foolishly she had believed that the sharing of her war-time difficulties and triumphs would help to bring them closer together as they were about to pick up the threads of their normal peace-time life. Instead it had immediately widened the gulf between them.

This gulf had started when she had unexpectedly arrived in London on a business trip and called on Donovan to give him what she had thought would be a pleasant surprise. He had not been in his digs nor on duty at the film studio. She had, by dogged persistence and bribery, (with the promise of nylons and bars of chocolate), learned about his night-club haunts and tracked him down to one where he was enjoying himself in a four-some with a fellow army officer and two ATS girls.

'What the hell do you expect me to do?' he asked later, not apparently feeling in the slightest guilty or contrite. 'Live like a monk?'

'Why not?' she had shouted at him. 'I live like a bloody nun!'

This was not strictly true, she often had occasion to have lunch or dinner with men, but it was all in the line of business. That night in London, after she had a fight with Donovan that had actually come to blows, she had stormed away from him hell-bent on revenge. If she had been able to see Matthew Drummond she would have slept with him. He would have welcomed her with open arms, she was sure. A lifetime ago in their youth they had enjoyed a passionate affair. Matthew had eventually betrayed her and married Victoria who had been her best friend at the time, but she had long ago forgiven him for this. Their relationship had deepened into a friendship that she knew Matthew continued to value, despite the fact that they only saw each other very occasionally now. Sometimes not only months had elapsed between meetings but, since he was based in London, often a year or more would pass before he would drop in to see her at the shop on one of his visits home. Or, if she was in London, she might ring him up and meet him for lunch. As often as not Donovan would also be present at these meetings. Matthew was a strange unsocial sort of person and Donovan was, as far as she knew, his only male friend. Even then he and Donovan only met when she was there, except on a very odd occasion like the time Donovan needed to do some research in the Commons and Matthew had helped him and bought him a drink in the Commons bar afterwards.

As far as she knew, and she felt she knew Matthew better than anyone did, even – or rather – especially Victoria, Matthew remained faithful to his wife. Why, she could never fathom, because Victoria had always been frigid. Granted she had lost touch with Victoria over the years, but she could not imagine her suddenly (or even gradually) turning into a passionate sex-pot. Matthew, on the other hand, was a very passionate man. He was also a man of principle and very high ideals – to the point of being a pompous bore. Matthew, she felt sure, would never stoop to having a casual affair just to give himself sexual relief. She believed that he would not consider his one-time lover and all-time friend, Rory, as anything casual. He would have sex with her all right if she offered it and she was never nearer offering than that night of her confrontation with Donovan. Unfortunately or, in retrospect, fortunately Matthew was in the House at a late-night sitting. There was an important debate going on in which Matthew was taking part. Even if sexy Mae West had invited him to come up and see her he would have refused. Politics, with Matthew, had always come first.

'You haven't been the only one to cope with difficulties,' Donovan said. 'Most people have had to "make do and mend" or do without, but not you, of course. It would take more than a war to put a spoke in *your* wheel. I'll tell you what will, though. Being found out.'

'Don't tell me, let me guess,' she acted the part of a wide-eyed innocent, enjoying a game. 'You're going to do an exclusive *exposé* about me in the *Evening Citizen*!'

'Don't tempt me.'

She felt a secret tremor of apprehension. The range of Donovan's ruthlessness was something she could never feel quite sure about. After all, he had had no scruples about trying his damnedest to ruin her by *exposé* journalism before their marriage. She shrugged, 'You know your trouble?'

'Surprise me.'

'You've got a newspaper man's headline mentality. I tell you something that to another business person would seem astute and show a capacity for survival; to you it just means a dramatic story with the headline – "Saleswoman Saboteur!" '

'Not bad,' Donovan said.

'Or – "How Stockwell Street stocks well!" '

'Clever,' Donovan admitted. 'But, in this instance, I prefer a plain factual heading, like – "Glasgow business-woman jailed for five years." '

'Very funny,' she said.

'No,' Donovan fixed her with one of his cold stares. 'Not funny at all.'

5

Mrs Agnes McDade was Victoria's best friend and very proud of her Victoria was too. Mrs McDade's husband, like her own, was a collar-and-tie man. He was a clerk in the Ministry of Food office in the Candleriggs, but Hector McDade was not as important as Matthew Drummond and his wife Agnes would be the first to concede this. 'No job in the land,' Agnes often assured Victoria, 'is more important than a Member of Parliament.'

Being wives of collar-and-tie men made them both a cut above most of their neighbours. Although neither of them would openly admit to believing this. They were ardent Labour supporters. Hector had definite precedence over Matthew in one respect. His special claim to importance was the fact that he could, from time to time, lay his hands on extra coupons. Not only food coupons either. Hector knew some obliging people in other offices. Of course one had to be discreet. Government snoopers were everywhere. Victoria believed in fair shares for everybody and in fair play, and no one could be more indignant at newspaper reports of rich people buying coupons or getting all sorts of luxuries that were denied to ordinary folk. Only the other day a titled lady had been fined an enormous sum of money.

'And quite right too,' Victoria had told Agnes. 'Although one can't help thinking that if it had been some poor factory girl she would have been flung in the jail.'

Agnes had wholeheartedly agreed.

Life was unfair. Life was a terrible struggle. These were two of their favourite sayings. Between them they struggled as hard as they could. Agnes was very clever with her needle. She had done wonders for both Victoria and herself in creating garments without coupons. For instance, when Victoria had a special engagement singing and playing the piano at a posh evening 'do' in the City Chambers, Agnes had excelled herself with a hospital-bed sheet given to her by her daughter Lizzie who was a nurse. Agnes had snipped off the edge, then cut out a halter neck-line. The material was pinned together at the shoulder with Mrs McDade's gilt brooch. The result was impressive, a heavy white dress gathered in at the waist and falling in folds below it like a Roman toga.

'With your noble carriage and your nose,' Agnes had enthused, 'you could pass for a Caesar's wife any day!'

A discussion had followed on what the word was for the wife of a Caesar. Neither of them could think of it and Victoria said she would ask Matthew when he came home. It was an unspoken agreement that Matthew knew everything. Although of course Victoria would never have divulged this opinion to Matthew. Victoria was extremely touchy about Matthew knowing more than her. In this as in everything else connected with Matthew, she believed attack was the best method of defence.

The hospital sheet's transformation was nothing to the uses to which black-out material was put, and Agnes was not alone in being able to do this. Black-out material covered as many women as windows. Agnes had that extra touch of genius. She had made for her daughter, Lizzie, a very attractive black skirt decorated with rows of brightly coloured tape. She bleached the rest of the black-out material to make a top to wear with it. Lizzie had also benefited by petticoats, knickers and bras made out of curtain net, butter muslin and cheesecloth which were also unrationed.

Hector and Agnes would never forget the day of Victoria's windfall, however. It had come as the result of Victoria being kind to a family whose undertaker's business and adjoining house had been bombed.

'I only did my Christian duty,' Victoria modestly protested, her head lifting with pride, and pleasure sparkling in her eyes. She had taken the family in and given them shelter and a share of what food she had until they 'got themselves organized' as they said. Her reward had been the windfall – a large roll of purple material salvaged from the wreckage, along with another of white muslin. The purple had been used to cover coffins that were going to cremations. The white muslin was used for lining coffins. Victoria had presented both rolls of material to Agnes who had been so overcome she had burst into tears.

'I'll never forget this as long as I live,' she sobbed. 'There must be at least fifteen yards altogether.'

After soaking, the purple material came up quite a nice shade of blue-grey and was made into two long-sleeved winter dresses, one for Agnes and one for Victoria. The white muslin served as much needed pillow-cases, handkerchiefs and curtains.

Nearly as exciting as this acquisition was the tracking-down of surplus service blankets that occasionally appeared in the shops. This was Victoria's forte. This was what she enjoyed most, getting out and around the shops chatting to neighbours, friends and strangers she stood next to in queues, and then, if she was lucky, coming home in triumph with an army blanket, a quarter pound of liver, a pound of cooking apples or, treasure of treasures, – an onion. The praise she received and the excitement her success caused kept her going through the most difficult days. These were the days when she could stand in a queue for two hours only to find there was nothing left in the shop when it came to her turn. Empty shelves or the perverse advertisements on them for what they did not have, were an all-too-familiar sight, depressing for most, but to Victoria a challenge. As she often said to an admiring and much less tenacious Agnes, 'Nothing on the shelves there might be, but nobody's going to tell me there's nothing under the counter.'

Victoria was kind to shopkeepers. She invited them to her parties and soirées and entertained them with music and song. She pressed Agnes into service to make garments for them. One shop assistant said she would be eternally grateful for Victoria organizing her wedding dress which Agnes had made out of Victoria's net curtains. Her gratitude had taken the form, from time to time, of a tin of sardines, a little extra dried egg, and, on one exciting occasion, – a *real* egg.

There was no use wooing anyone in a fruit shop, at least not for fresh fruit. Fresh fruit had become a fond memory, and sometimes not even that. Few children could remember what a banana looked like, far less what it tasted like.

Skill in acquiring goods from above or below the counter was not Victoria's only talent. Agnes often said, 'You're an absolute genius in the kitchen, Victoria. I don't know how you get some of your ideas.' Victoria had never been lacking in imagination in any sphere. Now, because of all the scarcities, she had turned this creativity to good use. Her 'mock haggis' made with bacon rinds, oatmeal, bicarbonate of soda, one leek and vegetable water, although nothing like haggis, was nevertheless very tasty. To eke out jam, she grated swedes into it. For lemon juice, she used rhubarb juice; for pepper, grated turnip. Once she had hit on the idea of cooking tinned apricots in bacon fat and serving them egg-like on toast. She refused, however, to take the Ministry of Food's advice and cook crow, rook or seagull pies, and she and Agnes both thought it a disgrace when a neighbour was fined for wasting bread by throwing a few crumbs out to the hungry birds in the back green.

'They're God's creatures, the same as us,' Victoria said. 'And it's our Christian duty to be kind to them.'

Victoria was always very positive about her duty and about everything else she believed in, and determination showed in her strong proud face. Agnes on the other hand was never sure about anything. She was an anxious wisp of a woman who only reached to Victoria's shoulder. Her mousy, finger-waved hair was tightly rolled up at the ends, kept in place by several kirbygrips, and covered indoors and out by a brown felt hat with a turned-up brim. Agnes was 'cold-rifed' and slightly arthritic, and she often worriedly told Victoria, 'They say that most of our heat leaks out the top of our heads. Don't you think you should keep your head covered, Mrs Drummond?'

Victoria never wore a hat indoors like Mrs McDade, or while she was hanging out her washing or running out to empty her rubbish pail in the middens in the back green.

Agnes always tutted and disapproved when she saw her bareheaded. This was the only disagreement they ever had, if disagreement it could be called.

It was surprising in a way because, apart from differences in appearance, there were several dissimilarities in their natures. Agnes tended to be pernickety in her habits and picky with her food. As a result no doubt of all the sewing or 'close work' as she called it, she needed to wear spectacles all the time, as well as a hat. Even so, she felt nervous of steps or crossing roads, and was glad to hang on to Victoria's arm when they went anywhere together. Unlike Victoria, Agnes did not enjoy 'stravaiging about' and seldom ventured a foot over her doorstep where she lived in the next close to Victoria, unless bullied into doing so by Victoria.

Victoria got Agnes's 'messages', as shopping was known in Glasgow. Victoria was also the carrier of all the local news and views. Mrs McDade's daughter Lizzie had an impatient and unsympathetic attitude to her mother. She was seldom at home because of her long shifts in Stobhill Hospital, and when she was at home she seemed to give her mother nothing but cheek. Many a time Victoria and Agnes spoke about the crosses they had to bear in the shape of their respective daughters.

'You don't need to tell me about what you've to suffer at Lizzie's hands,' Victoria said with feeling. 'Believe me, Mrs McDade, I know exactly what you're going through. Amelia is her daddy all over again!'

Agnes shed quiet tears when discussing Lizzie's lack of filial affection, although in fact Agnes's eyes often watered with weakness and she had a habit of wiping her eyes even when not sighing over Lizzie. Agnes did not have her troubles to seek with Hector, her husband, either. Hector was from the Highlands originally. He had been forced to come to Glasgow for work, but his heart was still up north.

As Victoria often said, 'Hector would be more at home in a kilt than a navy suit and brandishing a broadsword rather than a pen.'

Agnes always sighed her total agreement. Agnes and

Victoria's husbands were the other crosses they had to bear, although this was something they would never dream of divulging in any detail to another living soul. Victoria had never even told Agnes about her worries regarding Matthew's animal instincts. She had made it perfectly clear to him that his behaviour disgusted her when he allowed his instincts to get the better of him. Nevertheless he still sometimes tried to touch her bosom and other places which she never touched or even looked at herself. In her weekly bath she used a thick sponge in quick guilty strokes and with nothing but distaste for these private parts of her body. Fully clothed it was different. She carried herself with pride, her head held high.

It was a terrible harassment when Matthew was at home, having to be on her guard from this side of his nature. She did not mind all the buzz of his agent and secretary coming and going, or the people who came with their problems. It was only when she and Matthew were alone that her troubles started. She was forced to dress and undress hurriedly in the kitchenette or bathroom. It had become a source of impossible-to-bear resentment and anger, as well as shame, to have Matthew watch her undress. It was bad enough him seeing her in her nightdress before she hurried to cover herself with blankets. Experience had taught her that she could not afford to take any chances, so even if Matthew tried to kiss her goodnight now she froze and turned her face away. Although, once he had retreated to his side of the bed and she felt the danger was over, she always bade him quite an affectionate 'goodnight, dear'. Or sometimes she would chat to him about the day's happenings. She believed she was a good and loving wife and, despite Matthew's many faults and failings, she had remained over the years passionately loyal to him. Outside her own home, or to anyone outside her immediate family, she would not countenance a word against him. Even within the family, although she could accuse Amelia of having faults like her daddy and had no hesitation in bringing up the subject of her daddy's moodiness or bad temper, she was outraged if Amelia ever uttered a word of criticism.

'How dare you say a word against your good daddy!' Her eyes would widen with shock. 'Him that's been nothing but good to you, and kept you in food and clothes, and never a word of complaint when you stayed on at school after you were fourteen instead of finding a job. You wicked, ungrateful girl!'

'Mind you,' she once confided in Agnes, 'I've never quite forgiven Matthew for depriving his children of their proper station in life.'

Since Matthew had become a Member of Parliament and therefore provided them all with the best of stations, she no longer worried about that side of his refusal to acknowledge wealthy old Forbes-Cunningham as his real father. Alexander Forbes-Cunningham had got Matthew's mother into trouble when she worked as a skivvy at the big house. His mother had married John Drummond, a miner in the Forbes-Cunningham pit. John Drummond had been a good man and the only father Matthew had known. Then out of the blue, while Matthew had been serving as a fellow town councillor with him, Forbes-Cunningham had told him the truth. This was after his legitimate son Edgar had been killed in a motor-bike accident and Forbes-Cunningham had become a broken man. His wife had died shortly afterwards. For years Victoria had been so bitter she had hated Matthew for his stubborn refusal to have anything to do with the mine owner. Now, as she told Agnes, 'We are working-class folk and proud of it, and it says a lot for my man that he can mix with and hold his own with the top people in the land. He's far above the likes of Forbes-Cunningham now. But all the same. . . ,' she could not help adding wistfully, 'we could be doing with some of his money. An MP's wage is hardly enough to keep body and soul together.'

'Maybe he'll leave your man something when he dies,' Agnes had tried to be of comfort.

'No,' Victoria sighed. 'He's got that nephew and his toffee-nosed wife never off his doorstep now. They'll get everything. Wait till you see.'

At the beginning she had been desperate for the money so

that when Jamie grew up they would be able to put him through university and give him everything he wanted. But as it turned out all Jamie had ever wanted was to be an engine driver like his daddy. Now he was a fireman, getting driving turns and as happy as a lark. Happiness was the main thing, Victoria had decided. As long as Jamie was healthy and happy, that was all that mattered. For a time she had wondered if he might continue following in his father's footsteps, work his way up in the union, join the Labour Party, fight elections. Jamie however, had shown no more aptitude for this than he had done for studying for his School Leaving Certificate. In a way she was thankful. As things were, Jamie was not only happy and content, he was at home. Maybe he went too often to football matches. He played football a lot too and he went to the pictures and to the dancing. But he always came home for his meals and his bed. Home was his base. 'And long may it continue to be so.' She often expressed this fervent wish to Agnes.

'Has it never occurred to you,' Agnes said, 'that different and unusual things have happened to you? My life in comparison has been so dull and ordinary.'

'How do you mean?' Victoria was intrigued.

Agnes nibbled uncertainly at her lips. 'Perhaps it's because you've such a dramatic personality. You attract dramatic things.'

Victoria's head tipped up and pleasure hovered around her mouth. One of the things that endeared Agnes to her was the fact that her friend had such a keen appreciation of the finer points of her character. 'Och, don't be daft!' she said.

'You being connected like that to a man like Forbes-Cunningham is like something you'd see in the pictures or read in a book. And didn't you once know that woman who owns "Rory's"?'

'Huh! I knew her when she was running about in her bare feet and looking a right wee tramp in parish clothes.'

'No!'

'I'm telling you.'

'You see what I mean?'

41

'I think I can truthfully say,' Victoria patted her hair and pushed up the deep waves that flowed majestically over her head, 'that I had a small part in setting her on the right road. Her father was a petty crook, you know.'

'No!'

'And her brothers were proper little gangsters.'

'Oh my, who would credit it? And her such a posh lady.'

Victoria was tempted really to cause a sensation and tell her friend about how Rory had got herself into trouble and pleaded with her to help with her abortion. Neither of them had known what an abortion meant at the time. Sid somebody-or-other, who had got Rory into trouble, had given the assurance that all that was inside Rory was a wee bag with a spot or two of blood, and if she burst the bag the spots of blood would come away and she would be all right again. It still made her shudder to think of how she and Rory secreted themselves in her mother's wash-house in the back green one night and how Rory had struggled to get a steel knitting needle up inside her. But the real horror had been the rush of blood and flesh that had suddenly flooded over the wash-house floor. They had both been hysterical with terror. Somehow, however, she had managed to wash the floor clean and to help bind Rory up.

It had been the first time she had seen a woman's private parts and to see them stained in such a ghoulish manner had shocked and horrified her. She felt sick even now, remembering. She decided not to mention anything about the incident to Agnes. Apart from her revulsion at the mere thought of what had happened, her sense of loyalty to Rory remained, although she had long since lost touch with her. They were both still in the city of Glasgow, yet they lived in different worlds.

'She used to go with Matthew,' she told Agnes.

'No!'

'Before he met me, of course.'

'Fancy!'

'Och, yes,' Victoria made a nonchalant flick of her hand. 'And even after we were married, they remained friends – off and on – for years.'

Agnes's thin bespectacled face creased up with anxiety. 'Dear, dear,' she murmured in sympathy.

'Och!' Victoria laughed. 'There was nothing like that. My man would never look at another woman in a wrong way. He has his faults, but he's a good-living modest man and always has been.'

6

'What's your name, hen?' The old woman did not seem to
fit into a bungalow in posh Bishopbriggs, her big gaunt
frame and cadaverous face had a leathery toughness totally
unlike the owners of the other houses at which Amelia had
called. There was also a piercing directness in the faded eyes
that increased Amelia's uneasiness.

'Amelia Drummond.'

'I knew it! I'm Annie McElpy. Come on in.'

'I'm awfully sorry . . . but you see, I've still all these
pamphlets . . .'

'Och, you've plenty of time for that. Anyway, nobody
reads them. The Tory ones get flung straight into the
bucket. After a quick shifty at your da's photo it goes the
same road. He hasn't changed much, by the way. Come on.
Don't just stand there like a frightened rabbit.' One of the
woman's bony hands grabbed Amelia and hauled her into
the house. 'I've got a pot of tea ready made. I was just
having a cup.'

'No, really, Mrs McElpy, I . . .'

'Sit down and I'll pour you one.'

After being marched into the kitchen at the back of the
house Amelia was pushed none too gently down on to a
spar-backed chair.

'I'm glad of anybody coming to the door these days. I
miss having a blether with my neighbours in Cowlairs
Road. Gems of neighbours they were. You could be dead
and buried here and nobody would know or fucking care.'

Amelia's cheeks burned scarlet. It was the first time she
had ever heard a woman swear. Indeed the only time she
had heard this word uttered by anyone was when passing a
derelict piece of ground where some men were hunkered
down playing pitch-and-toss. One of the players had
shouted, 'Fuck that!' and another man had nudged him and

44

said, 'Watch your tongue in front of the wee lassie.' She had blushed then too.

'My daughter forced Scrap and me to come out here.' Annie McElpy continued, oblivious to Amelia's embarrassment. 'Cowlairs Road isn't good enough for her now. She used to know your mammy and daddy. Thick as thieves your mammy and her were when they were young.'

'Were they?' Amelia forgot her confusion in an upsurge of curiosity.

Annie poured a black-looking brew into a cup and put it on the table in front of Amelia. 'Help yourself to milk and sugar, hen. Och aye, thick as thieves they were.' She shook her head, remembering. 'Right from the primary school. Rory used to think your mammy was that clever. It was Victoria says this and Victoria says that. I used to get sick to my back teeth hearing about bloody Victoria.'

'Rory of "Rory's" big department store, you mean?' Amelia could hardly believe her ears.

'The very one. Now she thinks she's the bees' knees. She went with your daddy at one time. Thick as thieves they were as well until yer daddy ditched her and married yer mammy.'

Amelia had heard her mother boast about once knowing Rory, but she'd never taken her seriously. Her mother could tell so many stories, and mix facts and fiction until the facts became confused and lost altogether in the creation of a dramatic tale. Amelia never knew where she was, either with what her mother said or did.

'Daft about yer daddy she was.'

'Was she?'

'God, aye!'

Amelia had taken an unconscious sip of the tea while still gazing hypnotically at the older woman. Now she coughed and grued at its tarry taste.

'Forgot the sugar, did you, hen?' Annie sympathized. 'She got married to a newspaper man in the end. Tough as old boots is Donovan. Scrap and I hope he'll put the brakes on her.'

'Scrap?'

'My man.'

'That's a funny name!'

'Och, he was called that as a wean because he was such a wee scrap of a thing. Then when he grew up. . . ,' her pendulous breasts jerked with sudden laughter. 'Mind you, he never grew over five feet. He was still called Scrap because he was always in a scrap. He's led me a merry dance all my life that man. In and out of Barlinnie like a yo-yo he was. He's got too old for fighting and thieving, though. If he nicks anything now it's just out of habit.'

Amelia felt as if she was sitting through a dream. She often experienced this sense of unreality when things got beyond her. Sometimes she thought she was going mad. Like when she sat in company listening to her mother say to people, 'Oh yes, Matthew is a wonderful husband. We have a perfect relationship. Never one angry word has ever passed between us.' Had she imagined the unholy row that had just taken place behind the closed doors of 23 Hilltop Road? Was the background of constant bitterness and conflict only a dream? She had, it could be argued, an even more vivid imagination than her mother. Not that she ever verbalized these imaginings, but they lit up her head like beacons every time she was alone, curled up in her daddy's big chair. Sometimes she even wrote things down.

'You've a look of your daddy about you,' Annie said, then enjoyed a slurp of tea. 'As soon as I saw you at the door I said to myself, that's the Drummond lassie.'

'I haven't got black hair like mummy or daddy,' Amelia said.

'You've his look. And you're pale and thin like him. But its yer look, hen. I mind him as a young man. An odd sort of bloke he was. He never knocked about with any pals. It was just politics with him. Always very serious he was. But between you and me, hen, I had a soft spot for him. He was an odd sort of bloke right enough, but he was a perfect gentleman to me, that man.'

'He's home just now,' Amelia said.

'Aye, I know. For the election. No harm to your da, hen,

46

but if a bloody donkey stood for Labour here, he would get in. Springburn's always been a Labour place.'

'But this ward . . .'

'Bishopbriggs? Och, they'll never swing it. He's got *my* vote anyway, hen. And my man's.'

'Thanks very much. Now, I really must go, Mrs McElpy.' She rose and was somewhat taken aback by the momentary disappointment revealed by the older woman's expression.

'Och well. I suppose I can't keep you here all day. I'll maybe go and see my old pals in Cowlairs Road later on. I'm not so able now to climb on and off the trams. My legs are letting me down.'

'Oh, dear.'

'The worst of it is, my man's still like a wee ferret and I can't catch him now.' She gave another heave of laughter. 'Stupid wee bugger. Have you got a fella, hen?' She kept talking all the way behind Amelia to the outside door.

'No.'

'Aye, you'll be a loner like yer da. You've got that same look. He got hitched in the end though and so will you, hen.'

Amelia lowered her eyes and tried to smile. 'Cheerio, Mrs McElpy.'

'Cheerio, hen.'

Annie kept standing at the open door, arms folded across her chest, her eyes following Amelia's progress as she went along the street pushing pamphlets through letter-boxes. Amelia was both annoyed and embarrassed at being watched. She quickened her pace until she was practically running, getting more annoyed and harassed by the minute.

Only later when she was safely in her bedroom did she think calmly of the incident and realize that Annie McElpy was lonely. She felt sorry for the woman. She imagined herself returning to keep Annie company, and Annie welcoming her with open arms and being eternally grateful and telling her how wonderful she was. At the same time, Amelia knew she would never be able to bring herself to set foot in the place again. It was always the same, part of her wanted to be sociable and outgoing, and also to believe she would be made welcome and be acceptable in social situations. In her day-dreams, she was. The other part of her, however, was agonizingly shy and gauche, a cauldron of insecurities and uncertainties. Still, she told herself, she *might* go back and see Annie McElpy one day. Meantime she wrote about the incident in one of her old school jotters. She enjoyed describing the woman in detail, from her head with its hair twisted on top like a sheaf of withered grey corn, down to her big feet encased in red checked woollen slippers with a fawn cuff round the ankle and a fawn pom-pom in front. Then she tried to describe what the feelings of Annie McElpy had been. She replayed every expression on the woman's face over and over again in her mind, as if she was watching a film, with the eyes especially in close-up. She ended up again with mixed feelings. First there was the strange pleasure at having captured something on paper. There, before her eyes, in her school jotter, was Annie McElpy. There was also the increased vulnerability she always experienced after such an exercise. She *felt* for Annie McElpy. But in getting under the skin of the other woman she had peeled away a skin of her own. She prickled and tensed all over with anxieties and exposed nerve endings.

'Oh, there you are, Amelia.' Suddenly her father was standing in the bedroom. He looked like a stranger. He had always been particular about his appearance and regularly pressed his suits and brushed his shoes. Now, however, there was not just a look of neatness about him, he had an air of elegance. Hastily she hid the jotter under the pillow. She was sitting on the edge of the bed and had not realized until now that the room had become shadowy and very cold.

'Are you all right?'

'Yes, I'm fine thanks, daddy.'

'Why are you sitting through here by yourself in the cold? Your mother has lit a fire and made hot cocoa.' He took a few steps towards her. 'Are you sure you're all right?'

'I'm fine.' She jerked to her feet and pushed past him. 'Are Jessie and Bridget there?'

'No,' he said, following her out. 'They're exhausted and no wonder. It's been a hard day for us all. I walked them home.'

'Where's Jamie?' She had detected the sigh as she passed him. Now she heard the bitterness in his voice when he answered.

'Oh, he'll be away enjoying himself. He'll be squiring a girl to some dance or other place of entertainment, no doubt.'

They were through in the living room now and her mother immediately snapped, 'And why not? Who do you think you are? Are Bridget and Jessie and Amelia and me and the army of helpers you've had not enough for you?'

'Amelia asked me a question,' Matthew said coldly. 'I answered it. That was all.'

'No, that was *not* all.' Victoria's eyes were sparkling with indignation. 'Every chance you get you pick on Jamie. Dear knows why, because a more decent better-doing lad nobody could meet.'

'And the apple of his mummy's eye,' Matthew said.

'It's a mercy someone cares about him for all the love or attention you've ever given him. You're too busy being Mr Wonderful to outsiders, people who don't care a tuppenny toss about you.'

'Why don't you just give it a rest, woman?'

Silently but fervently Amelia seconded Matthew's request. Sitting at the table, her head bowed over her cup of cocoa, she marvelled at how her mother never gave up. Usually her father never gave up either. He battled back, often going wild with temper, his eyes staring out of his deathly white face like a madman. Tonight he was too tired. Or at least she hoped he was too tired. Sometimes she wondered if they had argued and fought from the first moment they were joined together in unholy matrimony. She knew intuitively that they had shouted in anger and hatred at each other while she had been in the womb. There had never been a moment, even in her unborn existence, she felt certain, in which she had not suffered the miseries of conflict, not been in the process of having her life force chipped away.

49

'Oh, you'd like that, wouldn't you?'

'Indeed I would,' Matthew agreed in his polite Anglicized tones.

'Oh yes, oh yes,' Victoria was beginning to get into her stride. 'You'd like me to shut up and forget all the wicked, selfish things you've done. Well, I won't. Not while there's a breath left in my body. You talk about Jamie? That's the boy, don't forget, that you condemned to live in poverty.'

'Victoria, don't talk nonsense. Jamie is earning a living wage, and he's perfectly content and happy with what he's got. Indeed, if anything, that's a fault in him. He never gives a thought either to trying to better his own lot or that of his fellow workers.'

Amelia knew by this time that they would go on for hours. Her father had made the fatal mistake of commenting on Jamie. Jamie had always been their main bone of contention and an immediate trigger to Victoria's overdeveloped maternal defence mechanism. After finishing her cocoa, Amelia decided to go to bed and pull the blankets up over her ears.

'Goodnight, mummy. Goodnight, daddy.'

Neither of them heard her.

7

'Matty!'

Drummond looked round. A silver grey Rolls Royce was kerb-crawling beside him. The driver was an expensively dressed woman in an olive green suit, beige blouse and pillbox hat. 'Rory?'

'Who else?' She gave a sarcastic lift to her brows, but only for a second before her perky face broke into a grin. 'As soon as you saw the Rolls, you should have known it must be me.'

'There's no need to ask how you're getting on then.'

'For Christ's sake, get in. Do you want me to get arrested?'

He eased himself into the seat beside her and he was immediately enveloped in the heady aroma of expensive perfume. He noticed that her leather-gloved fingers kept tapping restlessly on the wheel. 'You haven't changed, Rory.'

'*You* have!'

He gazed thoughtfully out at the busy thoroughfare of Argyle Street. Then the car plunged into the echoing shadows of the 'highlandman's umbrella', the part of the street which went under the railway and was so nicknamed because it had become a meeting place for people from the Highlands who had come to work in Glasgow. 'No, I don't think so,' he murmured.

'In appearance, at least.'

'Ah, my grey hairs. I notice yours is still as vibrant red as ever.'

'No, I didn't mean that. You look much more sophisticated than you used to.'

He smiled. 'Perhaps you would be more accurate to say "mature". It's a long time since I was the gauche young man that you're remembering.'

She lightly touched his knee. 'You were an experienced lover though.'

His dark eyes slid her a sidelong glance. 'Thank you.'

'How's the election going?'

'We've had some well-attended meetings.'

'I was passing through Springburn to visit my mother in Bishopbriggs yesterday and I heard you shouting the odds through your loud-speaker. Could you not get something better than the Co-op bread van to tour the streets? Maybe I could have loaned you the Rolls if you'd asked.'

'I can't think of anything more incongruous for a Labour candidate.'

'You're still a firebrand then?'

'I've never thought of myself in those terms.'

'Don't kid yourself. You know as well as I do that you're as passionate in politics as you are in love-making.'

He laughed. 'You've always been positive and forceful in your views, Rory.'

'I've always known what I wanted and made damn sure that I got it.'

'You've worked hard and overcome a great deal of adversity. I admire you for that even though I cannot agree with your politics.'

She groaned. 'Even Donovan's gone bolshy on me now.'

He laughed again. 'Poor Rory. You never were very fortunate with men.'

'I'm taking you home for a drink. Donovan's there at the moment. I've been having a hell of a time with him. Maybe seeing you will put him in a better mood. God knows what it'll be like when he comes home for good.'

'There's bound to be a period of adjustment. It hasn't been easy in London, you know.'

'Has the Blitz affected you? Do you keep finding fault with Victoria and interfering with what she's trying to do? And don't forget we've had our share of hardships and bombing here too.'

'Oh, nothing like London, Rory. Except perhaps Clydebank. The people of London have suffered terribly.'

'Not Donovan,' she said bitterly. 'All he wants is to make me suffer.'

'I find that very difficult to believe.'

'You don't know him.'

'How are the twins? They must be – what – seventeen now?'

Rory's face immediately brightened. 'They're fine. They're on holiday from art school. Both of them are very talented. I'll show you some of their work when we get home. Douglas especially is a really good painter.'

'They did exceptionally well at school, I remember. They were always a couple of classes ahead of their peers.'

Rory was radiating pride. 'And they got into art school younger than anyone else has ever done before.'

'Life's a puzzle, isn't it? I have always been very serious about education and tried to encourage both Jamie and Amelia to study and improve themselves intellectually but . . .' He sighed and looked away again.

'Knowing you, you've been *too* serious,' Rory said. 'You do go on a bit, darling. Your son's on the railway?'

'Yes.'

'Maybe he's aiming to follow in your footsteps.'

'He has no political inclinations, if that's what you mean.'

'And your daughter – what's her name again?' She stretched and stiffened her arms, arching her body for a second before relaxing her grip on the wheel again, and it occurred to him how well she had kept her lithe youthful figure. There had always been, he realized now, this barely suppressed energy about her, much of it sexual.

'Amelia.'

'What's she doing?'

'Nothing at the moment. She's just left school. It doesn't matter so much about her, of course.'

For the first time Rory took her eyes off the road and stared round at him. 'Oh? And why not?'

'Because she's a girl and the chances are she'll get married eventually. Meantime I'll be quite happy if she stays at home and is a help to her mother. Amelia wanted to look for a job, I believe, but her mother told her she was needed in

53

the house. Victoria is kept so busy organizing fund-raising events for the party and all her other activities, she hasn't time for housework.'

'Christ! You're worse than Donovan. These aren't bloody Victorian times.'

'Not every woman is like you, Rory.'

'What's that supposed to mean?'

Matthew smiled. 'You're as tough as most men, at least in spirit. And you're as hard-boiled and ambitious as anyone in the business world. Amelia's not like that.' His gaze became thoughtful. 'Although I sometimes detect an element of stubbornness about her despite her timidity.'

'She's probably just perverse like you.'

'The sins of the fathers. . . .'

'Something like that.'

'Poor Amelia.'

'There you go, being too serious again. Nobody's perfect. Victoria's not perfect.'

'It's sad how everything can go wrong though. I had such dreams of perfection when I was young.'

'The trouble with you is, you're an idealist, Matthew.'

'Damn it! You've known me longer than anyone else. How can you of all people say that?'

'Because it's true.'

'No, it is not true.' His voice angrily clipped out the words. 'You know my background.'

'Your background wasn't all that worse than mine. But if I discovered, as you did, that Alexander Forbes-Cunningham was my real father, I would have welcomed him and his money with open arms. That's being a realist.'

'I disagree.'

'I know you do. You're too bloody class-conscious, Matty. You've too much class loyalty. What has your precious fellow working man ever done for you?'

'From the Tolpuddle Martyrs through Keir Hardie and . . .'

'Oh, don't give me a lecture on politics or dig up people who are dead and gone long ago. Forget them. You're too much affected by the past. You're stuck in it.'

'We're what our past made us. And I refuse to forget the debt I owe to working men, including John Drummond, the man who *was* a father to me. I refuse to forget how they have been exploited and their lives reduced to miserable existences . . .'

'But it's the present you're supposed to be concerned with. Is this all you do in Parliament? Keep dragging up the past? You must bore the pants off them all.'

'I try my best and I believe I succeed in being a good parliamentarian.'

'Now you're in a huff. Never mind, I'll give you a good belt of whisky when we get in. That'll cheer you up. We're nearly there.'

'I never drink when I'm at home now.'

'Why not? You always did before. It was one of Victoria's major gripes, if I remember.'

He hesitated, then, moving his gaze around to the side window, he said, 'Anything for a peaceful life, I suppose.'

'Not you!' Rory scoffed. 'Pull the other one.'

He shrugged. 'All right. I accept the invitation to have a drink with you and Donovan.'

She stopped the car. 'Here we are then. What do you think of it?'

Drummond unfolded his long legs from the Rolls and stood up. The substantially built villa towering at the top of a steeply sloping driveway was typical of the dwelling places of successful Glasgow businessmen. Pollokshields was a favourite residential area for such men because of its spacious well-planned streets, lined with mature trees, and the facility with which the district could be reached from the city centre. 'In one way,' he said, 'I find it hard to believe. But . . .'

She interrupted him in her breezy cocksure voice. 'That a cheap floosy from the slummiest part of Springburn could end up owning a big villa like this?'

'No.' His tone grew gentler and he touched her arm. 'You were never that.'

'You thought I was that when you ditched me.' They walked together up the sloping driveway, her high heels stabbing into the gravel. 'Not that it matters a damn now, of course,' she added.

'The point I'm trying to make is that, although it seems incredible that a girl from such a poor background could acquire all the wealth and position that such a dwelling house symbolizes, knowing you it is not surprising. You're a fighter, Rory. And a survivor.'

She had taken out a gold cigarette case and selected a cigarette. After lighting up with a matching lighter she sent a jet of smoke piercing upwards, then said, 'At the moment I'm having to fight Donovan and that's never been easy.'

'I was just remembering how the two of you conducted a strange kind of battling courtship in public in the *Evening Citizen*.'

'I can't use those tactics this time. He's still got this idiotic obsession about my business methods, but he's criticizing how I've brought up the children as well.'

Drummond drew down his brows. 'In what way does he believe you have erred?'

Rory jabbed her key in the door. 'God knows!'

Donovan was half a head taller than Drummond and heavier-built. Indeed no two men could have looked more different. Donovan's head was a thick crown of springy curls whereas Drummond had longish straight hair. It was Donovan's ruggedness and his hard chips of eyes, however, that made the sharpest contrast to Drummond's lean sensitive appearance.

'Drummond!' Donovan bounced up from his seat and strode forward, his big spade of a hand outstretched. 'Good to see you. How long's it been?'

Drummond smiled. 'I believe the last occasion was when you visited the House of Commons.'

'Yeah! For the film. Sit down, Mat. Make yourself at home. You'll have come up to Glasgow for the election?'

'That's correct. Are you still making films, Donovan?'

'I just do the research and write the scripts. Propaganda shit most of them. They'd be worse, though, if some of the old generals got their way. It was a hell of a job trying to make them see sense. I wasn't allowed to talk to them until I

56

was commissioned, of course. Before that I had to go along to discuss each project through a lieutenant or captain who knew nothing about the subject. He just had to come along because it wasn't the done thing for someone in the ranks to speak on equal terms with a general. A load of shit!'

'Whisky?' Rory asked.

Drummond nodded his acceptance, then he said to Donovan, 'You'll be looking forward to returning home for good.'

'Yeah. Shouldn't be long now.'

'You think not?'

'I bet you a fiver the Jap war will be over before the end of the year.'

'Let's hope your prophecy will prove correct.'

'Cheers!' Donovan lifted his glass, and Drummond said, 'I wish you a happy return to civilian life.'

Rory laughed. 'You knocked that back as if you needed it, Matty. Have another. Let's all have another. Let's all get pissed.'

Drummond eyed the bottle that Rory was holding out. 'You surely had a great stroke of luck getting a bottle of whisky, Rory.'

'Not luck. Black market.' Donovan's voice hardened. 'She's got enough booze stacked away to keep a publican happy. And that's not all. The war has made no difference to our Rory. Except to make her richer.'

'That's a lie,' Rory said.

'Not black market?' Donovan queried in mock surprise.

Drummond shook his head. 'If this *is* the case, Rory, you could find yourself in serious trouble.'

'Save your breath,' Donovan lit a cigarette and leaned back in his chair. 'She won't listen. But I've warned her. As soon as I'm demobbed and back home for good, the first thing I intend doing is sort her out whether she likes it or not.'

'Oh, shut up!' Rory said. 'The pair of you!'

8

Contrary to the normal belief about what twins felt about one another, Helena didn't like her brother Douglas very much. He was a spoiled conceited brat. Although what he had to be conceited about she could not imagine. He wasn't that good-looking. He was the same height as her and had the same dark auburn hair, only his was cropped short. He was also stockily built, not slim like her. Although she had a shapely figure that she was accentuating at the moment with a new uplift bra that pushed her breasts into high peaks underneath her cream-coloured sweater. It was Douglas's air of insolence that irritated her most.

He had talent, she had to admit. Everyone said he had astonishing originality. Sometimes, though, she thought it was more nerve and conceit than talent and originality. He was the same in everything and he had been the same as far back as she could remember. He had to be the first to blow out the birthday candles. He had to have the first slice of the cake. He had to have something different and better than she did as a present. At school he always had to be first in exams and the winner at every sport. She had tried her damnedest to keep up with him but he had always pipped her at the post. He had been dux of the school eventually. She would not have minded his obsessive competitiveness; she enjoyed a challenge. If only he didn't gloat. It was his main and most unlikeable characteristic. Not that he indulged in this with everyone all the time. He could be exceptionally charming when it suited him. He boasted ad nauseam about his sexual conquests. All virgins, of course. She might have thought he was lying, and have put it down to something that most young men did to hide their inadequacies and prop up their male egos. However, Veronica, to mention but one friend, had admitted that she had lost her virginity to Douglas. Veronica in fact had been crazy about him and been broken-hearted when he had tired of her and began looking around for another conquest.

'You're a rotten selfish bastard,' she had raged at him on Veronica's behalf. 'I hope you end up with somebody exactly like yourself.'

He had only laughed at her and said. 'Impossible! I'm unique!'

'What obnoxious conceit! I hate you!'

Her mother complained as usual. 'Twins are supposed to be close. What the hell's wrong with you two? I can't understand the pair of you.'

Her mother was never around much to do any understanding. Her shop kept her occupied most of each day and often she was out wining and dining business contacts in the evening. Winnie, the housekeeper, had looked after them most of the time since childhood and both she and Douglas could twist Winnie round their little fingers. Rory gave each of them as much money as they wanted and everything that money could buy, which was fine as far as they were concerned. Specially considering that she never questioned them on how they spent it. Douglas in particular spent a lot on drink and Donovan had been criticizing him about this. For once she had been in agreement with Douglas when he had said, 'Father's got a bloody cheek trying to tell me what to do. Look at him and that crowd of drunken journalist bums he calls friends!'

It was their one area of total agreement. Their father was unfair and, of course, dead boring. 'I usually managed to avoid him before,' Douglas said. 'But now he's here nearly every week-end it's absolute shit.'

'I know,' Helena sympathized. 'And just think what it's going to be like when he's here all the time. I mean, can you imagine?'

'He's got a bloody cheek. After all, we're nearly eighteen. We're old enough to do what we like.'

'Not until we're twenty-one, according to him. We're not even supposed to get the key of the door until then. I mean, honestly, did you ever?'

'Our only hope is his job,' Douglas said.

'How do you mean?'

'Well, he used to work all sorts of hours and often he was sent away on assignments, sometimes abroad.'

That cheered Helena up. She was by nature an optimist anyway. 'I forgot about that. Oh well, it shouldn't be so bad.'

It was not that she did not love her father. She did. And she was sure that Douglas did too. Donovan had been fun when they were small. He had played games with them. She remembered him throwing them up in the air and catching them and swinging them about, making them squeal with laughter. She remembered him telling stories and taking them for walks, and generally spending more time and giving them more attention than her mother ever had. Looking back, it occurred to Helena that what had started her parents fighting had been the fact that Rory was devoting so much time to the shop and not enough time to her family. Certainly this was so after the war started. Before the war, as far as she could recall, everything had been all right. They had gone as a family to the seaside then and to the zoo and for picnics in the country. She could remember Rory and Donovan holding hands or clutching each other round the waist as they walked, or gazing into each other's eyes like lovers.

Her mother said the war had brought difficulties for her business. She could not get staff, and then rationing and all sorts of other irritations meant she was 'up to her eyes in it'. Her mother had to be admired for making such a success of the shop despite the war. And nobody in 'Rory's' was allowed to be cheeky and act like little Hitlers either. Not like in other shops. It was awful to go into a shop for things like notepaper and envelopes in order to write to a boyfriend in the forces, only to be met with an impudent 'Do you not know there's a war on?' If it was not that, it was 'Do you not know what "It's in short supply" means?' or 'Our quota's been sold long ago!'

Clothes were not so bad because her mother could usually help out. There were many other things, however, like make-up and sweets and cigarettes where she was not any help at all. It was a terrible nuisance having to search round all the shops looking for her favourite pancake make-up or a dark blue and silver bottle of Evening in Paris perfume. As far as cigarettes were concerned she was sick to death of the taste and smell of Pasha cigarettes. She was sure they must be made of sweaty old socks. The worst of it was the way shopkeepers flung them at you and had the cheek to tell you that you were lucky to get anything. Winnie, who did most of the shopping for food, hated shopkeepers and could not get used to being given purchases such as fish unwrapped. Winne was a tiny, ladylike person with grey hair neatly plaited into earphones. Douglas and Helena had collapsed laughing one day when, on their way home from art school, they had met her walking along the street, her nose screwed up in disgust and holding four kippers by their tails as far as possible from her clothes. The iniquity of shopkeepers was Winnie's favourite topic of conversation, although she had never been brave enough to put her criticism into words in front of the actual offenders. Butchers included too much bone in one's shillingworth of meat. Grocers included rind in one's miserable two ounces of cheese. Far from openly criticizing people like those, however, Winnie, along with most customers now, pleaded to be allowed to buy anything from them.

Winne was just as worried about Donovan coming home as they were but for different reasons. 'How am I going to find enough food to feed a big man like your father?' She had a habit of worriedly shaking her head and muttering to herself. The problems caused by food rationing were making her do this in an absent-minded way nearly all the time now. 'Your mother always manages the miracle of getting bottles of whisky. I wish she'd try a bit harder and work some of her magic in producing extra food,' she kept telling Douglas and Helena.

'My main worry,' Helena confessed to Douglas, 'is what he will do once we go back to art school. I mean, it'll be just awful if he tries to spoil our all-night parties. Do you think he will?'

Douglas's mouth primped in readiness for his mimicking

61

voice. ' "It'll be just awful if he tries to spoil our all-night parties. Do you think he will?" What a damn silly question,' he added, reverting to his normal tone. 'Do you think he's going to let you stay out all night drinking and fucking?'

'Oh, you are coarse,' she said, but laughing at the same time. 'Well, if he thinks he's going to spoil my fun, he has another think coming.'

'What are you going to do? He's bigger than you, remember. And he's the type who would resort to violence. He'll have you over his knee, what do you bet?'

Helena laughed again. 'He'd have to catch me first.' All the same she felt uneasy. She knew from past experience she could not twist her father round her little finger. Even her mother had never been able to do that. 'You just worry about yourself and leave me to take care of number one.'

Douglas shrugged. 'Oh, I wasn't worried about you. On the contrary, the more father guns for you the less he's likely to notice what I'm up to.'

'Oh, thanks very much.' Helena strolled over to gaze out of the sitting room window, her flared skirt undulating out with the sensuous movement of her hips. She could hear a loud speaker's hollow echoing cry in the distance. Pushing back the port-wine-coloured curtains she pressed her face closer to the glass. 'It's the Tory candidate's car. It's just turned into our street.'

'Not interested.'

'Did you know that mother knows a Labour candidate? She's known him for ages. Since she was young.'

'You're joking!'

'No, honestly. He was here the other day when I came in. A tall slim man. Handsome in fact, quite striking and distinguished-looking.'

'A Labour candidate?' Douglas scoffed.

'I wonder if mother and him ever had a love affair?'

'You've a one-track mind. Do you ever think of anything else?'

'Why shouldn't she have? I wouldn't mind one myself with a man like that.'

'If he's of mother's generation he must be old enough to be your father.'

'So what?'

'Is that why you're mooning about at the window? Are you expecting him to arrive for another visit?'

'No, I'm waiting for Eddie.'

'Don't tell me, let me guess, Eddie's a Yank!'

'What's wrong with Yanks?'

'Nothing, I suppose, as long as we realize they're foreigners. Or so the paper says.'

'What paper?' she giggled. 'Let me see.'

He tossed a newspaper in her direction and she picked it up from where it landed at her feet. The paper advised:

Remember that:

1   Americans are foreigners. Only a small percentage have British forebears.

2   The similarity between our languages is misleading.

3   They are all young in spirit as well as body and that the mistakes they make are likely to spring from too quick enthusiasm and too little 'background'.

4   Though we may be spiritually far more civilized, materially they have the advantage.

5   Like all children they are very sensitive. They mistake our British reticence and reserve for the cold shoulder and positive dislike.

'How bloody patronizing,' Helena said.

'Anyway,' Douglas relaxed back in his chair and put his feet up on the coffee table, 'they'll not be worrying about your cold shoulder. They'll be far too busy with your hot arse!'

Normally she could stand any amount of teasing from anyone. Anyone that is, except Douglas. There was a nastiness about him that was seldom funny. 'Do you know something?' she said and meant it, 'I'll be really sorry for the woman who eventually gets you.'

9

'Here's to the future,' Jessie McGregor, her chipmunk cheeks flushed with triumph, raised her glass of parsnip wine. 'It's in good hands with men like Matthew Drummond as our newly elected Labour Member of Parliament.'

A wild burst of cheering hit the roof of the Springburn Public Hall. Amelia lifted her glass and took a sip. She did not cheer. Cheering or any unbridled show of emotion either made her squirm with embarrassment or nudged her dangerously near the brink of tears. She was pleased and relieved that her father had succeeded. She was also in her own way enjoying the party celebrating his landslide victory. She and her mother, Mrs McDade, Jessie and Bridget, had worked a miracle in producing a spread of cakes and sandwiches on the long trestle table. Jessie, despite being shaped like a plum pudding, was light on her feet and enormously energetic. Bridget was slimmer, slower-moving, and much more ladylike. But it was her mother, as Mrs McDade put it, who 'took the biscuit'. Her mother had nerve enough for anything and had not only gone round all the shops persuading shopkeepers to give her extra bits of dried egg and fat and sugar, but even went knocking on doors asking the residents of Springburn to help out.

Her mother used a variety of methods to obtain what she needed or wanted. She used charm, something she had in abundance. This encompassed kindliness, like saying, 'That's an awful cold you've got, Mrs McAskill. I'll take your turn of washing the stairs this week. No, dear, I insist.' Or sometimes it was 'Amelia will take your turn of the stairs. Of course, dear. She'll be delighted!' Or she'd be a sympathetic listener to someone's long tale of woe, eventually dispensing confident words of encouragement like, 'God is our comfort and our strength, Mrs Saunders. Have faith in Him and He'll help you through these dark hours.'

It wasn't that her mother was being hypocritical. On the contrary, her mother's belief and faith in God were totally sincere. She said her prayers every night. At some part of every day she sat reading her well-thumbed Bible. She often said to Amelia, 'God will provide,' or 'The good Lord will protect us.' It was as if Victoria had a personal knowledge and a long-standing relationship with God. She was especially convinced that God was on her side in any conflict with Matthew. 'God will punish you for that,' she'd warn him. 'In his own good time, he'll wreak vengeance.' Or she'd worriedly confide in Amelia, 'Fancy your daddy saying he didn't like hymn-singing and switching off the wireless like that while people were singing God's praises. He'll have a bad end yet, that man.'

The election, however, had come to a good end and even Drummond who was normally stiff and ill at ease in any social situation seemed tolerably relaxed. He smiled through his protective air of dignity, and clinked glasses and talked to his helpers, charming the women especially, with his polite and obviously sincere words of thanks. Amelia experienced a sense of pride as she watched him. She had always felt like this. At least, pride was one of the strands in the tangled skein of her emotions for him. As if sensing her gaze he turned and, smiling, came towards her.

'Are you pleased?' he asked.

'Of course.'

He put an arm around her shoulders and drew her affectionately close to him. 'Thank you for all your help, Amelia. You worked extremely hard on my behalf.'

She allowed herself to be embraced but only for a second before she willed herself to shrink smaller until she was able to wriggle away. 'I'm so glad you had such a good win, daddy,' she said in a desperate attempt to make up for the hurt she detected in his eyes. 'I really am. But you deserve it. You're the best MP in the whole of the Labour Party.'

65

His laughter made the hurt retreat into his inner eye. 'I doubt it, Amelia; but as long as you think so.'

She hated hurting him and hated herself every time she did so. Confusion and regret added to the jumble of her other emotions.

'Is that you away in a dream again?' Her mother's voice shook her muddled mind like a terrier. 'Don't just stand there like a knotless thread. Go and help pass the sandwiches round.'

Obediently she moved about the hall holding out plates of grey-coloured bread filled with mock banana and mock meat paste. She prayed that no one in the happily chatting crowd would try to draw her into their conversations. Nobody did. The sandwiches disappeared. Then the victory sponge cake; the siege cake and the sour milk pancakes. The Red Flag and finally Auld Lang Syne were lustily sung before people began drifting contentedly away. Only Amelia, her mother and father, Mr and Mrs McDade, Bridget Dunbar and Jessie McGregor were left to clear up the debris. The women busied themselves stacking dirty plates and cups and saucers, and wiping crumbs from the tables and sweeping the floors. Mr McDade and Drummond stood talking, Mr McDade in his usual loud and expansive way, while Drummond was smiling, an expression of polite interest clinging to his face. His back was to the door, however, as if ready at the first possible moment to make his escape. Amelia couldn't blame him. He had done his share of talking these past three weeks, both publicly and socially. He deserved some peace and quiet on his own now.

'That's it, then.' Victoria surveyed the cleared hall. 'Now we can get home to our beds. I don't know about you but I'm ready for mine.'

'Not me,' Jessie said, still bouncing about shifting chairs. 'I could've danced all night.'

'Well, I couldn't have played the piano all night. I don't know where you get all your energy. Especially with you being so fat.'

Amelia cringed at her mother's lack of sensitivity but

Jessie was made of tougher stuff. 'I'm not fat, Victoria. I'm generously moulded.'

Victoria laughed. 'Don't be daft. Come on. Leave these chairs alone. I've away up the hill to Balornock to go, remember? Matthew!' She raised her voice. 'Are you going to stand there talking all night?'

Drummond slid her a look of dark disapproval before smiling and continuing to speak to the sedately adoring Bridget, who always wore her best hat with her mother's pearls and gold watch when in Drummond's company. She also wore her home-knitted twin-sets with her best black skirt, and Matthew's words of praise on her smart appearance never failed to bring a flush of pleasure to her sallow cheeks. Both she and Jessie lived in Springburn within a step or two of the hall.

'And none of your black looks.' Victoria's voice forced its way over his. 'Talk about Dr Jekyll and Mr Hyde!'

One part of Amelia's mind told her that her mother and father could not possibly quarrel tonight. For one thing they were bound to be far too tired. Another part of her knew that nothing could stop them. At the moment, because Mr and Mrs McDade would be walking up to Balornock with them, the quarrel had the appearance of light-hearted banter. Only once their own front door was shut did it twist into bitter earnest. Jamie had been at the party but he had left earlier to take a girl called Fiona Marshall home.

'I don't know what he sees in that girl,' Victoria had said, 'and he seems to be going steady with her now.'

Amelia, remembering the stunning blonde with the starry eyelashes and rosebud mouth, wondered if her mother was needing glasses.

It was not until after her father had returned to London next day that Jamie and Fiona dropped their bombshell. They were going to get married. Worse, they *had* to get married. Her mother was shocked and stunned. She rallied bravely, however, and after heaving a big sigh she said, 'Oh well, what's done's done. With God's help we'll just have to make the best of it. Do your mother and father know?' she asked the saintly smiling Fiona.

'My mother's a widow and she knows. She was naturally worried at first about how we'd manage, but I can manage on a fireman's pay and I wouldn't mind if we couldn't get a house to rent because of the housing shortage. I'm not a worrier like my mother.'

'What do you mean "at first"?' Victoria asked. 'Is she all right about everything now?'

'Oh yes. After I told her about Jamie's grandfather, she was.'

Victoria looked puzzled for a minute. 'Jamie's grandfather?'

'Mr Alexander Forbes-Cunningham, or rather,' Fiona's smile reflected like a beacon of triumph in her eyes, '*Sir* Alexander Forbes-Cunningham as he is now.'

'I see,' said Victoria.

Amelia saw as well. Later she could not help but agree with her mother who kept wringing her hands and repeating, 'I knew it! I knew it! That girl doesn't care about my Jamie. She's a right little gold-digger if ever I saw one.'

Now her mother said coldly, 'Oh, him? We don't recognize that branch of the family.'

'Why not?' Fiona asked sweetly.

'It's a long story,' said Victoria, and the disapproval on her face added 'and none of your business.'

'Oh, but now that I'm going to be one of the family I think I ought to know.'

Jamie intervened then. 'Och, I told you, Fiona. It's dad!'

'My husband,' Victoria said with dignity, 'was very sorely used by Sir Alexander Forbes-Cunningham.'

'Really?' Fiona's large blue eyes widened.

Jamie said, 'I told you. Grandma Drummond used to work in the Forbes-Cunningham house. That was when Sir Alexander was a young man and he took a fancy to her. Dad was the result.'

'Is it *really* true?' Fiona asked breathlessly.

'Would I lie to you?' Jamie laughed. 'Of course it's true. Not only that, my grandpa Drummond worked in Sir Alexander's pit.'

'Yes,' said Victoria grimly, 'and that was the death of him

more than anything else. A man that brought my husband up without one word or brass farthing of help from Sir Alexander. A man who was a real father to him. My husband has never forgiven Sir Alexander Forbes-Cunningham and I don't blame him.'

Amelia thought this was incredible. It was one of the countless times while listening to her mother she could hardly believe her ears. Victoria had been blaming Matthew unceasingly as far back as she could remember.

'It's the Christian thing to do,' Fiona said, 'to forgive those who ill use us and to turn the other cheek.'

Amelia trembled inside. It was the wrong thing to say to her mother if Fiona wanted to get on with her. But maybe she did not. Her mother drew herself up to her full height.

'I don't need a slip of a girl like you to tell me how to be a Christian, Fiona. I was a good Christian woman long before you were born or knew the meaning of the word. What we're talking about here is true love and loyalty. My husband loved and was loyal to the man who brought him up. My husband was and always will be a good man. A man of high principle. He was not tempted by power and riches.'

'Yes, Mr Drummond is a wonderful man, isn't he?' Fiona fluttered her lashes. 'And a wonderful speaker. He had me absolutely spellbound at his last meeting.'

Nothing more was said about Sir Alexander Forbes-Cunningham. But as Victoria remarked later and Amelia could not help agreeing with her, 'That two-faced little gold-digger is up to something!'

10

Drummond could not get over the thrill of being summoned to number 10 Downing Street after the election. His mind reeled with the excitement of the visit and his impressions of the place. It was as if a brightly coloured film kept running and re-running through his brain. In the cramped bedroom of his digs he sat motionless in a chair by the unlit gas fire, his dark eyes seeing nothing of his shabby surroundings.

He was reminded of how he had felt the first time he had entered the Palace of Westminster and taken his seat in the House of Commons. He had a strong sense of history and he had been deeply affected by Parliament. After all, the British Parliament was the Mother of Parliaments and her offspring were to be found all over the world. This was because at the British Parliament bitter battles had been fought and won. The battle against the absolute rule of the monarchy, the battle for free reporting so that the country could know what the legislators were doing, to name but two.

He had stood in Westminster Hall on that first day and thrilled to the history of the place. Here had also stood Sir Thomas More, one of the highest in the land. Here in 1535 More had been condemned to death because he would not recognize Henry VIII's divorce and marriage to Ann Boleyn. Here Guy Fawkes was tried and then hanged, drawn and quartered in the 'new' Palace Yard. Here Charles the First was tried and condemned to death.

Here for centuries were the headquarters of the law courts. Here was where the saying 'Men of Straw' originated. They were the 'Witnesses' who were willing to swear to anything, and they wore a wisp of straw in their shoes to show it. The anger and bitterness of all the injustices that had been suffered down through the centuries, mixed with

Drummond's pride in the fact that men had continued and were still continuing to struggle tenaciously for freedom and justice. Now he was part of that struggle. He wished his father could have known and shared his pride. And oh, if only his father could have known about Prime Minister Attlee summoning him to 10 Downing Street. Matthew Drummond, ex-railway man, son of a coal-miner, had entered these famous portals. His eyes took everything in so that he could later make a meticulous record of the visit in his journal: the entrance hall with its black and white marble tiles, its Chippendale hooded chair, gilt table, sunray clock and paintings. The staircase with its handsome iron balustrade and its wall lined with engravings and photographs of Prime Ministers from Walpole to the present day.

There was no picture, he had thought wryly, of George Downing. Like so much of the British Empire over which successive officials of 10 Downing Street presided for so long, the house was the creation of an unscrupulous speculator. Pepys had called George Downing a 'niggardly fellow', 'a mighty talker' and 'a most ungrateful villain'. Downing had betrayed his comrades and ever since anyone who was not to be trusted had become known as 'an arrant George Downing'.

In the white-pillared drawing room Drummond sat under the crystal chandelier, gazing at the multi-coloured Tabriz carpet with its Persian inscription. 'I have no refuge in the world other than thy threshold. My head has no protection other than this porchway. The work of a slave of the holy place Maqsud of Kashan in the year 926.'

This was the Muslim year corresponding to 1520 AD. He had read about it in a book somewhere but it had not meant all that much to him at the time. However, actually seeing the beauty and artistry in the work of some poor fellow human being, who had lived out his life under the yoke of slavery, both touched and angered him. Life was so bloody unfair. Yet here he was, Matthew Drummond, being invited to be Minister of State at the Ministry for Education. He would never forget the moment when Prime

71

Minister Clement Attlee approached him with hand out-stretched to welcome him. Attlee was a small mild-mannered schoolmaster of a man, with dark hair and neat moustache. Only his shrewd eyes gave any clue to the real man, who was surprisingly strong-willed for someone not physically robust. Attlee had called him 'Matt' and invited him to respond with 'Clem'. This made Drummond embarrassed and uneasy, and he had a struggle to accept the informal address.

He had no trouble in accepting the post Attlee offered him. What could be more important than education in the new socialist Britain. He would change the whole concept of education from the three Rs to the three As, age, aptitude and ability. He would have the marvellous reputation of Scottish education behind him. John Knox had been the first advocate of comprehensive schools. The doctor's sons, the laird's sons and the crofter's sons all went to the same school. Drummond did not believe, however, that it was just a case of lumping everyone together. He would push for a comprehensive system that meant grammar school *quality* of education at every level from the mentally handicapped, physically handicapped, right up to the high flyers who would get on regardless of what kind of education they had. It was the *quality* of education that mattered.

Matthew Drummond, Minister of State for Education. It had a good ring to it. He had an office in Whitehall across the river from the Palace of Westminster and a new London-based secretary. This meant dispensing with the part-time services of Bridget Dunbar. Bridget had not been at all pleased at this, nor indeed had Victoria. She had acted as if he had stabbed Bridget in the back. 'After all that woman has done for you,' Victoria kept saying. 'After all her loyal work on your behalf you suddenly turn round and stab her in the back!'

It was no use trying to explain how and why he now needed a full-time London-based secretary. Victoria's sense of drama had been aroused and she was caught in the scenario of tragic betrayal. Nothing could stop her making the most of it. At least Bridget was *quietly* furious.

The new secretary's name was Caroline Ridgeway and she was an extremely able and intelligent person. Right away he had felt a rapport between them. Pleasure in talking to her soon grew into a need. It was as if a dam in him cracked and a lifetime's unspoken conversation began to pour out. He struggled at first to quell his eagerness and to support a wall of dignity and business-like impersonality, but the need for communication was too strong.

They got into the habit of going for a coffee in the cafeteria of the House and sat for ages discussing, for instance, what was best for tomorrow's children. In retrospect he could see that on this subject they allowed their imaginations to run away with them and at times became rather idealistic. He had to remind her that they were not dealing in dreams but realities. It was easy, though, in the euphoria of the Labour victory, to get carried away. Talking to Caroline was like a great adventure. More and more he looked forward each day to the stimulation of it. She had told him she had never experienced so much pleasure conversing with anyone before. He wondered what age she would be. She had a slim girlish figure but was probably in her early or mid thirties, about ten or fifteen years younger than him. It turned out she had a first from Oxford in English Literature. He sighed in admiration tinged with envy at this. How he would have savoured the experience of studying literature among those 'dreaming spires'.

The more they talked the more his admiration for her grew. They discovered they were both members of Gollancz's Left Book Club. They discussed the Gollancz list in enthusiasic detail and other books they had found they had in common. Not that they agreed in everything but even their disagreements were enjoyable, a stretching and sharpening of the mind that was totally absorbing. He had never felt so happy in years.

Sometimes, when she was working in his office, he would steal a look at her. She was well-dressed but not in the same way as Rory or Victoria. Caroline never appeared in the latest fashion looking like a professional model as Rory did.

73

Nor did she dress in modestly priced but extravagantly coloured clothes like Victoria. Victoria had the panache to wear things like an emerald green or large floral-patterned dress with a large scarlet tammy. She could not bear dark clothes and had an especial aversion to black. She had never even donned black at the funeral of either her mother or her father. Caroline had a careless way with clothes. She looked as if she had flung on her fawn sweater and tweed skirt without a thought to appearance, only comfort. Everything she wore seemed to have an easy elegance. It was the same with her hair. It hung carelessly loose and flicked up at the edges. While she was absorbed in her work, she had a habit of tucking a stray brown lock behind her ear, or absently pushing at the bridge of her horn-rimmed glasses with one finger.

They had been going as usual to the House cafeteria, when one day he suddenly said, 'I'm not in the mood for House of Commons' food today, are you? Would you care to accompany me to an outside restaurant?'

'What a good idea!' Caroline said, and continued with the conversation they had been having on Sir Thomas Erskine May's *Treatise on the Law, Privileges, Proceedings and Usage of Parliament*.

Then, out of the blue, as if it was the most natural thing in the world, she invited him to come home with her for the week-end to meet her parents. He had arranged to go home to Glasgow, after first attending to some business in the Scottish Office in Edinburgh, but she said, 'Oh do come, even if it's only for one night. After all, it is on your way home. Mother and father live in Peebleshire, border country. We could have time for a long walk, exploring around. It's a very interesting historic area. But apart from that, some fresh air would do you good.'

He could not resist the temptation. Caroline's car was out of commission so they travelled by train to Edinburgh and took a bus from there to Innerleithen which Caroline said was the nearest village to where she lived. Caroline's father met them at the bus-stop in an ancient battered van. They sat in the back in darkness and in a stench of petrol and dogs, and he worried about getting dog hairs or worse, petrol stains, all over his best suit. He had only managed a cursory impression of Mr Ridgeway, who was tall and thin and dressed in a shabby tweed jacket. He seemed in a tearing hurry and had given them the barest nod of recognition before bundling them into the van and careering off. The vehicle had no windows at the back and so Drummond could not see where he was going. He began to feel somewhat apprehensive about his destination. He was a fastidious man and did not relish the prospect of spending even one night in some isolated cottage that might be far from clean if the state of the van was anything to go by.

'Father's shy,' Caroline explained, 'until he gets to know you.' That was the sum and substance of their conversation until the van lurched to a halt. Drummond had the definite impression that Caroline was even more apprehensive than him. He groaned inside at the ordeal that no doubt was to come. The van doors were whipped open and Caroline clambered out in front of him. He followed her, carefully dusting down his suit. When he looked up he froze.

Caroline's father was saying, 'I don't want to take the van into the drive. You don't mind walking from here, do you?'

'Of course not,' Caroline said. 'See you later.'

Drummond could not believe his eyes. Immediately in front of him were high wrought-iron gates topped by a family crest in gold. Beyond the gates were two wide sweeps of driveway with a velvety green forecourt in the centre. Beyond that was an enormous castellated building constructed of ancient grey stone, its towers and turrets of remote antiquity, its rows of deep dark windows, giving a fairy-tale look of a French château. Vaguely he was aware of Caroline linking her arm through his and leading him towards the gates and up the driveway to the massive, iron-studded entrance. Their feet echoed into a cool shadowy hall and it took Drummond a second or two to adjust his eyes to the change from the bright sunlight. A row of brass servants' bells dangled from the ceiling and against the wall were rows of ancient swords and shields and pistols.

Pushing at her glasses, Caroline said, 'I'll take you to

75

your room first and you can dump your case.' She led the way quickly up a winding turnpike stair to the first floor. 'Mother's put you in the white room. Here we are. There's a bathroom just along the corridor if you want to freshen up. Come downstairs when you're ready.' She gave him a hasty peck on his cheek before leaving.

He deposited his case on the floor and stared around. A four-poster bed draped in white and with white matching bed-spread dominated the centre of the room. The curtains were of the same colour and material and were looped back, trapping gauzy sunshine with bands of delicate blues and golds. The blue and gold were reflected in the colours of the carpet. He went over to stare out of the window. It looked out from the back of the house and afforded a glimpse of a terraced garden. It was a peaceful hollow, sheltered by a high wall of trees and bushes. Sunshine was held there undisturbed, a golden haze shimmering over flowers. The window was open and from the distance he could hear the faint humming of bees.

Suddenly, for no apparent reason he thought of his mother. Different memories of her came flashing before his mind's eye, proud and erect but gradually being worn down by grinding poverty. She loved books and he could see her, in the miner's hovel in which they had once lived, sitting beside the black grate under the gas mantle. She was patiently struggling to read the small print of *Pride and Prejudice* or *Mansfield Park*. After his father's accident which meant he lost not only his job but his home, they had been forced to move to an old barn up the back road from Balornock to Auchinairn. The Mortuary Road it was called because that was where the mortuary for Stobhill Hospital had been built. The barn had no gas and no water and a rough earth floor. His mother had tried to make a home of the place but the effort had killed her. They said the operation had been successful and what she had died of was malnutrition. That was bad enough, but worse he knew she had been dying for a long time of the hopelessness and ugliness of her surroundings. The lack of beauty in her life had killed her as much as anything. She would have found

76

peace and beauty here. Here she would have blossomed like the flowers and been fulfilled and happy.

He felt so angry at the unfairness of the world he could have laid his brow against the window and wept.

11

'Isn't it a right disgrace?' Victoria lowered her voice dramatically.

Drummond shrugged. 'They're getting married, aren't they?'

'I don't suppose anyone will twig in the circumstances,' Victoria answered herself. 'Before the war people always had long engagements. It was definitely the done thing. But since the war everything has gone to pot.' Despite her self-assuring words, she felt anxious and ashamed. Her emotions, in fact, were in painful confusion. Her loyalty and love for her son were unshakable but, at the same time, she felt acutely distressed at the situation he had got himself into.

'I agree the war has caused a lowering of moral standards,' Drummond said. 'It has affected marriage too. The divorce rate in England and Wales has risen from 9,970 couples in 1938 to 24,857 this year.'

'People have been marrying within a week of meeting one another. Marrying foreigners as well. So I don't suppose Fiona and Jamie getting married after knowing each other for a few months will look *that* bad. Although what we're all going to do for clothes, I just don't know.'

'If anyone can manage it, you can.'

Victoria looked pleased. 'I've met her mother, you know.'

'Oh? What is she like?'

'A terribly highly strung kind of person.'

'She's a widow you said.'

'Yes, but not a poor widow. Her house is better furnished than mine. I've got rugs for instance and I'm not complaining about them. There's nothing wrong with my rugs. My mother made those rugs and I wouldn't change them for all the tea in China or for any of Mrs Marshall's big carpets.

She's got a carpet square in her living room, her front room *and* could you credit it? *A carpet in her bedroom!*'

'Her husband must have earned a good income when he was alive and no doubt she was thrifty.'

'Are you suggesting that I'm extravagant?' Her distress returned, this time bringing an inward tremble. She tipped up her chin, determined to reveal no sign of vulnerability or weakness. 'I'd be hard put to it to be extravagant with the pittance I get from you.'

'No, I was not,' Drummond retorted irritably.

'I suspect she's downright mean and you would have known all about it if you'd had somebody like that to contend with.'

'I take it she's providing the wedding.'

'She was going on so much about the cost of it and getting into such a state, I offered to help. It was only going to be a registry office affair, but I said if they were properly married in the church I'd rustle up some extra clothing coupons and do a bit of baking for the reception.'

'What does it matter as long as they're legally married?'

'That's so like you!' Victoria's mouth twisted with bitterness as she recalled the many times that her husband had dismissed in the same impatient tone things that had been of the utmost importance to her. 'You wouldn't even have had our children christened if you'd had your way.'

'How do you propose to get extra coupons?' he said, ignoring the bait of the christening controversy. 'Or for that matter, attain the materials necessary for baking? You surely cannot go around the doors cajoling people to part with their butter and sugar rations as you did for the election victory celebration.'

She turned, as she always did, to her Maker for comfort and protection. 'The good Lord will provide. He has never let me down before.'

'I fail to see how your good Lord is going to come up with clothing coupons.'

'Don't you dare take the Lord's name in vain, you wicked man.'

'I made a simple statement of fact . . .'

'I know sarcasm when I hear it.'

'Oh, forget it.'

'No, I will not forget it. I blame what's happened on you.'

'What nonsense are you talking now, woman?'

'It's not Jamie's fault. He must have inherited your strong animal instinct and of course he would be sorely tempted by that girl. She'd do anything to get him.'

He sighed. 'If you must blame something, blame the war. I told you, there's been an almost complete breakdown of moral standards.'

'Right enough,' Victoria agreed, slightly mollified. 'Look at Mrs McGregor across the road.'

'What about her?'

'Didn't I tell you? We're all in a state waiting for her husband to come home. He's due home from France or some such place.'

'I fail to see . . .'

'She's had a baby, oh, she had it ages ago. I think Benny must be two now. A nice wee chap. But what Mr McGregor will think of him, I don't know. He's been away for over four years.'

'The McGregors won't be the only ones in that situation.'

'I know. Isn't it terrible! I could tell you of at least half a dozen in Springburn alone. There's one woman in the next close to my mother had, could you credit it, a *black* baby. Another just down the road had *twins*! It's the poor wee mites I worry about. I blame the Americans, of course.'

'Well, you know the saying.'

'What saying?'

His mouth twitched into a smile. 'They're overpaid, oversexed and over here.'

'My poor mother would turn in her grave if she heard you saying that word.'

'Well, we can be sure of one thing.' Drummond sighed, his voice acquiring a twist of bitterness. 'The lowering of moral standards has not in the slightest affected *your* attitude to sex.'

'I should think not!' Victoria was indignant at the mere

idea. 'I'm a good-living Christian woman and always have been, as you well know.'

'Indeed. Indeed.'

'And I hope you're going to be here by my side, where you belong, when Jamie gets married. It's the least you can do. I don't want to hear about how you're needed by strangers in London. Your son ought to come first. Not that he ever has. None of us ever has. It's always been strangers first with you, but you'd better be here to do your duty at your son's wedding.'

She would have managed better if he'd stayed away but then, as she confided in Mrs McDade, 'What would people think? But he's such an awkward, unpredictable man, Mrs McDade. He's just a worry at any social occasion. It's a case of whether to put up with the showing-up he's likely to give us if he's here, or the showing-up he's likely to give us if he's not here.'

'He's awful good at public-speaking,' Mrs McDade sought to allay her friend's fears. 'So I expect he'll make a good wedding speech.'

'I know. I know. And he's a good man underneath. It's just this awkward bit about him. It's a heavy cross to bear, Mrs McDade. A heavy cross to bear.'

Soon, however, Victoria was busy with the wedding preparations. Matthew and his eccentricities were completely forgotten. Until, that is, Fiona dropped the bombshell about the invitation she'd sent to Sir Alexander Forbes-Cunningham. Victoria was in Mrs Marshall's house having tea at the time and thinking what a dry, untidy fuzz of hair Fiona's mother had, like a wig that had tipped slightly askew. It took her a few seconds to switch her thoughts from Mrs Marshall's mousy head to Fiona's blonde one. Mrs Marshall gave one of her bursts of hysterical laughter, a habit Victoria found very irritating.

'I told her. I told her. Oh, she'll be the death of me yet. Fiona you will! Fancy having the nerve to ask one of the gentry.' Another burst of laughter trilled out. 'That means we can't have the reception here. A man like that couldn't come to a place like this. It's only a two-bedroomed semi.'

81

Mrs Marshall had originated from the country and had 'touching the forelock' ideas that never failed, as Victoria put it, 'to get my dander up!'

'There's nothing to be ashamed of about your home, Mrs Marshall. And you're as good as that man any day of the week. But if it'll make you feel any better I've no doubt we could get the use of the Labour Party Hall for next to nothing.'

Mrs Marshall's laughter wilted into a wail. 'You can't think she's right in doing this, Mrs Drummond.'

'No, I don't think she's right, Mrs Marshall, but not for the same reasons as you. My husband hates that man and with good reason. Oh, I know it's not right to hate anyone but there it is, hate him he does, and Fiona knows it.'

'Oh!' A squeal of hilarity seemed to bring even more disarray to Mrs Marshall's hair. 'Bad feeling at a wedding. It won't be lucky.'

'Just leave everything to me, mother,' Fiona said, with an infuriating calmness that made Victoria nurse unchristian longings to box her ears. 'Why worry? He might not even come.'

'Oh, he'll come all right,' Victoria said. 'If that old rascal doesn't come, my name's not Victoria Drummond.'

'Oh!' Mrs Marshall's tragic eyes were a terrible contradiction to the giggly sounds she was making. Her face had become a mass of red blotches and Victoria wasn't sure if they were caused by nerves or a skin disease.

'Look at the state you've got your poor mother into,' she rounded on Fiona. 'You ought to be ashamed of yourself. Have another cup of tea, Mrs Marshall. It'll help steady you.'

She refilled all the cups and passed the scones as if she was in her own house and completely in charge.

'Thanks, Mrs Drummond,' Mrs Marshall said humbly. Then with a trill of laughter, she added, 'I haven't even anything decent to wear. His servants will be better dressed than me. I *was* a servant before I was married.'

'There's nothing to be ashamed of in that either, Mrs Marshall. You worked hard for your money I've no doubt,

82

which is more than what can be said for folk like Forbes-Cunningham. People like that are just gamblers but, instead of gambling a few shillings on dogs or football pools like the working man, they gamble fortunes on the stock market. You should hear my husband on this.'

'But he's the gentry. What could the likes of me say to him?'

'I'll not be stuck for something to say to him, I can tell you. But I agree with you he should never have been asked. It's put me in a terrible position. Now I don't know whether to tell Matthew or not. If I do tell him he won't come to the wedding. His own son's wedding, he won't come. Either way he's going to be terribly hurt.'

Fiona enjoyed a mouthful of scone. 'I don't see why.'

'I know you don't, Fiona.' Victoria eyed her severely. 'That's because you're young and haven't yet developed the maturity and sensitivity that your mother and me have.'

'Oh!' Mrs Marshall gave a despairing giggle. 'I'm dreading the whole thing. I'm sure it's going to be an absolute disaster.'

'Nothing of the kind,' Victoria said firmly. 'Not if I've anything to do with it. Drink up your tea!' She enjoyed a challenge and already she was bracing herself and girding her loins.

12

'Look at this!' Rory flung the card across the breakfast table to Donovan. He was lighting up a cigarette and reading his own mail.

'What is it?'

'A wedding invitation from some girl who's marrying Jamie Drummond. You know, Victoria and Matty's son. I suppose she's after a decent wedding present, knowing I've got the shop.'

'Trust you to think like that.'

'What else can it be except a girl on the make? I don't know her from Adam. I've never seen Victoria for years.'

'I doubt if I'd recognize her now,' Donovan admitted. 'I'd certainly not know the son.'

'Victoria's not responsible for the invitation, that's for sure. Jamie must have told the girl about us and she's after the main chance.'

'Do you fancy going?'

'Do you?'

He shrugged. 'I'm easy.'

Helena spoke up. 'I'm not going, anyway.'

'You'll do as you're told,' her father said.

'But dad, we don't know them and they sound dead boring.'

'We're all included in the invitation and if your mother decides you should go, you'll go.'

'We're eighteen,' said Douglas. 'We can please ourselves.'

'Not as long as you're under my roof, you can't. You're still wet behind the ears. You're not earning a penny, so shut up!'

'What a reasonably minded, charming father we have, Helena.'

'Shut up, you birk!' his father repeated.

Rory lit up a cigarette. 'I don't suppose it would do any harm to go. For one thing, it would show our two how the other half live.'

'True. True.' Donovan agreed.

'Mother!' both Douglas and Helena groaned, and Helena added, 'As it happens, mother, we're much more sophisticated and knowledgeable about life than you and dad. We don't need lessons about anything or anybody.'

'Really?' said Donovan.

Rory could not help grinning over at him. 'They're young, darling. Didn't we know it all at their age?'

'One thing I do know, I was never as spoiled as them. Nor were you.'

Rory blew a quick stream of smoke upwards. 'Life was tougher, I must admit.'

'What?' Helena squealed. 'How can you say that, mum? My youth has been spent during a war. I've had to suffer terrible shortages and deprivations. When did I last have any rouge or a decent French perfume?'

'My heart bleeds for you,' Donovan said. Then, 'My God, Rory!'

'All right, all right,' Rory said. 'Maybe I *have* spoiled them a little.'

'A little?'

'Give me back that invitation. I'll write and accept for all of us. No doubt it'll be a bore as you say, Helena, but you'll be nice to everyone, do you hear? You'll behave yourselves, both of you.'

'It's about time they learned to do that,' Donovan agreed.

'I think *I* should go, anyway,' Rory said. 'For old times' sake. Victoria and I used to be very close friends. My God, when I think of it . . .' She shook her head. 'It seems a lifetime ago now.'

'Are you sure it's just Victoria you're going to see,' Douglas sneered, 'and not her husband?'

The words were hardly out of his mouth before Donovan's big hand shot across the table, caught him by the throat, and dragged him across his plate of porridge. 'Don't you dare speak like that to your mother!'

'You're choking me,' Douglas howled.

'That's right,' Donovan said. 'You'd better be quick with your apology.'

'I'm sorry, mum!'

Donovan let go of him and Douglas collapsed back in a fit of coughing. Worriedly Rory got up and made as if she was going towards him but Donovan's warning tone diverted her.

'Off to work, honey? On you go then. I'll call for you at twelve and take you to lunch. OK?'

'OK,' she said unhappily, with another backward glance at the still coughing and spluttering Douglas. She was afraid that Donovan was going to the opposite extreme from herself and being much too harsh with the children. Although she was having to admit more and more that they were getting completely out of hand. Even Winnie, who normally believed the children could do no wrong, was beginning to express concern.

In a way she was dreading the Drummond wedding and could not think now why on earth she had said they should all go. She sensed it would be the first big test of authority between Donovan and the children, her and the children, too, for that matter. She had flung down the gauntlet in telling them they must behave and, as if that was not asking for enough trouble, she had done it in front of Donovan. Knowing Donovan, he would make it his business to see that they obeyed to the letter. Even if she had had enough time to think of and arrange some business important enough to take her out of town, and so give her a believable excuse to cancel their attendance at the wedding, it would not have been so bad. But it was, like most weddings nowadays, a double quick affair. She had hardly posted the acceptance when the wedding day was upon them.

'I was wrong,' Donovan admitted. 'I would have recognized Victoria anywhere. She's put on a bit of weight, otherwise she's much the same.'

It was true. Victoria had the same regal posture that they remembered. She held her head as high as ever. It was as if she genuinely believed that she was the most beautiful woman in the room. Despite wearing not a scrap of make-up and having a Roman nose and strong chin, she was undeniably handsome. Rory was not sure if it was her queenly posture or fine dark eyes that did the trick, but she reckoned that anyone would only need to be five minutes in her company to forget her cheap, badly cut clothes, rough red hands and pungent smell of carbolic soap.

As a matter of fact, Rory had always suspected that there was an element of self-defence, even fear behind Victoria's over-confident facade. She felt it again now. They used to embrace warmly when they met and they embraced now. Yet there was a hint of stiffness, of prickliness about Victoria's attitude. It was as if she was saying to Rory, 'You may have gone up in the world and made yourself a lot of money, but I'm still every bit as good as you and don't you forget it.'

As Rory watched Victoria and Matty together at the reception, she had never been so clearly aware of how ill-suited they were. Despite her proud bearing, Victoria looked the cheaply dressed, solid working-class woman that she was. Matty looked every inch a gentleman. Rory smiled ruefully to herself. She had often seen men in the train travelling down to London in the same first-class carriage as herself and the twins, and she had on more than one occasion astonished the twins as well as the men by correctly guessing that they were delegates for the union going down to some executive meeting or other.

She had explained to the twins afterwards that she had thought that, despite being dressed up in well-pressed suits and pristine collars and ties, the men did not look right. To her it was obvious that they belonged in dirty dungarees and comfortable open-necked shirts. She sensed they felt like aliens in the first-class compartment.

Matty had obviously long since overcome this aura of inferiority. He looked as intriguingly intense as ever. Yet at the same time he had an air of sophisticated elegance. It was not surprising that he looked elegant, of course. He was wearing one of the two suits her tailors had made for him when he had first become an MP. She had, unknown to

Matty, ordered them to use the very best, the most expensive cloth in the shop. She had charged him the same price as he would have paid for an off-the-peg suit in Hoeys in Springburn. She had even let him pay the bill in instalments and thrown in a Harris Tweed sports jacket for good measure. Those suits and that jacket would last him for a lifetime and still look good.

Suddenly, as she watched Matty, anger darkened his face and he turned on Victoria as if about to strike her. Rory could not hear what they were saying but she knew the air had become electric. Then she saw the reason. 'Oh, Lor',' she nudged Donovan. 'Look who's just come in!'

'That can't be . . .'

'It can.' Rory said. She had come to know Sir Alexander Forbes-Cunningham very well over the years. Her tailors made his suits and shirts, and she always had a chat with him when he came in for fittings, to make sure everything was to his satisfaction.

'I'd better beat Matty and Victoria to it. Either of them is capable of buggering this up.' She made it despite Victoria starting off first. She had always been quicker on her feet than Victoria. 'Sir Alex! How nice to see you. Come and meet my husband, Captain Donovan. I remember how interested you were when I told you about his film-making for the army.'

Sir Alexander Forbes-Cunningham was a tall man but more heavily made than Matty. He had the same brooding look about his eyes, however. He came with her without a word and shook hands with Donovan and the twins. 'The Army Cinematograph Corps did you say, Captain Donovan?'

'No. The Army *K*inematograph Corps. We needed the "K". Otherwise we'd have been confused with the Catering Corps.'

Forbes-Cunningham laughed then.

'Who's the Dresden china blonde, mother?' Douglas asked.

'You mean the bride?'

'No, of course not. That girl over there.'

'Oh. That must be Amelia, Jamie's sister. Definitely not your type, darling.'

Just then the bride and groom came across. The bride was wearing a long white dress cleverly fashioned out of her mother's lace curtains and was carrying a glass of whisky. She made straight for Sir Alex and fluttered her lashes up at him. 'Sir Alexander Forbes-Cunningham, isn't it? My husband and I are so glad you could come. May I offer you a glass of our best whisky. It's an excellent malt.' The malt whisky had in fact been part of Rory's present.

Sir Alex accepted the glass but stared past Fiona to her husband. 'So you're Jamie.' he said.

'Yes, sir,' Jamie gave him one of his happy grins. He had an open good-natured face that even the most ill-natured person would have found difficult to dislike. 'Pleased to meet you.'

'And I am very pleased to meet you.' Sir Alexander Forbes-Cunningham stuck out his hand. 'You must be more like your mother, Jamie. I don't see much of your father in your face. Is he here, by the way?' Although the old man's voice was nonchalant, Rory detected a glimmer of pathetic hope in his eyes as he glanced around.

'Yes, of course he is, Sir Alexander,' Fiona said. 'Come with me. I'll take you over to him.'

Rory followed, aching to wring the girl's neck and at the same time feverishly trying to think of something to avert the confrontation Fiona seemed hell-bent on precipitating.

'Father-in-law,' Fiona said, 'dear Sir Alexander was asking about you. Now the two of you can have a lovely chat. I'm so glad that both of you could come to my wedding. It *really* made it the happiest day of my whole life!'

Rory held her breath as Sir Alexander put out his hand to Matty. The resemblance between the two men had never been so obvious. Both were tall and distinguished-looking with the same dark eyes and brooding expression. There was a few seconds' pause before Matty accepted the older man's proffered hand and said stiffly, 'Good evening, I hope you are well.'

But Sir Alexander had barely replied, 'Very well, thank you,' when Matty murmured a polite 'Excuse me' and turned away.

13

Amelia was fast becoming caught up in a giant bubble of excitement. It had been growing all day since the announcement it was a holiday to celebrate the victory over Japan. Now it was about to explode in a kind of madness all over the city. She had managed to get a seat on top of a packed tramcar but crowds were blocking the aisles, the stairs and the platform. People were even climbing up and swinging monkey-like on the brass pole. The conductor, throwing to the winds all thoughts of collecting fares, flung his arms round the driver's shoulder and accompanied him in belting out a duet. The rollicking crush of passengers lustily joined in:

'I belong to Glasgow, dear old Glasgow town,
But there's something the matter with Glasgow,
For it's going round and round.
I'm only a common old working chap,
As anyone here can see,
But when I get a couple of drinks on a Saturday,
Glasgow belongs to me. . . .'

All the way down the Clyde, steamers blared forth their joyous song. Searchlights from a great fleet of warships and merchant vessels combined to give a dazzling display. Occasionally ships would join in making the 'V' sign with their searchlights. Multi-coloured flares, rockets and star-shells added to the scene, making a blazing panorama of light and colour.

Every one of the vehicles that crowded all roads leading to the centre of the city was a mass of figures clinging on to running boards and luggage racks. Flags flew. Bugles blared. Trumpets tooted. Even on normal days the drivers of Glasgow tramcars drove aggressively, fearlessly and at exhilarating speed. On this day, no exception was made and

91

no quarter given. The Glasgow tramcar was king of the road and motor vehicles blocking the track were impatiently gonged out of the way.

Amelia clutched at the metal grip of the seat in front to steady herself against the pitch and roll of the tram. She was wearing her brown bar sandals and last year's summer dress, the one she had worn at the school outing. Mrs McDade had made it out of an old cotton bed-spread. It was a faded fawn colour with brown piping on the short puff sleeves and Peter Pan collar. If she had been worrying about her appearance, which she was not, she would have been aware that her dress was too near the colour of her hair and made it appear faded. She looked in fact like a delicate little girl of no more than thirteen or fourteen years. Her appearance, however, was the last of her thoughts. She was too overwhelmed by everyone else and everything that was going on around her. She was huge-eyed with wonder. Her mother had given her permission, if very reluctantly, to go and see the fireworks in town. Her mother and Mrs McDade had been invited to a special party in the Temperance Hall at which her mother had promised not only to sing and play the piano, but to organize the games.

'You can go to see the fireworks if you must.' Her mother had eventually succumbed to her pleadings and assurances that half the girls she had known at school were going too. 'But you be at Temperance Hall for ten o'clock sharp, do you hear?'

'Of course, mummy.'

'And don't speak to any strange men, remember. Don't speak to any strangers. You never know!' Her voice lowered meaningfully, mysteriously. Her mother was an authority on the white slave trade and often told fearsome stories of girls being injected by drugs and dragged off to awful dens of evil out East, never to be seen or heard of again.

Amelia shivered at the thought. Nevertheless it was a terrific adventure being out on her own. She enjoyed her own company whether it meant adventuring into a make-believe dream-world in her mind or actually moving about in the real world. Being alone meant having peace to observe and store up more food for thought. To be on her own on such a day was good fortune indeed. It would feed her imagination for days, weeks, months, years to come. It never occurred to her that she was probably the only human being on the streets of Glasgow who was on their own. Her happiness was total and intense.

The tramcar stopped nodding and rocking along, jangling through junctions and lurching round curves. Hurriedly Amelia rose and crushed her way towards the stairs. People were dancing together in the streets. Others were singing at the pitch of their voices, heads thrown back:

> 'You are my sunshine, my only sunshine.
> You make me happy when skies are grey.
> You'll never know, dear, how much I love you;
> Please don't take my sunshine away. . . .'

People were laughing and hugging one another. Others were holding bottles up to their mouths. A crowd perched on top of a car were screeching:

> 'Give me land, lots of land under starry skies above.
> Don't fence me in.
> Let me ride through the wide open spaces that I love.
> Don't fence me in.
> Let me be by myself in the evening breeze,
> Listening to the murmur of the cottonwood trees.
> Send me there for ever, but I ask you, *please*,
> Don't fence me in. . . .'

The words of both songs became a confused jumble and were drowned in the louder wave of noise that hit her as she approached George Square. The ribbon-bedecked car was swallowed up in the multitude-thronging streets leading to the square. High above them was a bright vermilion glare, a reflection of hundreds of street bonfires strung around the city. The sky was also a-dazzle with fireworks, and George Square, usually a quiet dignified area of sooty buildings and grey statues, had been completely transformed. Now it was

93

a brilliant island of light, noise and hysterical abandon. Bagpipes, whistles, mouth organs and kettle-drums vied with the explosion of squibs and rockets. Accordionists were prancing about playing wildly to dancing crowds.

Amelia tried to see everything, to take everything in, to miss nothing. She would write it all down when she got home. Capturing things on paper was her secret delight, her bonus of pleasure. She hoarded impressions like a miser, recounting them over and over again. Gazing wide-eyed at the scene, she thought, 'This is the most wonderful night of my life. This is my shining night.' This was the point where fantasy and reality came together. This was where dreams came true. Then, just at the peak of her happiness, she suddenly found herself jostled into being a participant instead of an observer.

She was sucked into a frightening whirlpool. She was grabbed round the waist and swung wildly into high-kicking frolics. Men bruised her lips with kisses. Someone pushed a bottle to her mouth and fiery liquid poured down her throat. In panic she fought to escape, but it was impossible because of the press of the crowd and the strong arms jerking her this way and that. She made a feeble wailing attempt to laugh as the others were laughing but nothing quelled her acute apprehension. At home there was only verbal violence and it could reduce her to palpitating confusion. Here there was every kind. She was a helpless prey to physical assaults. Her arms were bruised; her feet were trampled on. Her emotions were assailed by the mad abandon of the mob and the noise which had become a high-pitched yell, like a locomotive whistle that never died down. She could not free her arms.

Half-weeping now she kept saying no to drunken proffered drinks. But nobody heard her. She shook her head from side to side but there was no escape from the bottles forced against her mouth, making her choke and splutter. Her chest and stomach burned and she began to feel sick. Whisky flowed out of her mouth and dribbled down her chin and neck, making the front of her frock cling wetly to her skin. The madness, the noise, the violence spun wildly out of control. The dream had become a nightmare. She thought she must be crying but could not hear herself. She began to spin round. And round. And round. A numbness crept over her face, then her body, then her legs. She had a foggy awareness of lolling helplessly about, of being jerkily unfolded, of being laughed at like a puppet on strings. A velvety curtain of blackness kept coming down and only lifting occasionally to allow the locomotive whistle of noise to penetrate through.

Gradually the noise faded into the distance. There was darkness and quietness even when she opened her eyes. An intimate quietness, a quietness that wrapped closely around her, shutting her off in some strange suffocating island on her own. At least she thought she was on her own. For a few seconds, as she lay sinking and surfacing, she thought she had strayed into one of her erotic dreams. She felt the furtive twitching and throbbing. But through her dream came, not the safe nest of her daddy's chair with its pleasing aroma of leather and its soft velvet cushion, instead there was the pungent stench of smoked fish and male sweat. A weight like an iron girder crushed down on top of her. Her chest and stomach could not heave to be sick. She welcomed the panic now. It helped in the struggle to clear her mind, to move her numbed limbs. A sharp pain stabbed between her legs and, as it did so, she heard herself cry out. Soon afterwards she realized the weight had gone. She felt so ill the release of the pressure made no difference. All she managed to do was crawl over to crouch against a wall and vomit until she wanted to die. Such was her nightmare she had no idea how she eventually managed, in the early hours of the morning, to struggle home. Her mother came to open the door in answer to her knock. Victoria's face twisted and drew back at the sight and smell of Amelia.

'You filthy, disgusting animal,' her mother said. 'Get out of my sight.' She was still in her night-clothes, and she turned and strode back to her bed-settee in the living room, her white flannelette nightgown flurrying out behind her.

Somehow Amelia managed to feel her way to the bathroom, splash her face with cold water and drink some from her cupped hands. Then she struggled out of her dress, her vest and her knickers. They were all stained and stinking but it was the blood stains that caused her, for the first time, to break down.

14

Donovan grinned over at Beer Bailie. They were lolling back at their desks enjoying a cigarette in a reporters' room awash with discarded pieces of crumpled paper. Hardly an inch of floor was visible. 'You know what they say, "Do right and fear no man, don't write and fear no woman!"'

Beer Bailie laughed, then ruefully shook his head. 'You're too late with that advice, pal.'

'Don't tell me you've already committed yourself on paper.'

'Fraid so.'

'Christ! You of all people?'

'I must have been pissed at the time.'

'That won't get you off the hook.'

'I know. I know.'

'You've left yourself wide open for a breach-of-promise suit.'

'I don't need you to tell me that. It's all very well for you. You've been away living it up in London in your fancy uniform, having as much nooky as you like and no strings attached. Us poor bastards of civvies had to promise the moon.'

'My heart bleeds', said Donovan, 'for all the newspaper men like you, slaving away on the civvy front with only a few cash bonuses to keep you going. You deserve a medal, especially for the devoted work done during the election.'

'Don't blame us for that. Blame Beaverbrook! I knew he was going over the top in the *Express* with his warnings of bloody revolution and trade union bogey men. God, that man must hate the unions!'

' "Whose finger on the trigger?" ' Donovan mocked. ' "The end is nigh!" Stupid bastard. I hope he realizes he killed the Tory Party. When we heard the final landslide

97

result, me and a crowd of my army mates were in our favourite pub, The Dog and Duck; do you know it?'

'Don't think so.'

'In Soho, near our headquarters in Curzon Street. Anyway, a crowd of us were there and when we heard the result we lifted our glasses and said "To the founder of the feast, Lord Beaverbrook!" '

Just then Crab McKay, the sports-writer, woke up from his alcoholic haze. 'Shumbody shay they were going to the pub?' As well as his weakness for alcohol the sports-writer had a weakness for crabs, thus the nickname. It was his habit to send his boy assistant out to Whites in Gordon Street to get him one. He could sit most of the day while he was awake, chewing it. He'd eaten so many crabs, in fact, he'd come to look like one, with his bald pink head and broad pink face.

'Yeah, why not?' Donovan stuck his hat on the back of his head. 'I'll need to get in a few extra before I go home today.'

'How's that?' asked Beer Bailie.

'There's a party on tonight.'

'Never heard you complain about a party before.'

'It's the kids' birthday and God knows what kind of little hairy monsters they've invited from that art school.'

'At least your boy's clean-shaven and respectable-looking. I hear he's a bit of a genius as well.'

'Whassat? Who says Guinness?' Crab surfaced, realized his mistake, and promptly sank back into a deep slumber.

'So they say.' Donovan agreed. 'But have you seen any of his stuff? OK, maybe I'm an ignorant slob and know damn all about art, but to me it's one big fraud.'

'You're right,' Beer Bailie agreed. 'You *are* an ignorant slob! You'll be telling me next you don't think your daughter's a raving beauty.'

Donovan sighed. 'Don't get me wrong. They're both great kids. They've got a lot going for them and I'm proud of them. It's just . . .'

'Just what, for Christ's sake?'

'Oh, the war, I suppose. Rory having her hands full

keeping things going. Me being away most of the time. The trouble is I'm worried about them. All of them!'

'The truth is you're a suspicious bastard. You're always ferreting about looking for something behind every stone.'

Donovan got up, grinning. 'What you're saying is I'm a damn good journalist. I can't argue with that.'

'At least you're wide awake.' As he passed Crab he gave him a punch and yelled in his ear. 'Partick Thistle's beat Rangers twelve nil!'

'Pish off.' Crab mumbled without opening his eyes.

There were already some of their colleagues propping up the bar when they sauntered in, and Beer Bailie was hailed with, 'Come to drown your sorrows, eh, Beer? My God, you've done it this time.'

'Aw, give it a rest for Christ's sake.' Beer took his glass over to a corner table and sat looking morose. Donovan left him after a couple of quick drinks and drove home just in time to see a little fair-haired girl being ushered into the house by a smiling Douglas.

'Is that the Drummond girl just come in?' he asked Rory once he had tracked her down to the big tiled kitchen.

'Douglas insisted on inviting her, so I suppose it was. In fact he asked for this party solely as an excuse to get together with her. Odd, isn't it?'

'If you mean it's odd for him to keep chasing her after she did her best to avoid him at the wedding and since, no, I think it's only too natural. Her playing hard to get will make her seem all the more desirable. Especially to Douglas.'

'I still can't help feeling she's not his type. She's such a little mouse. Although Matty once said he thought there was more to her than meets the eye. Don't touch those yet!' She smacked his hand. 'We're just about to take them through to the dining room. You can help if you want to.'

'Like hell I do! Where's Helena? She's the one who should be helping.'

'It's her birthday, too, remember.'

'I thought you said she didn't want a party.'

'I know, but she's decided she might as well join in.'

'How many are there through there?'

'Only half a dozen, plus Douglas and Helena.'

'He must be really serious about the Drummond girl.'

'I know. He's never had a party of less than thirty before.'

'Maybe she'll be good for him.'

Rory gave him a quick kiss. 'You really do care about him?'

'Idiot! Of course I care about him. He's my son.'

'And Helena?'

'She not half the woman her mother is, but she'll do.'

Rory kissed him again. 'You'd better go through and see what they're up to.'

'That's sure to increase my popularity.'

'Tell them supper's ready.'

He turned at the door. 'I'm surprised what's her name . . .'

'Amelia.'

'. . . Amelia came tonight.'

'Knowing Victoria, she probably frog-marched her here. Amelia would have no choice if her mother decided she ought to accept the invitation.'

Winnie came bustling into the kitchen carrying an empty tray. 'That's just the sausage rolls and mock oysters to go through.'

Rory sighed. 'God knows what they'll taste like.'

'I know what the sausage rolls will taste like. Horse, that's what they'll taste like.' Winnie said. 'That rascal of a butcher's capable of anything. Do you know what he said to me yesterday after I'd waited for nearly two hours in the queue?'

'Yes, I know, Winnie,' Rory interrupted hastily. 'You told me. Let's get these through. They'll be waiting.'

As the evening progressed Rory became more worried about her son's apparent obsession with Amelia Drummond. He seemed to have eyes for nobody else. And the more Amelia spurned him the more desperate he seemed to become. She showed not the slightest interest in Douglas. Indeed his charming attentions were met with ill-mannered rebuffs. What Douglas saw in her, Rory could not fathom. Getting himself mixed up with somebody like

100

that could mean nothing but heartache and trouble for him. Somebody like that might undermine his confidence, instead of helping and encouraging him along the brilliant path in the artistic world that he deserved. She was neurotic to say the least. Even her mother knew that. Amelia had refused to dance with Douglas at Jamie's wedding and had only done so after her mother had lectured her for being stupid, moody and bad-mannered.

'She's even worse than Matthew,' Victoria had confided. 'She'll be the death of me yet, that girl!'

No wonder Victoria kept pushing her into Douglas's arms. Victoria wanted rid of the worry of her. Well, Victoria Drummond was not going to burden Rory Donovan's son with her problem daughter. Not if she could help it. She was polite to the girl, of course, but she did not like her. There was something secretive, almost furtive about Amelia's manner. Nor did she appear very bright. She seemed so slow and stupid at times. It was difficult for Rory to hide her impatience. Her son, her brilliant son, deserved better than that. She wasted no time in telling him so despite Donovan's warnings that it would only make Douglas worse. It infuriated her to find that Donovan was right. The more she criticized Amelia the more Douglas defended her and praised her. At the same time she could not help herself. She had made such plans for Douglas. He was to have every opportunity. She had promised him, for instance, that he could spend his next holiday time in Florence to study the art there and sketch and paint. He had everything in life to look forward to. Why on earth did he need to get mixed up with a neurotic little oddity like Amelia Drummond?

'She doesn't even want you,' she had burst out in exasperation to Douglas.

'She will,' Douglas assured her with that flinty determination in his eyes that reminded her of Donovan. 'She will!'

15

Amelia felt distraught. Douglas Donovan's persistent attention had confused yet sharpened every emotion. She felt so grateful she would have laid down her life for him. Yet how could he like her? It was impossible. She was utterly and totally convinced of the impossibility of anyone having any regard for her, far less a good-looking talented young man like Douglas Donovan. She was afraid to have anything to do with Douglas or anyone in case they found out what she was really like.

She realized now that her knowledge of herself had been growing like a bad seed in her subconscious mind ever since she had been a baby. She remembered one particular incident. Nothing was clear-cut. It was just a feeling of being in a cot. Through the darkness of time she caught a glimpse of wooden cot bars. She was aware of being near an old-fashioned black grate with a gas mantle above it. Close at one side was a high set-in-the-wall bed. On that bed lay the humped figure of her mother. She had not so much the sight but the impression of these things.

She did not feel any pain or remember any sound but she knew she was crying. Then she had the sensation of a man bending over the cot, lifting her out and dressing her in a tiny velvet frock. It was dark red in colour. The memory was not in colour. Everything was still in shadow. She just felt that it was dark red in the same way that she knew the man was her father. The clearest thing was the wave of hatred she felt coming towards her from the bed. It was more than hatred. It was repulsion. That first engulfing wave of hatred and repulsion had receded from time to time but it had never gone away. It came overflowing back on innumerable occasions in her childhood, like the time when she was to have a compulsory examination in the primary school by the school doctor. The day before the examination her mother was forced to give her a bath. She remembered sitting in the bath and looking askance at the dirt ingrained into the skin of her body. Her body was a different colour from her hands. Her hands were a soft pink. Her body was a dark gritty grey. She remembered being jerked about by the force of the scrubbing brush her mother was using to try to get rid of the shameful evidence of neglect. That is what Amelia realized it was now. Although even then she instinctively knew that the sight of her disgusted her mother and that was the reason for the neglect.

What happened on VJ night had confirmed in herself that she was completely beyond the pale. If she had been a food she would have been labelled 'not fit for human consumption'. She certainly was not a fit person for Douglas Donovan to have anything to do with. The trouble was that her mother, because she wanted rid of her no doubt, was doing everything in her power to force her into an association with Douglas.

'I cannot understand you,' Victoria kept saying. 'If you'd any sense, you'd be glad of the chance to get yourself safely settled with a decent young man. After all the worry you've caused me. I'll never forget you staying out all night for instance and coming to my door stinking with drink and vomit. I'll never get over that, never! If your daddy and your brother knew. . . .'

Amelia tried not to think of the horror of her mother telling her father or her brother. She shrank and shrank inside, closing off doors in every layer of her mind as she retreated, desperate for oblivion.

'Why don't you want to be friends with that nice respectable lad?' her mother kept asking. 'You'll never get another chance like this again. I know his parents. He comes from a good home. You'd lack for nothing. You're just being perverse like your daddy. Just because a nice boy wants to court you, just because I give you my permission, you go into one of your black moods and dig your heels in.' Her mother was so used to fighting her father's perverseness she had taken up the cudgels automatically. Amelia had experienced enough of her mother's determination to know that she would never give up. That was why, despite her head-splitting resentment at her mother's road-roller tactics, she had gone to Douglas's party.

Victoria and Mrs McDade really enjoyed the few days beforehand. They never stopped talking about the party. They had long earnest conversations about whether or not Amelia should wear any make-up and what dress she should put on, one of her own, one belonging to Mrs McDade's daughter, or one belonging to Mrs McDade herself that could 'soon be altered and made quite presentable with a bit of coloured tape and a few bright buttons.'

Amelia was never included in any of these discussions although she was always there. When she expressed an opinion she was, as she had known she would be from previous experiences, completely ignored.

'Her skin's perfect, dear. She takes after you in that,' Mrs McDade said. 'So she doesn't really need face powder but maybe a wee touch of lipstick.'

'No, no,' Victoria shook her head. 'She's not going to give me a showing-up by going to Pollokshields looking like a painted hussy.'

Amelia thought this was typically tactless of her mother. Mrs McDade's daughter, Lizzie, regularly wore lipstick.

'Lizzie's got a bottle of Californian Poppy. Do you think maybe a wee dab of that?'

'Yes,' Victoria agreed. 'That would be all right. Just a wee dab behind each ear.'

'And how about jewellery?' Mrs McDade enquired.

Amelia immediately determined that if it were decided she should wear her mother's Woolworth's 'ruby and diamond' brooch, she would unpin it and hide it in her pocket before reaching the Pollokshields house.

Victoria's head lifted with pride and pleasure. 'There's my ruby and diamond brooch.'

'Very nice, dear.' Mrs McDade nodded sagely.

'And my beads.'

'I've always liked you in these beads, Mrs Drummond.'

104

'Yes, I suit green, don't I. And they've a nice sparkle about them. They'll help brighten up the look of her.'

'You're very kind, dear. I was just saying to my Hector the other day, "Mrs Drummond's a right gem." '

'I'm just as God made me, Mrs McDade. Now, have we decided about the dress?' In the end there had been a general consultation with all the neighbours from Mrs McDade's close and from their close which was the next one along.

'It being such an important occasion,' her mother told Mrs McDade, 'it's only right that every offer of help should be considered.'

Eventually the loan of a blue satin party dress was accepted from Kate Milligan who lived on the top flat in Mrs McDade's close.

'Although where she got that dress,' Victoria confided in Mrs McDade, 'I'll never know.'

Everything Kate Milligan had was suspect because she was friendly with so many Yanks. Mrs McDade's close had become at times like a miniature America. Gum-chewing Yanks of every variety had been seen trooping up and down the stairs.

'Ah well,' Mrs McDade said about the acceptance of Kate's dress, 'any port in a storm, Mrs Drummond.'

The shining dress and the hooded cape, also donated by Kate, had made Amelia stand out against the drabness of the other girls at the party in their made-up black-out curtains and air force blankets. Amelia felt sorry for them and did not blame them for their barely concealed hatred. In a way she was glad she had come. It was fascinating to see inside a big house. The hall alone, panelled in rich rosewood, could have accommodated the whole of their council flat with room to spare. The furniture in the lounge was made of equally beautiful wood and Amelia longed to examine more closely the contents of the glass-fronted book-case. She was led straight over, however, to sit beside Douglas on the settee. It was upholstered in plum-coloured velvet like the armchairs and matching velvet curtains.

Never in her wildest dreams had Amelia imagined such

opulence. The dining room proved equally impressive with its long table covered with a white linen table cover and real bone china. There had even been napkins. She savoured the experience of all these things, but what moved her and confused her most was the flattering attention that Douglas Donovan lavished on her. She retreated behind a far-away expression that could have been interpreted as cool and uncaring. Later he had taken her home in a taxi. It was the first time she had ever been in a taxi in her life. He had come into the close with her and up the stairs. It was then she experienced flutterings of fear. In a quick stiff voice she had said, 'Goodnight, Douglas. Thank you for accompanying me home.' Then she had knocked at the door.

'Wait,' Douglas sounded as if he could hardly believe his ears, 'when can I see you again?'

She shrugged, impatient with herself for being so unable to cope with the situation, just desperate to escape from it. 'Oh, I don't know. I want to go now, Douglas. I hear my mother coming.'

He grabbed her hand and kissed it. 'I'll call for you tomorrow.'

'But tomorrow's Sunday.'

The door opened then and Victoria said, 'Hello, son. It's kind of you to see Amelia safely home. I'd ask you in for a cup of tea but it's after eleven and time decent folk were in bed.'

Douglas said, 'Would you mind if I called tomorrow afternoon and took Amelia for a walk in the park, Mrs Drummond?'

'What a good idea. She needs a bit of fresh air and exercise to get some colour into her cheeks. Her daddy's pale-faced the very same. As long as she goes to church and doesn't miss her bible class, that will be all right, son. Call about three o'clock. I'll have afternoon tea ready. I'm a dab hand at making soda scones.'

After he had gone, Amelia bitterly complained, 'You shouldn't have done that, mummy. I'm not a child. It was up to me.'

'Don't be daft,' Victoria gave a dismissive flick of her

hand. 'If it was left to you, you'd never get anywhere. I wonder if I've enough lard for the scones? I'd better get up early tomorrow and see what I can do.'

Amelia burned with resentment about her mother as she so often did these days, even when she believed her mother to be right.

'And I'll have none of your daddy's black looks either,' Victoria flung at her in passing. 'Away you go to your bed!'

Lying wide-eyed in the dark Amelia tried to sort out her impressions. She came to the conclusion that in retrospect she intensely enjoyed the evening's experience. Gone was the trauma of having to deal with the reality. Now she could enjoy all she wanted in her dreams. She could hold the evening for ever in her mind, shining, perfect, and safe. Her dreams were no long erotic. She felt sick at the mere idea of physical contact. Romance had taken over. She floated ethereally with Douglas to the beautiful strains of violin music. She wore long gauzy dresses and Douglas was elegant in black tie and tails. He told her how beautiful she was and how much he loved her. Occasionally his lips, like the most delicate feather, might brush the back of her hand. All the time he was gentle and sensitive and charming. He took her to all the best places and always in taxis. The best places were usually no more than vague shadowy backgrounds. She had never been to any in real life and so did not know what they looked like. Sometimes, however, she utilized what she had seen in films. Sometimes film performances also merged into the dream. Often, for instance, she and Douglas danced with the exact expertize of Fred Astaire and Ginger Rogers.

Douglas always went down on his bended knees and pleaded with her to marry him. They were married in a church with a holy hush and tall stained-glass windows. She wore a long white shimmering dress and Douglas had never been more proud of her. Love and pride were shining in his eyes. His eyes remained forever like that in their happy marriage as he praised her, for keeping the home so beautiful, for being such a wonderful cook, for entertaining his friends so charmingly. They lived happily ever after, dancing, floating in a delicate dream of love.

Amelia fell asleep hugging the corner of her blanket as she'd always done to comfort herself since she was a child.

16

'It can't be true!' Helena sounded incredulous. Her sea-green eyes stretched wide, raising her brows. 'I mean, honestly, you can't be *in love*. Not you!'

Douglas sparked a lighter to his cigarette. 'What do you think of her?'

'To be quite honest, I don't know what to make of her.'

Douglas looked not merely pleased. He had an eagerness about him that almost amounted to vulnerability. 'Yes. She's different, isn't she? Enigmatic. A blonde Mona Lisa.'

'She's a virgin. That's all that turns you on.'

'The trouble with you, dear sister, is that you're jealous.'

'What? No, honestly, I'd far rather look like sexy Rita Hayworth than a blonde Mona Lisa.' She flicked her fingers up through her hair, admiring in her mind's eye its burnished copper colour and the way it fell in careless curls onto her shoulders.

'You and mother might at least pretend to like her. Not that I care a fuck whether you like her or not.'

'So?'

'It might put her off, that's all. I'm having one hell of a job as it is.'

'Don't lie. I've never seen you getting such a kick in years. How long do you think this one will last?'

Douglas took a long, pleasurable drag at his cigarette before answering, 'She doesn't know it yet but I'm going to marry her.'

For a moment Helena was stunned into speechlessness. Then she managed, 'Marry her?'

'You heard.'

'Isn't that putting too high a price on sex?'

'She's absolute perfection,' Douglas ignored her question. 'I'm longing to paint her.'

'As an angel, no doubt!'

He grinned, 'A nude angel. I will, you know.'

'Well,' she shrugged, 'the best of British luck to you! But have you told mother and father about how you feel?'

'God, it's a wonder you didn't hear mother from Greens Playhouse, or wherever you were cavorting last night.'

'You didn't say you were going to marry her?'

'Why not?'

'You're barely eighteen; that's what *they* said, I bet.'

'Father, of course, in his usual charming manner just said I was an idiot and to stop talking shit.'

'You are planning to finish your course at art school and take your diploma first, though?'

'Wait for years? Fuck that! Why shouldn't I be married while I'm still at art school? And don't say because I can't afford to. Mother's already nagged on about money ad nauseum. Why should money be a problem?'

Helena mocked innocence. 'Because you haven't got any?'

'Mother's got more than enough to go round.'

'You didn't say that, did you? Not in front of dad. He's a bit touchy about that subject. Have you noticed?'

'I simply said that society, and parents in particular, had a duty to support the artist.'

'Dad would love that. I suppose he trotted out his story about fighting his way up from the Gorbals.'

'Not to mention mother's equally boring rise from the cesspit of Springburn.'

'I thought there was a frozen atmosphere at breakfast this morning, but I was still half asleep and didn't care.'

Douglas laughed, 'They're in a cleft stick.'

'How do you mean?'

'They know I have talent and mother especially is fiercely proud of the fact. She *has* to keep me on at art school. She won't cut off my allowance.'

'Maybe not, but I can't see her or dad giving you permission to marry. You'll have to wait at least until you're twenty-one.'

'That's what they said. They've obviously forgotten about Gretna Green.'

Helena's eyes sparkled and her hand flew up to her mouth to catch a giggle. 'You wouldn't! Anyway, I can't imagine you succeeding in persuading Amelia to do anything so rash. To tell you the truth, I can't imagine you persuading that girl to do anything!'

'Want to bet?'

Helena could hardly wait to tell Veronica, who was staggered at the news, then quietly malicious. 'She's a right little cow. A stupid one at that. She can hardly open her mouth.'

'That gives Douglas a chance to talk about himself without interruptions,' Helena said. 'He enjoys that.'

'I couldn't stand her on sight, could you?'

'I can't make up my mind,' Helena said thoughtfully, 'whether she's cold and aloof, or pathologically shy.'

'What're your mum and dad saying to all this?'

'Mum tried to nip the whole thing in the bud by going to see Victoria Drummond. Victoria took it as a personal affront. I mean, honestly, it *was* a daft thing for mother to do. What did she expect Victoria to say? "I agree with you absolutely. My daughter isn't good enough for your son." '

Veronica glowered through her half-curtain of hair. 'They're obviously on the make.'

'Exactly what mum said. Dad told her she didn't mean that and she was getting everything out of proportion. He accused her of taking an absolute hatred to Amelia.'

'I don't blame her. Sly little bitch!'

'Douglas, of course, is enjoying being the centre of all the drama. And he's doing some of his best work. One minute dad's saying he's a right shit and needs a kick up the arse. The next he's saying in that sarcastic kind of way he has that Douglas will go far because he has a definite talent for turning everything to his advantage.' Helena enjoyed a chew at her gum. 'That absolutely infuriates mum. Honestly, Veronica, I'm glad to get out of the house for a few hours.'

She and Veronica were on their way to a party in a fellow student's basement flat in Argyle Street. Their high heels clicked a cheerful accompaniment to their conversation and

111

Helena's taffeta skirt added swishing sounds like cymbals glancing against each other. They were each carrying a bag of beer cans and it was obvious by the smell rising from the converted cellar when they arrived that it was already crowded with people. Descending the steps the two girls were immediately cut off from the light and air of Argyle Street. A fog enveloped them. It stank of smoking candles, beer, Pasha cigarettes, crotch sweat, hot hairy armpits, paint-stained corduroys, Brylcreem and talcum powder. A gramophone record was blaring out, 'All of me, Why not take all of me . . .'

Both chewing energetically, Helena and Veronica began dancing with one another so that, for a few more minutes at least, they could continue with their conversation.

'As mum said, it's not as if she's clever at anything or has a sparkling personality. What help would a girl like Amelia ever be to Douglas, she keeps saying. Of course, she's tolerably pretty, if you like that type.'

'She's not pretty!' Veronica scoffed.

'Fancy having her for a *sister-in-law*,' Helena rolled her eyes. 'I mean, honestly, have you ever known anyone so *dead boring*!'

Amelia's trust in Douglas was gradual and extremely cautious. It was his lack of judgement in liking her that made her suspicious more than anything else. She wanted to trust him. She wanted to believe all the wonderful things he said. She needed his love. Yet love seemed to her such a dangerous, treacherous thing. In a way, she felt safer and more able to cope without it. But it had a magic side to it, too. At least with Douglas it had. He made her feel so happy she wanted to sing and dance. Not just in day-dreams but actually sing out loud and swirl round the house. Until one day, she seemed to overdo her display of happy exuberance because she suddenly felt dizzy and sick. The feeling soon went away, only to return next morning in waves of acute nausea. She didn't mention it to her mother. Her mother would only have accused her of another ploy of trying to get out of seeing Douglas. Although she had been seeing him

112

more and more often recently. He never seemed to be off the doorstep. Sometimes she suspected he watched her all the time. More than once he had suddenly confronted her in the street when she had been out shopping for her mother, or just out alone walking and thinking. She was beginning actually to believe that he liked her company. The belief was a drop of pure water in the desert of her soul. Gratefully, she opened up to one seed of trust after another. She had faith in him. Her gladness was so all-consuming no sound was needed to express it. No sound, no song could do justice to the joy inside her.

Victoria said to Mrs McDade, 'He's besotted with her, you know. Absolutely besotted. He can't take his eyes off her. If he's done one sketch of her, he's done a hundred and one. He says he's taking notes so to speak – for the painting he's going to do.'

'Didn't I tell you, dear,' Mrs McDade said, 'unusual and dramatic things are always happening around you. First it was Jamie getting married and Fiona inviting all those posh people, and then her telling you she wasn't having a baby after all. Now it's Amelia going with an artist, and the son of Rory Donovan, too,' she added hastily, because Fiona's trick to get Victoria's cooperation for her marriage was something that still enraged Victoria.

Douglas had sketched Mrs McDade. A few rapid strokes and there she was on paper – anxious pixie face with its half-moon specs, close-fitting felt hat with its turned-up brim, tiny trembling mouth.

'One of these days, Mrs McDade,' he said, as he presented it to her, 'that's going to be worth a lot of money, especially now that I've signed it. Take good care of it.'

'Oh I will, I will,' Mrs McDade breathlessly assured him.

'*Such* a nice lad,' both Mrs McDade and Victoria agreed afterwards.

He'd sketched Victoria too. He'd caught exactly the aura of defensive pride about the tilt of her head and quirk of her mouth, and the expression of mixed defiance and apprehension in her eyes.

Amelia was enormously proud of Douglas. She had not

reached the point of self-confidence, however, that could provide her with the courage to tell him so. Indeed she seldom said very much. He did most of the talking. They walked arm-in-arm now or hand-in-hand, and that felt the most natural thing in the world, and the most delightful. Her mother seemed to take vicarious pleasure in this. She would watch them from her window and when Amelia turned to wave, her mother would smile and wave back. Then, in an eager, childishly expectant kind of way, she would keep watching until they disappeared from sight. It was an extra bonus of happiness that at last she had done something that met with her mother's wholehearted approval.

Then suddenly Douglas had suggested they elope. She was thrown once more into doubt and confusion. 'Don't you want to marry me?' he had asked.

'Your mother is against us even seeing one another.'

'There's nothing she can do once we're legally married. She'll soon get used to the idea. She'll have to once it's a *fait accompli.*'

'I'll ask my mother and see what she says.'

'Better not, darling. Your mother will only beard the lion in its den and you know what happened the last time the two lions, or rather lionesses, got together. You don't want that again, do you?'

Indeed she did not. The quarrel between Rory and her mother had been painfully distressing to witness.

'Darling Amelia, your mother will be delighted. We'll leave her a note explaining why we thought this way would be best and easiest for all concerned.'

Amelia was not at all sure, especially after the awful way Fiona and Jamie had deceived Victoria. No doubt they had convinced themselves that it was the easiest way at the time. The trauma of such a course of action as Douglas proposed, especially the long journey now that Amelia was feeling far from well, apart from whether or not it was fair to her mother, was not something she felt capable of rushing into. Feeling so nauseated every morning, sometimes even being sick down the lavatory pan was proving very weakening.

'Darling,' Douglas assured her, 'your mother will be delighted and I'd be so proud to have you as my wife. Not in three years' time, but now. Right now.'

She wanted to please him. She wanted him to be proud of her. That was why in the end she murmured a worried, 'All right.'

17

'Damn Victoria!' Rory shouted brokenly, as soon as Winnie had brought in the coffee and cleared away the rest of the lunch dishes. 'She was always a bloody romantic. This has been her idea!'

'Calm down,' Donovan said. 'You don't know that.'

'I'm telling you I do! I've known her since we were kids at primary school. This is exactly the kind of thing she'd dream up.'

'Douglas is eighteen years of age . . .'

'A mere boy! Hardly more than an innocent child.'

'Don't be ridiculous,' Donovan snapped. 'He's a man, and more experienced than he ought to be at eighteen if you ask me. By the look of Amelia she's the innocent one.'

Rory's face hardened. 'This is Victoria's doing . . .'

'Face facts. Douglas wanted to marry the girl and we disapproved of her. If anyone's to blame we are.'

Helena came over and put an arm round her mother's shoulders, 'Mum's upset, dad.'

Donovan drained his cup of coffee and wiped his mouth with a napkin. 'It's been a shock for all of us but losing our heads won't help. There's nothing we can do. It's too late. They've posted this from Gretna Green. They're married and that's that!'

'What gets me,' Rory reached for one of the big crystal ashtrays and jerked it towards her, 'is how it's all been carefully planned beforehand and not a word to anyone. He's even organized a flat to come back to.'

'In my book, that's in his favour. At least he's not just coming back here and dumping all his responsibilities onto us. Flat and studio, the letter says, so he's meaning to work. He'll be OK, Rory. He's got the kind of ruthlessness that will get him through anything.'

Rory viciously stubbed out her cigarette. 'It's the way it

happened. And he could have done better than Amelia Drummond. Girls from some of the wealthiest families round here were after him. He could have had any of them.'

'He probably had all of them,' Donovan said. 'We'll just have to make the best of it, Rory.'

'It's Victoria bloody Drummond behind this. I'll never forgive the stupid interfering cow. Never as long as I live.'

'Christ!' Donovan groaned. 'I give up. I'm going back to work. See you tonight.'

'Are you all right, mum,' Helena asked after Donovan had left. 'Can I get you a drink?'

'Make it a large brandy. She was always like that, you know.'

'Who?'

'Victoria. Her head was always full of romantic ideas. But at the same time she was frigid. Still is. She's given Matthew Drummond one hell of a life. I'm really worried, Helena. I'm afraid it'll be like mother, like daughter. Didn't you get that impression? Amelia isn't easy-going and natural like the rest of you.'

'Right enough,' Helena was intrigued. 'At the party – remember? She seemed to shrink back when any of the blokes touched her – even Douglas. How do you know her mother's frigid?'

Rory took a swig of the brandy Helena had poured out. 'Her mother before her, old Mrs Buchanan, was the very same. She used to be always going on at us and warning us about men's "animal instincts" and the dangers of "human nature". She always said those words as if she needed to hurry and wash her mouth out afterwards. She would have died rather than say the word "sex". Victoria and I used to giggle behind her back.' She watched the brandy slop around in the bulbous glass for a few seconds before going on, 'But Victoria soon became like her mother, worse I'd say. Much worse. At least Mrs Buchanan recognized her husband's needs. She did her "duty" as she called it. Not Victoria. She's always regarded it as Matty's "duty" to control his animal instincts. She's probably never forgiven him for Amelia's conception. As far as I understood it – after Jamie, that was to be the end of it.'

'Gosh, I'm beginning to feel sorry for Douglas, as well. You've just got to look at Amelia!'

'Victoria would have been the death of Matty – they fought like cat and dog, you know, always have. I know him better than anyone. He would have been dead by now if he hadn't had his politics. All his passion and his reason for living have gone into that.'

'Gosh! Victoria doesn't know how lucky she is. I mean, he's so handsome and clever.'

'So is your brother, Helena. Do you think Amelia Drummond realizes how lucky she is?' Rory shaded her eyes with one hand. 'I can't bear the thought of seeing the same pattern happen all over again with my boy. Damn Victoria and her bloody daughter!'

Everything had happened too quickly for Amelia's mind to take it in. Douglas had proved himself to be an enthusiastic and efficient organizer and, used to a lifetime of being organized and told what to do by her mother, it was in a way as if nothing had changed. Life was just muddling along with the same puzzling confusion. Yet now, above and beyond the familiar layer of her existence, was pure joy. She had to keep pinching herself, shutting and opening wide her eyes to convince herself that it was true. That Douglas was true, that his feelings for her were true, that they were actually *getting married*. Surely at any minute she would wake up only to discover it had all been a dream? Even when Douglas kissed her after the ceremony, it had a dreamlike quality. She was dazed with happiness. On the way to the hotel he had kept his arm around her and kept whispering words of love to her. All through dinner he had gazed at her as if she was his most precious, most beautiful possession, and the one of which he was most proud. Indeed he had told her that over and over again. She became hypnotized by his words and, helped by the relaxing effect of the wine, she began almost to believe them. She believed them enough to be able to come, cautiously at first, like a timid tortoise, out of her shell, until she was able, once in the privacy of their own room, to undress with shy happiness at being given the opportunity to give him pleasure. She was able, despite her timid flutterings and tremblings, to allow him to caress her breasts and private parts. Kissing her deeply, tenderly, he carried her over to the bed and as he moved on top of her he put out the light. And the light went out of her life. The moment he plunged inside her she knew all the love and tenderness had gone. If it had ever existed in the first place. There was a quick vicious climax then he rolled off her to lie at her side, his head back against his linked hands.

After a long silence in which she sank into an abyss, she managed to ask dully, 'What's wrong?'

'Aw, shut up,' Douglas snarled. 'You know damned well what's wrong.'

She was a baby in her cot again, sensing her mother's revulsion and hatred. She was five years old, sitting hopelessly on the tenement steps. She was an alien-skinned eight-year-old being scrubbed out of existence. She was a sixteen-year-old reflected as a maggot in her mother's eyes. She knew that Douglas was going to look at her like that. She had known it all along.

In the morning she crept out of bed not knowing what to do or where to go. In the bathroom she was sick, and retched so violently and for so long she thought she was going to die. Douglas glowered all through breakfast and never spoke to her all the way back to Glasgow. She tried to take comfort from the flat, her own home, her refuge and her strength – that is how she had thought of it. It proved no refuge, however, from Douglas's fury at her, especially once he found out about her morning sickness.

'You sly little slut,' he was almost weeping with rage. 'You've tricked me into marrying you to give your bastard a name. You'll be sorry for this. Nobody takes me for a mug and gets away with it.'

'I don't understand,' she said.

'Don't come the innocent with me any more. It won't

119

work. I know you are having another man's baby and you know you are having another man's baby. What happened? Did he refuse to marry you, or have there been so many men you don't know who the father is? Or was it a case of I came along and I was the best catch?'

'I don't know what you're talking about,' she said. But she could not meet his eyes because she did know. Or thought she did. VJ night and all its terrors came flooding back to her. Hastily she dodged the memory and began tidying up the flat. It used to be that her escape was to retreat into immobility and day-dreams. Now she found day-dreams to be of no use. Physical activity was the thing. She kept the flat spotless, which was not easy after some of Douglas's parties. He reminded her of her mother in the way that he could be two different people. To outsiders he was the same life and soul of the party, and it amazed her how he could laugh in apparent pleasure at his friends' ribald jokes about his randy virility and compliments on getting her pregnant so soon. Only when they were alone did he seethe and glower and sneer and snap and do everything possible to prove how much he loathed and detested her. As her pregnancy progressed he never tired of telling her how fat and ugly she looked.

'You're like a fat, flat-footed duck the way you waddle about,' he would say. Or 'You look bloody enormous in that bell-tent of a coat. How many air force blankets went into that?'

Right from the start they had separate beds. She slept in the bedroom and he slept on a divan in his studio. This was the worst cut of all. Even her father and mother, who seemed to have nothing in common and who fought all the time, still shared a bed when he came home. It was a matter of a basic need for comforting contact with another human being. It was belonging to someone no matter what they were like. Her mother gave the impression without needing to say it (although she often did) that Matthew was 'her man' and she was content and secure in the rightness of her status.

'No matter what he's done,' she had said to Amelia before

120

plunging wholeheartedly into working on his behalf in the election, 'he's my man and it's only right that I should stand by him.'

Douglas did not want her to stand by him. He did not want her to do anything except get out of his way and keep out of his sight. If he was in the sitting room, she sat in the bedroom all evening. She would knit for the baby or she would write in one of her notebooks. In the notebook she tried to pin down each nuance of feeling. In a strange way it helped keep her sane, because it was not just the feelings she was concentrating on when she was writing. It was the actual words. The words became a diversion, a challenge, something positive to latch on to. Finding the right words and structuring them, acquiring the instinct to impose a shape to the expression of her experience began, despite the struggle, to give her pleasure. A notebook became a secret bolt-hole. And it was hers. And hers alone.

18

Drummond had to face the fact that the Ridgeways were nice people. He liked them. He supposed that his intelligence had always accepted that not all wealthy business tycoons or landed aristocrats were wicked exploiters of the poor. It was the system that was at fault; and the vagaries and weaknesses of human nature. Greed, for instance, and the lack of experience of living and working conditions other than one's own, and therefore the lack of understanding. There had to be a system that protected the weak against the greed and ruthlessness of the strong. But one man's freedom must not be another man's prison. Freedom had to be zealously protected. In his view 'everyone for himself', 'free for all' was the kind of freedom not worth having. He had long since, however, grown out of his wild beliefs of bloody revolution. The trouble with revolution was another group of strong and ruthless people could take over. The ordinary man in the street could still be oppressed and made to suffer, although perhaps in different ways.

He was a firm believer in democracy while at the same time being aware of its weaknesses. He remembered only too well the poor attendances and the thankless struggles he had had at union meetings. The Communists always conscientiously turned up to put their point of view and to register their vote. That was their democratic right. In those early days he only wished he had had such fervent and conscientious men among his Labour Party so-called supporters. It came down to the human factor again. Instead of taking their part in the democratic process from the grass-roots, most men could not be bothered. They stayed at home with their families. They put their feet up and listened to the wireless, or they relaxed over a pint of beer in the pub. They did not value democracy enough even after witnessing what happened in Nazi Germany.

It was a person's holding to principle, it was the taking the trouble to keep oneself informed, it was the acceptance of personal responsibility, it was conscientiously applying one's self to the most mundane and thankless tasks at grass-roots level, that laid the foundation on which democracy either stood firm or crumbled.

It turned out that the Ridgeways (Lord and Lady Ridgeway, to give them their proper title,) were Liberals. He had long since discovered that most Liberals were nice people, too nice, that was their problem. In one of his many discussions with Alan Ridgeway, he more or less told him this and added, 'Politics depends on power and unless you have men who have a ruthless streak and are schemers like Gladstone or Lloyd George, the Liberals are never going to get power.'

He had discovered that Alan Ridgeway enjoyed an argument. He had been a professor at the Dragon School at Oxford, but when his elder brother was killed during the war he had inherited the title and the estate. It had meant giving up his career and coming north from Oxford to Innerleithen. He obviously missed the debates and dis-cussions at Oxford and the stimulation and challenge of mixing with people of widely differing views. Drummond could well imagine that the local hunting, fishing and shooting types would not be on a par, to put it mildly, with Ridgeway's enquiring intelligence. Drummond realized that it was for this reason more than any other that Ridgeway welcomed his now quite-frequent visits. He was able to visit Innerleithen House at least once a month as he only returned to Glasgow every fortnight for his surgeries and to see Victoria. Ridgeway's pleasure at having him as a guest was guarded, of course. Caroline had once said her father was shy but his shyness was of a different type from Drummond's.

Lord Ridgeway had the 'born to rule' expression that seemed to perpetually look down from a great height. His eyes never lost their look of distant appraisal. He was the type of man who could command instant attention and first-class service without needing to ask for it. It was obvious by his face and his bearing that he expected the best and believed it to be his right. Drummond had met similar 'born to rule' types in London and their aloof appraisal had never failed to trigger off a spark of defiance in him. His eyes had always responded with the signal – 'I'm every inch as good as you. Indeed I am intellectually your superior.'

Alan Ridgeway did not have this effect on him. Nor did Lady Ridgeway, a quiet but elegantly spoken woman, who always looked comfortable and casual during the day in flat shoes, long loose cardigan and a silk scarf tucked in the open neck of her blouse. Her distancing of him was more subtle and tempered by a sensitive and gentle nature. Drummond believed it was also the sensitive intelligence he detected in Alan Ridgeway that took the edge off his cool and aristocratic manner.

On his first visit, he received from Lord and Lady Ridgeway impeccable politeness and hospitality, but he could have been a creature from outer space. They were not sure what to make of him. Indeed it could be said Drummond felt much the same about them.

At first he had sat in their dining room taking in the scene with a somewhat cynical eye; the table laid with the silver punch bowl inscribed with the family coat of arms, the *Famille Rose* plates, the Bristol glass finger bowls and eighteenth-century knives and forks. Caroline told him the names of her ancestors depicted in the portraits hanging in heavy gold frames around the walls. There were more stern-faced portraits (Lords, Earls and Honourables) in the lower drawing room. This room led off the dining room and both areas, he noticed, were hung with the same hand-blocked French wallpaper. The paper alone, he reckoned, must have cost a fortune, even back in the days when it was first put up. Despite his initial cynicism he found it all too easy to relax in the lower drawing room with an after-dinner brandy and cigar. He warmed to the place as well as the people. It was very civilized reclining back in one of the comfortable chairs beside the log fire, its aroma spiced with the smoke from one of Lord Ridgeway's cigars. It was wonderful not to feel crowded or hemmed in. Here there was room for the soul to grow. Here one could wander alone down corridors, or browse to one's heart's content in the magnificent library on the second floor. Not even Caroline distracted him; earnest, intelligent Caroline, who seemed to know instinctively what he had always needed. After a time he went searching for her and together they strolled outside in the grounds. It seemed as if there was no one else in the world except the two of them. The back of the castle with its terraced garden and pavilions was always visible through the trees. Its old walls were yellowed by sunshine, but no movement or shadow reflected the slightest sign of life. He consciously impressed the scene on his mind so that he would never lose it. Later he would capture every sight and sensation in his journal. Where it was clear of trees, the sun, shimmering and breathless, showed the path a mere thread through the grass. Then there was the shade of the yew trees, where they were awakened out of their mesmerized silence by the startled flight of some roe deer.

'You're happy here,' Caroline said.

'How could anyone help being happy in a place like this?'

'Lots of people would hate it. Even some of our relatives find it incredibly boring and can't wait to dash back to the city.'

He sighed and gazed up at the sun winking spasmodically through beech, elm, red cedar and sycamore. He had never seen anything so beautiful. He wished he was a painter so that he could capture everything on canvas. But he would do the next best thing and paint the scene with words.

Caroline said, 'Let's sit down by the stream.' Here the foliage was so dense only ghostly fingers of light filtered through. Water splashed and frolicked with a muted sound and the occasional shy sparkle.

'Tell me about your wife,' Caroline said unexpectedly.

Drummond was silent for a time. Eventually he said, 'Victoria would not like it here. I believe she would not only feel restless, but depressed and afraid.'

'Afraid?'

He shrugged. 'Nervous then. Or tense. She is happiest and most at ease with noise and bustle and people around her. After my daughter got married, she took in lodgers rather than be in the house on her own.'

That was part of the reason why whenever possible he avoided going home now, despite his pleasure in seeing his grandson, Amelia's little boy. The small council house was so crowded it was claustrophobic. There was a navy man and his wife and a young child in the front room. They also had the use of the two bedrooms, one for themselves and one for the child, and of course the kitchenette and bathroom. He had to remain in the cramped living room all the time, even trying to shave there with a brush in a mug in front of the mantelpiece mirror. Victoria, bustling past, would knock his elbow and make him cut himself with his razor. He invariably lost his temper as a result and she immediately lashed back with a catalogue of all his faults and every despicable thing he had ever done, but always in a low voice in case the lodgers would hear her.

'Oh, Matthew!' Caroline put her hand over his. 'I can't bear you to be unhappy.'

He smiled round at her. 'I'm happy here with you. Come to think of it – I'm happy anywhere with you.'

He was not sure if Caroline made the first move or he did, but their arms reached round each other in a comforting, nursing kind of way at first. Then passion grew with their rocking motion until they were moving with it and, in that beautiful private place, he became more intimate with her than he had ever been with any woman before. They strolled back eventually with arms around each others' waists. That night she came to him in the big four-poster bed and they made love until they were happily exhausted.

'Stay another night,' Caroline said. 'At least one other night. Why go to your wife when she obviously makes your life so miserable?'

'I have surgeries to attend to. I have a responsibility to my constituents.'

She had just sighed and left it at that. She had not gone into a huff. She had not been cool or angry or made him suffer. He loved her all the more for that. He loved her serious grey eyes. He loved her hair and the way it curled behind her ears. He loved her lithe, youthful body and the way it lapped up love-making like a thirsty kitten. He loved the way that, at other times, she could quietly distance herself.

It was only afterwards alone on his way to Glasgow to fulfil his responsibilities to his constituents that he remembered his responsibilities to his wife. Poor Victoria, with her middle-aged spread, greying hair and ever-recurring 'internal problems'. They had been married a long time and, despite their differences, there was still a bond. In a way he still loved her. He did not believe that such a precious thing as love could ever die. He loved the Victoria he had courted and married, and with whom he had set up house and shared such optimistic dreams. That Victoria was still there, entwined and overlaid with a lifetime of struggles, of happy and sad experience. They had grown up together through shortages of money, through the childrens' illnesses, through Granny Buchanan's heart attacks, through his pleurisy and double pneumonia. For better or for worse, Victoria was part of him and he of her. The operation of cutting themselves apart was neither going to be easy nor painless. He had no desire to hurt Victoria. Indeed he cringed from such a prospect. Victoria would be cruelly hurt if he told her that not only had he been unfaithful to her, he wanted a divorce so that he could marry the other woman. Victoria would not understand it. He was 'her man' and to Victoria that was that. 'Till death us do part' they had vowed and, to Victoria, that was that. She would never give him a divorce. At the same time he had to do his best to make her see reason. There was also the fact that he detested deceit.

Every time he arrived home now it shocked him with its shabbiness and lack of comfort. There was only linoleum on the floor of the windowless lobby and, as he entered it, he was nauseated by a mixture of smells: baby's soiled nappies, baby's vomit, boiling cabbage, chips and vinegar, and the bleach in which the bed-sheets were soaking.

Victoria in rolled-up sleeves, a floral wrap-around apron and checked slippers, greeted him with her usual peck on

127

the cheek, 'Hello, dear, had a nice journey?' She must have had her hands and arms in the bleach water while attending to the sheets because the smell was overpowering.

She was proud of the fact that she had managed to scrape up enough coupons to get him a piece of boiled beef to go with the cabbage. She had also been busy baking one of her apple tarts and had made a pot of custard for pudding. She enjoyed some of everything herself but enjoyed even more watching him eat.

'I queued for an hour for that beef,' she said for the second or third time. 'I was determined to get it for your tea.'

'It's delicious,' he responded mechanically. Admittedly it was true. Victoria had always been a good cook.

'You're enjoying it, then?'

'Yes.' He struggled to quell his irritation.

While he was still eating, the navy man's wife, who looked as if she had been built with Michelin tyres, came to stand in the living room doorway, nursing a baby in her arms and otherwise ignoring its lusty howls.

'It's his teeth,' she explained, grinning over at his plate. 'Enjoying your beef?' She raised her voice in competition with her offspring. 'Mrs Drummond waited over an hour along the road for it, didn't you, hen? Me and my man have been enjoying the smell of it cooking.' She gave a screech of laughter that sent the baby's sobs careering into screams. 'But never a taste for us. Our tongues have been hanging out, so they have!'

'Oh here,' Victoria said. 'I'm awfully sorry, Sadie, have a wee taste of mine.'

The navy man's head appeared over the mountain of his wife's shoulder. 'Don't pay any attention to her, Mrs Drummond. She'd take the bite out your mouth if you'd let her,' he shouted.

'What a cheek!' his wife laughingly protested. 'I was only kidding. Honest I was, Mrs Drummond.'

'I know, but all the same,' Victoria said, 'I'd be happier if you took just a wee taste.'

Sadie looked over at Drummond and yelled, 'She's a

right gem, isn't she? She'd give you her last farthing so she would.'

'Have a wee taste, just to please me,' Victoria insisted, holding out a piece of beef skewered on her fork.

It was as much as Drummond could do to prevent himself from throwing his own plate of food at them and striding from the cluttered room. He managed to remain glued to his seat through the nerve-jangling uproar, but gave himself acid indigestion and a blistering headache in the process.

Then Amelia arrived with little Harry, and he found some solace looking at the baby lying in his arms and gazing back at him with adoration. Amelia was too thin and had a strained look about her, and it occurred to him that her husband never seemed to be with her. He wondered if Douglas Donovan was being good to her. His suspicions were confirmed when he managed a moment's privacy with her in the lobby just before she left. 'Are you happy, Amelia?' he asked.

She avoided his eyes and looked down at the baby. 'As long as I've got Harry,' she said. 'He's my only reason for living.'

He had meant to confront Victoria with the fact that their marriage was over and that he wanted a divorce. Apart from anything else he had promised Caroline that he would. Now his mind was hedged about with worries about Amelia.

In the end it was Amelia and Harry and how Douglas Donovan was treating them that became the sole topic of conversation.

19

Amelia did not want to go back to live at Hilltop Road. She dreaded it. She had no choice, however. If it had only been herself to consider it would have been different. She no longer had any illusions about Douglas. He had long since stopped being a knight in shining armour. He hated her and she hated him. Before Harry's birth she had suffered every insult, neglect and cruelty from him, and felt neither hatred nor anger, only misery and guilt. Douglas's repeated attempts to be cruel to the baby, however, had brought ferocious hatred. She lived on her nerves since the first moment she had heard him slap Harry because he had been crying. She had run through from the kitchen and snatched Harry into her arms just as Douglas was raising a clenched fist. She had only to glimpse his swaggering figure and cropped red head coming along the road for her stomach to turn acid. She watched Douglas all the time now, never leaving him alone with Harry, not even for a minute. She had wanted to walk out for good a hundred times, but where could she go? She had no money and she could not bear the thought of Harry suffering in any way. At least in the flat the baby could share her warm bedroom and had all the material comforts he needed.

Then her mother found out about Douglas. She too became anxious. Only, her mother believed in making a fight of everything. Amelia's hatred smouldered in silence whereas her mother's emotions always needed to be expressed in positive action, usually in a verbal attack. She came regularly to the flat and told Douglas exactly what she thought of him. Even when Douglas, in answering fury, shouted at her that the baby was not his, her mother reeled, but only for a second.

'Harry's an innocent wee baby. Nothing excuses cruelty to an innocent child.'

Later, after Douglas had stormed out, Amelia had said, 'I keep telling you, mummy, you only make things worse. Every time you come you make things worse!'

'How dare you speak to me like that, you wicked girl,' her mother's anger had turned on her. 'Was that true what he said – the baby isn't his?'

Amelia lowered her eyes. 'Yes.'

'You wicked, wicked girl! Whose is it then?'

'I . . . I don't know.'

'You don't know?' her mother gasped incredulously. 'You don't know?' Then, half to herself, 'Is this not terrible? Not even your daddy's ever been as bad as this. Both your daddy and I have always kept ourselves pure.'

'It must have been on VJ night.'

'Oh, I can believe that,' Victoria said bitterly. 'The state you came home in. Is this not terrible? I don't know what your daddy's going to say about this.'

'Please don't tell daddy.'

'If I don't tell him, he'll want to murder Douglas. You know what a temper your daddy has. If I do tell him, he'll want to murder you.'

'Just don't tell him anything at all,' Amelia pleaded. 'Just let him think I'm happily married and everything's all right.'

'Don't be daft. It's obvious to anyone with half an eye that you're not happy and everything's not all right.'

As it turned out her mother had not told her daddy about the baby not being Douglas's, only about Douglas being cruel to them both.

'It took me all my time,' her mother said afterwards, 'to keep your daddy from dashing away over to the west end and getting Douglas by the throat. It's lucky for all of us that your daddy had to go back to London.'

It was then that the pressure started to get her to return to Hilltop Road.

'Do you not think you've done enough to make that child suffer,' her mother asked, 'bringing it into the world without a father, then putting it at the mercy of that monster? If you've a scrap of decency left in you or any love

131

at all for that child, you'll take it away from here at once.'

At other times she would take another tack. She would say in a kinder tone, 'You've no need to worry. You've always had a good home with your daddy and me, and you always will. Your daddy said he'd cut down on his expenses as best he can, so that he can send me a bit extra to cover the expense of having you and the baby at home. Your daddy says you've just to come home and not worry about anything. He's good that way,' she added generously.

It was tempting. She longed to unwind her taut nerves and feel sure that Harry would be safe. Yet to go back home was at the same time like walking into a quicksand. Harry would certainly be safe from being battered. Was there not a danger, however, that he might be driven down, suffocated and destroyed as his mother had been before him? Would she not need to keep her nerves equally taut and alert to this kind of danger, just as much as the other? More and more she felt caught between the devil and the deep blue sea. She did not know which way to turn. Her tension and anxiety were of course transmitted to the baby who cried almost incessantly during every night. She had to stagger about the bedroom nursing him, until she felt so fatigued she could have been violent to him herself. It was that fact and not her mother's increasingly bullying and aggressive tactics that persuaded her in the end that she had to return to Hilltop Road. Her sense of failure had never been so crushing. Yet it never ceased to surprise her how the steel in her soul kept her from going under altogether. She was like someone hanging above a precipice by her finger-tips and everyone stamping on her fingers to try to make her let go. She could not do anything to stop them but she could and did shut her eyes, grit her teeth and stubbornly hang on.

She had known right from the start that it was not going to be easy at home. It was not that her mother meant any harm. She remembered when she had first gone into labour, her mother had sat by her bedside in the flat tensing and screwing up her face in sympathetic pain at each contraction. Eventually the midwife had to insist that she left.

At first her mother did not pay any attention. Only when she was reminded that it was late and if she did not leave she would miss the last bus home, did she reluctantly rise from the bedside. The next evening, however, before Amelia had recovered from the utter exhaustion of the birth, she had returned and happily announced she had invited a few friends to come and see the baby. Amelia still had nightmares about lying helplessly watching a crowd of cigarette-smoking women crowding round and bending over the sleeping infant. Her mother had made a party of the occasion and brought tins of home-made scones and fancy cakes to feed everybody. The small bedroom was grey with smoke, and rattling with tea cups and plates and continuous exhausting chatter. It had wakened the baby who had screamed and coughed, and she had felt like screaming herself but had not enough strength.

She was not home for very long when the real problem started. Her mother had told the navy man and his wife they had to leave but got them temporary accommodation with a neighbour until they found a place of their own.

'Never let it be said,' she told Amelia, 'that I made anyone homeless.'

After the lodgers left, Victoria slept on her usual bed-settee in the living room. One bedroom (a tiny box room hardly big enough to hold a single bed and nothing else) was used as a 'glory hole' as Victoria called it, in which to keep the baby's pram and all the other 'paraphernalia' that Amelia had brought with her. The other, almost as tiny, room was for Amelia to sleep in. The baby's cot was put in the front room. Victoria always insisted that it sat in front of the gas fire, despite the fact that she also insisted the baby should be put to sleep dressed in as much clothing as it wore when taken outside in its pram, including its woolly bonnet. With only her instincts to go on – nobody had ever told her anything about how babies were supposed to be looked after – Amelia tried to move the cot to the other end of the room, tried to remove the bonnet from the pink sweating head. All to no avail. Her mother promptly moved it back again and retied the bonnet. She would try again, of course, and again and again. All to no avail. Her mother was a very determined woman. It reminded her of a million other battles of will between her mother and her father – battles that had long ago become part of the debilitating fabric of her life.

Her mother would switch on the wireless. Her father would switch it off. Her mother would switch it on, louder than ever. Her father would switch it off. On, off, on, off, while all the time a battle raged between them. A battle that even her father could never win.

Her father, however, could always make some sort of escape. He could stride off to the pub. Or to a union or council or Labour Party meeting. Now he escaped to London. She had no avenue of escape even if she had had enough strength and self-confidence left to take it.

Her mother never argued with her. She obviously did not think Amelia worth arguing with. She would get the baby's bath ready, humming and singing happily as she did so, completely ignoring Amelia's protests and even her attempts physically to take the bath from her mother.

'Harry's *my* baby,' she protested over and over again. 'I want to look after him. I want to bath him . . . I want to dress him . . . I want to give him his bottle . . .'

It did not matter in the slightest what she said or did, her mother completely ignored her and went on happily singing and concentrating her whole attention on busily looking after Harry – even taking him out in the pram to show off and use as a conversation piece while waiting in queues along at the shops.

Amelia began to feel worse than she had in the flat living with Douglas. It was one thing hating Douglas – a man who could inflict pain on a helpless infant. It was quite another hating one's good-living Christian mother. A woman who had always 'kept herself pure'. To hate one's mother had fearful overtones of wickedness and guilt that could not be excused or rationalized away. It said in the bible – 'Honour thy father and thy mother'. Far from honouring her mother, far beyond even hating her, Amelia had become obsessed with the desire to murder her. Or at least, one part of her longed to commit the act of murder. Another part of her was appalled at the mere idea. Indeed, she became terrified that she would black out and harm Victoria without knowing it. She had been having temporary blackouts recently. They had begun after she had gone into the front room to look at the baby and smelled gas. The fire had gone out for the want of a penny. Then someone had put a penny in the meter in order to boil a kettle for a cup of tea. The gas of course had started to hiss through the unlit mantle of the room fire.

She rushed to the cot, snatched Harry up and flew with him to the open front door. Then, oh thank you, God, Harry opened his eyes and smiled up at her. She would remember that smile and that look of love and trust until the end of her days.

'What are you doing with Harry at that open door?' her mother had come striding along the lobby. 'You'll give the poor wee mite his death of cold.'

For once Amelia had been glad of her mother snatching Harry from her. She had begun to tremble so violently she was physically unable to hold the baby herself. She was literally chattering as if from icy cold. Her legs could barely carry her through to the living room. Her mother was already there, laughing and happily dandling Harry on her knee, and singing out – 'Who's granny's clever wee boy, then?'

Ashen-faced, Amelia sank down on to a chair. 'He might have been gassed,' Amelia said, 'if I hadn't gone through just now, he would have been dead.'

'Don't be daft,' Victoria said. 'Who's granny's clever wee boy, then?'

Amelia thought – this is real. It's not my imagination. It is not a dream. I really am going to kill her. I'm going to kill her. I'm going to kill her.

20

Rory was just working her way round to forgiving Amelia (and Victoria) and taking Donovan's advice to 'make the best of it', when Douglas dropped his bombshell. She had seen, of course, that he was unhappy and she had said to Donovan, 'I knew it. That girl was just not the right one for him. Have you ever seen Douglas so miserable?'

Donovan was forced to admit that he had not. Before his marriage Douglas had a swagger about him and a noisy exuberance. He did everything with an enthusiastic and selfish panache. He drank too much with careless enjoyment. Now he drank too much with morose determination. He was miserable, all right. Nevertheless Rory was prepared to do her best for Amelia for the sake of the baby.

'I'll buy the pram and the cot,' she promised, 'I've contacts who I think can be persuaded to lay their hands on quite a few things for the baby.'

'Don't bother,' Douglas said.

'No bother,' she assured him. 'I'm used to wheeling and dealing. I enjoy it. And the baby's going to need a pram and a cot.'

'I don't care a shit what it's going to need,' Douglas said.

She had been both shocked and angry. 'How can you talk like that about your own child?'

'It's not my child.'

She had been stunned into silence. Eventually she managed, 'You mean she . . .?'

'If you say I told you so, mother, I'll swing for you. I swear it!'

'The sly little shit!'

'My sentiments exactly. But for God's sake, mother, don't tell anyone. I feel a right fool.'

'As far as I'm concerned, this won't go beyond the family. You can depend on it.'

'Thank you.'

She could not bear to see his young face soured with such bitterness. 'Is there anything else I can do to help, Douglas? You know you only need to ask.'

He shook his head. 'An artist has to suffer for the sake of his art.'

Normally she or Donovan, especially Donovan, would have laughed at this sort of remark. But even Donovan did not laugh when she told him. He groaned and shook his head. 'Kids! Why the hell did we have any? They're nothing but a worry.'

Right enough they had been worried about Helena as well. It had come to Donovan's notice that she was in the habit of staying out late and he had caught her one night the worse for drink. He had told Helena what he thought of her behaviour in no uncertain terms. Helena had the cheek to answer back and there had been one terrible row, more than one in fact because it happened again.

'You're a fine one to talk. The way you knock it back,' Helena had shouted at her father on the second occasion. 'Anyone would think that you had hollow legs.'

'None of your impertinence! What I do is my business.' Donovan snapped back.

'And what I do is *my* business,' Helena retorted.

'That's where you're wrong. You are my business. I'm responsible for you until you're at least twenty-one.' He had turned to Rory then. 'No more perks for her until she learns to behave herself, do you hear? I don't care if you get a hundred pairs of stockings into the shop, she's not to get any. She's to get not one thing out of your shop, do you hear?'

'All right, all right,' Rory had agreed. She was as worried about Helena's wild behaviour as he was. She was in fact at her wits' end with Douglas and Helena, and only too glad for Donovan to take charge and tell her what should be done. Not that anything either she or Donovan did seemed to make the slightest bit of difference. Secretly she worried herself sick in case Helena should get herself into trouble with some man. She had eventually plucked up courage to broach the subject of contraception, not that she knew much about it herself. 'The best way, of course, is abstinence until you get married,' she had advised.

As usual Helena just laughed at her. 'Don't worry, mother. I know how to take care of myself.'

'Well, I certainly hope so, Helena. It was more than I could do at your age, if I remember.' Not that she wanted to remember, especially the rape. She still shrivelled inside at the thought of that night in the dark stinking back close in Cowlairs Road. Every night now she sent up a prayer that Helena would be all right. She would close her eyes after she got into bed and think, 'Oh God, keep them safe, both Douglas and Helena. But especially Helena. Please God, don't let anything happen to Helena.'

Life had become emotionally fragmented. Bits of her seemed constantly turning this way and that, splintering her concentration even at work. Her mind had begun to wander down any path in her attempts to avoid the hopeless roundabout of worrying about her children. Sometimes, if Donovan was working late or away somewhere on an assignment, she would take the car and drive about the streets to keep herself from staying at home worrying. Helena would already be out, God knows where. It had not been so bad in the summer with the Victorian buildings of the city bathed in comforting sunshine. It was not so pleasant on dark winters' nights, despite being safely cocooned in her Rolls Royce. But anything was better than staying at home worrying about Helena, or about Douglas lumbered with the expense and responsibility not only of Victoria's daughter but also of another man's child. She was too restless, especially when Winnie was away visiting her married cousin and she did not even have her company. A great quiet filled the house then and seemed to take possession of it. In such a quiet, her worries grew to frightening proportions.

Outside now, rain was drizzling down and everywhere there was an odour of soot and coal smoke. At least the street lamps were lit. Unlike during the war when darkness was not only depressing but dangerous. You could quite

138

happily go into a cinema when it was daylight, and come out to complete blackness and not knowing how many steps it was down to the pavement and even less which way to turn in order to grope your way home. To make any attempt to hurry was fatal. Anyone who went any more than a shuffling, groping pace was liable to black an eye against a pillar-box or a baffle wall or a blacked-out lamp post. Or step out onto a road and be knocked down by a motor car.

Although often it was imperative to hurry. Crime in the streets, assault and theft were rampant in the black-out. She had always been thankful for the protection of her car, and she was still glad of it as she drove down by the river, then stopped to gaze absently at it for a while. The River Clyde was shimmering, trembling, rippling with the reflection of the rows of gas lamps on either side. It seemed alive, as if it were seething with fiery serpents. Even there she became restless and decided on impulse to turn the car north and go to visit her mother. She had to talk to somebody.

'Is that not fucking terrible,' Annie McElpy said when she told her about Douglas's predicament. 'She seemed a nice enough wee lassie to me.'

Rory stared at the older woman in surprise. 'I didn't know you'd met her. Did Douglas bring her here?'

'Eh?' Annie gave a sarcastic screech. 'He'd pass your da and me on the street if he could get away with it.'

'Don't be ridiculous, ma! How did you meet her then?'

'Last year when she was helping her da at the General Election. I had her in and gave her a cup of tea.'

'I wish you'd put poison in it!'

'What a way to talk. You've always been as hard as nails. It beats me who you take after.'

'She's a right shit, ma. She had it off with somebody else and never let on.'

'You were no angel when you were young and don't you forget it, milady.'

'I never did anything like her.'

'A right wee shit you were. Many's the time I thought you were going to be the death of your da and me.'

'God!' Rory cast her eyes heavenwards. 'You're not going

to drag up yet again how cruel I was to you and da, forcing you out of your lovely wee room and kitchen and lavatory on the stairs to this awful big bungalow with awful mod cons.'

'There was nothing wrong with our room and kitchen. The neighbours were right gems and it was that handy for the Co-op.'

Rory had heard it all before and it never ceased to infuriate and frustrate her. It didn't make sense, but neither her mother nor her father enjoyed, far less were grateful, for a share of her wealth. She stared at her mother in silence for a minute. Despite the fact that the hair knotted at the top of her head had gone white and the skin round her eyes brown-crapy, Annie was still as raw-boned and as tough as ever.

'I don't know what to do about Douglas,' Rory admitted eventually.

'He's a grown man,' Annie reminded her. 'Let him do for himself.'

'I can't just stand aside and do nothing.'

'Well, give him a kick up the arse!'

'Oh charming! Thanks very much, ma, for your usual helpful advice.'

'What I used to do with your da was give him a black eye.' Annie wiped away some tears of laughter with the corner of her apron. 'He was an awful man, your da. Many a good rammy we had.'

Rory cast her eyes upwards again. 'I know, I remember. Where is he just now? He's not getting into any more trouble, I hope.'

'Naw. He's half the man he used to be. He's out playing bools.'

'I'm glad he's found an interest apart from thieving.'

'You watch your tongue. He was always a good da to you.'

Rory was tempted to ask how, but refrained. Her mother was still more than capable of boxing her ears. She shivered. 'Ma, it's bloody cold in here.'

'I know. There's no heat in this place. It's like living in

the Kelvin Hall. When I think of my nice cosy wee kitchen in Cowlairs Road. . . .'

'For God's sake, ma. All it needs is background heating to supplement your coal fire.'

'I'm having no more of your fancy gadgets. I'm fair bamboozled with them already. That's the trouble with you. You think money solves everything. Well, you listen to me, milady, it doesn't. You lavished money and presents on your boy and girl, but it would have fitted you better to have spent more time with them. You wouldn't have the worries you have today, if you had.'

Scrap McElpy appeared in the room then, all five feet of him, topped with a big flat pancake of a cap. 'I'm just giving her a few home truths,' Annie informed him.

'A load of shit, you mean,' Rory said bitterly.

'Oh,' Annie sounded genuinely aggrieved. 'Is that not fucking terrible!'

21

Helena heaved her folder into a more comfortable position as she climbed the outside steps to the Glasgow School of Art. The building had been designed by Charles Rennie Mackintosh, and was regarded as a truly great work of architectural originality and one of Europe's first buildings in the 'Modern Style'. Helena had come straight from an unholy row with her father and was in no mood to appreciate Mackintosh's structural and decorative features of wrought-iron, the meticulous way he had detailed every aspect of the building, or the way he had created lofty spaces and excellent lighting inside. There were two swing doors, one 'In' and one 'Out', and both were unusually wide to accommodate students bashing through carrying drawing boards or large folders. Even so, the black paint was a bit scratched. The entrance hall was not what one had come to expect in institutions in a Glasgow that was widely recognized as the Victorian city *par excellence*. There was none of the usual Victorian grandeur. Instead there were elegant white-painted wood panels.

Helena passed the main staircase, which led to the museum, and went along to the narrow twisting stairway that went up to the studio in which she worked. The heavy grey stone-flagged walls with their narrow arches between each landing gave a sombre air of antiquity, learning and mystery that belied the building's fairly recent construction. To Helena, burdened with the unwieldy folder, the stairs seemed endless. The only thing to cheer her up was the thought of the party she was going to later that evening in the common room across the road in the 'new building'. Her father had forbidden her to go. But 'To hell with him!' she thought.

'You've been warned,' he had told her. 'And you've paid no attention. You've kept coming home at all hours and in a disgusting state. Well, no more, do you hear? From now on, you'll behave yourself. You'll do your work during the day and at night I want you here, where I can keep an eye on you.'

It was ridiculous. He could talk all he liked. He was not going to keep her in. She passed the Mackintosh tile design isolated in its lonely elegance, then the landing for the library, onwards and upwards until she finally burst out into the loggia at the end of the 'Hen-run'. Groaning to herself, she thought, 'You have to be a bloody Sherpa to survive in this place.' She turned to one of the arched window bays and dropped heavily onto a seat. 'My God,' she thought, 'what a view, though.' The tapestry of the Clyde Valley draped before her in grimy splendour. The setting sun, like an impressionist painter, was colouring the buildings pink and mauve. Giant cranes, back-lit, were strung across the horizon like a spider's web against cloud formations rolling upwards in waves of pewter and gold.

The echoing clatter of footsteps along the bare wooden floor of the Hen-run dragged her from her reverie. 'Veronica! Are you late as well?'

'No,' Veronica said. 'I had to run back down to the shop.'

'I suppose I had better go in.' Helena reluctantly lifted her folder. 'I'm exhausted before I start. I had such a helluva row with dad. It's put me right off my stroke. He's really had his knife in me since he's been at home. I wish to God he'd hurry up and disappear away on an assignment.'

'Do you think there's any chance?' Veronica asked, as they walked towards the studio.

'There's been talk about one to Russia. I'm praying he takes it because it would mean he would be away for absolutely ages. He would have to travel all over the country and keep sending home articles about the life over there and the people.'

'Do you think he will take it?'

'He's dead keen, but mum is furious. They had a row about it and she called him a right selfish bastard.'

'Work on *her* then. Try to make her keep quiet about it.'

'What do you think I've been doing? I reminded her it

143

was dad's job to travel about like that, just as it was her job to be out all day and every day at the shop.'

'What did she say to that?'

'Told me to mind my own bloody business.'

'Charming!'

'I know. But they can both do or say what they like. They are not going to keep me a prisoner.'

'You're going to the party tonight, then?'

'Of course!'

In the studio the model had emerged from behind the screen already undressed and wearing her dressing-gown. Old 'Santa' McQuillan, so called because of his matted wavy hair and beard, was waiting to arrange the model on the square box on wheels known as 'the throne'. From a panel covered with wire mesh on the side of the throne came hot air from a concealed heater. This prevented the nude models from freezing. Santa glowered across at Helena as she made her way to her place and began setting up her easel. He was a huge man in a red shirt, floppy paint-stained corduroys, and sandals. He wore greasy green socks and neither they nor the pungent smell of paint could conceal the sweaty smell of his feet.

The model was called Martha and she was almost as big as Santa. She dropped her dressing-gown to reveal voluptuous proportions. She seemed to fill the studio with flesh. Her breasts thrust out and drooped with their own weight and her belly hung in folds of fat. Santa took some time in arranging her. He was not satisfied until her chin was on her extended palm, elbow on one splayed knee, bottom sprawling all over the throne, pubic hair showing all its bushy luxuriousness. Then he roamed around the room examining and criticizing the work of each of the students. When he came to Helena, he said, 'When will you grow up?'

Helena caught Veronica's eye and barely managed to suppress a giggle. 'Eh?'

'You're always late,' Santa said, 'and you can't get away quick enough. All you think about is having a good time. You don't care a damn about your work.' He sighed. 'I

144

wouldn't care either. But I can see you have talent and it's such a waste.'

'I thought it was my brother who had all the talent,' she said.

'Not in my opinion. If you would just grow up and take your work more seriously, there's no telling what you might accomplish.'

He moved away then and Helena winked across at Veronica. They both thought Santa, despite his great age, had taken a fancy to her. He often made flattering and encouraging comments about her work. At other times, he would lose his temper and say things like, 'Do you not realize that that tube of cadmium-yellow you've just wasted cost over two pounds? That's a week's wages to some people.'

It was late when they finished and, as Helena and Veronica wiped the paint off their brushes on the hessian that hung on the wall over the sink, Helena grumbled, 'I wouldn't put it past that old sod to keep us this late on purpose, because he knows we're itching to get across the road to the common room.'

'Shh!' Veronica giggled. 'He'll hear you.'

After wiping their brushes on the wall, they cleaned them in white spirit, then washed them.

'Have you got your bevy?' Helena asked.

'A bottle of port and six cans of beer down in my locker. What did you get'

'A bottle of whisky.'

'Whisky? Lucky dog!'

'I pinched it from our drinks cupboard at home. Mum seems to have an unlimited supply.'

'Let's hope your dad doesn't find out. The way he's been raging on about your drinking, he's liable to kill you!'

'For God's sake, put up a prayer with mine,' Helena pleaded, 'that he'll take this Russian assignment.'

The common room was in the new building across the road and was tiny compared to the assembly hall upstairs where the big dances like the Christmas Ball took place. But it held a piano and one of the male students, Philip

Henderson, could fairly belt out boogy-woogy. After a while and a good few drinks, Philip was incapable and Sammy Peters had to take over. His favourite was 'Peg O' My Heart' and they all sang lustily to it as they danced, although the room was packed so solidly that it was getting difficult even to breathe, never mind move.

'Peg o' my heart,
I love you,
Peg o' my heart.'

There was a lot of squeezing, and crushing out and in from the corridor where the drink was served.

'Look what your cheap port's doing to the tumbler!' Helena, who by this time could hardly stand, screeched with laughter. 'It's dyeing the insides pink.' Sure enough the insides of the bakelite tumblers were vividly stained. 'Think what it's doing to our insides!'

Veronica's hair hung down over her eyes and her voice was slurred. 'Who cares? Anyway we can't all have rich mothers like you.'

Just then Gerald Smith and Keith Kerr joined them and Gerald said, 'How about going back to my place and really having a good time, eh?' Gerald had a studio further up Hill Street which contained, among other things, the biggest bed anyone had ever seen. 'Let's get our coats and go, eh?'

'OK,' Helena said. 'Come on, Veronica.'

The coats were among a mountain of garments which had been tossed onto one end of the shadowy corridor floor. The two girls and their partners passed couples glued against the wall intent on necking and heavy petting, and stepped over one or two others lying on the floor in their own vomit. They started to pull the coats about in search of their own. It was fortunate that theirs were near the bottom of the pile. Some of the coats on the top had been urinated upon. Normally it would have taken only five minutes to reach Gerald's studio but, in their inebriated state and taking up the full width of the road, it took them fifteen minutes. Once there, they lost no time in shedding their clothes and falling naked into the giant-sized bed.

146

★

Donovan missed them by less than half an hour. He had called at the art school and been directed across to the common room. There, despite howls of protest, he had pushed and pulled people aside in his search for his daughter. Eventually he had caught one terrified youth by the throat and threatened to strangle the life out of him if he did not tell him where Helena Donovan had gone. The youth had choked out that Helena sometimes went to Gerald Smith's studio after common room 'dos' and maybe she would be there. Donovan flung him aside, left the new building and strode along to the address the youth had given him. The sound of raucous laughter pealing from behind one of the doors was enough. Donovan's knee shot up, his foot shot forward and the door exploded open. Once inside the room he was faced with the sight of the bed and the tangle of limbs, beards and bodies. He made straight for his daughter's auburn hair and pulled her, screaming, out of the bed by it.

'Get your clothes on and get out of here,' he roared.

'Heh!' Gerald scrambled up and began tugging on his trousers. 'We were only having some harmless fun. This isn't the twenties, you know.'

'Oh, shut up, you little weed.' Donovan said.

'Hi, wait a minute,' Gerald protested and made the mistake of giving Donovan a push. 'You can't speak to me like that.'

The words were hardly out of his mouth when they were replaced by blood pouring into it. Donovan had immediately butted him in the nose with his rock-hard head. Gerald fell back on the bed in a welter of blood and before he could scramble up again, Keith squared up to Donovan. Keith prided himself on being a bit of a boxer in his spare time. He swung a punch at Donovan which the older man easily took on his left forearm and swung through with a right forearm smash up across Keith's cheekbone. The young man crashed back across a wooden chair, then landed on the floor dazed.

'Come on!' Donovan snapped at Helena, flung a coat

147

around her shoulders and, without a backward glance, dragged her from the room. Helena sobbed all the way home in the car and all the time in the sitting room while Donovan related to a horrified Rory exactly what he had witnessed.

'It's not going to work, is it?' Donovan said to Rory. 'We've both warned her, shouted at her, punished her every way we could think of. Nothing's done any good. She's ruining her life, Rory. At this rate she'll end up on the streets.'

Rory lit up a cigarette and took comfort from it and the whisky that Donovan had poured out. 'I knew she'd got into a wild crowd. But I never realized that it was as bad as this. We'll have to get her right away from there for her own good.'

'I agree,' Donovan said grimly. 'It's the only way. I've made up my mind.'

'What are you going to do?' Rory asked.

'She's coming with me to Russia.'

Helena was so shocked she stopped sobbing. 'You can't take me there!'

'Oh no?' Donovan said. 'Just watch me!'

22

Drummond propped himself up on his elbow on the pillow and stared at Caroline's sleeping figure. She looked vulnerable without her glasses and she had a habit of sleeping with one arm abandoned back against her pillow like a child. He loved her. He loved her long gangly legs and the soft moist crevices between them. He loved her tiny waist, her hazel-tipped breasts, her baby-soft neck. He loved her tender rose-petal mouth. He could have gazed at her all night. He could never get enough of her. All the time, night and day, he ached to touch her and not necessarily in a sexual way. Often they held hands or linked arms, just as friends or loving companions. Often he gave her a hug of affection. They got on *so well* together. It was such a joy. It was as if he had never lived before. It was as if he had been born again, been given a miraculous second chance.

They went to the theatre and came back to Caroline's flat. They had a glass of wine and earnestly discussed the play. Next day they read the critics and compared views. Sometimes they went to the cinema and afterwards enjoyed a similar critical discussion. Or they went to an exhibition of painting, or sculpture, or photography, or to a lecture on English literature, something they both were interested in. Caroline was quite an expert on Shakespeare and could quote extensively from the bard. He felt like quoting from the sonnets at this moment.

' "Shall I compare thee to a summer's day?
Thou art more lovely and more temperate." '

His enjoyment was intense, his happiness was so complete he could never sleep right away. He always lay like this staring at Caroline, not wanting to give up one moment, savouring his joy, unable to credit that it was really happening to him. His only regret was that they had missed so many precious years of knowing one another.

Caroline felt this way too. For each of them every minute was a jewel beyond price now. Eventually the overpowering weight of sleep made it impossible to keep his eyes open and he was forced to lose her from his sight. In the morning he awakened to find Caroline propped up on one elbow lovingly watching him.

After he had explained to her how he had not been able to tell Victoria of their love because of the crisis in the family over Amelia, she had not broached the subject again, but he knew that she longed, as he did, for them to make a life-long commitment to each other in marriage. He wanted the world to know that they belonged to each other as man and wife. Caroline deserved more than a hole-in-the-corner affair. The fact had also to be faced, however, that the scandal of a divorce would ruin his career. It would be the end of him in politics. Having a mistress would have exactly the same effect and they had to be extremely discreet, at least about the occasions when they slept together in Caroline's flat. At other times, it was an invaluable help that she was known to be his secretary. It was perfectly natural and proper that she should be seen with him. At first they had had no thoughts for the future, so caught up were they in the euphoria of the present. It still did not worry Caroline over much.

'I admit that it is bloody infuriating and unfair that you'd be forced to leave Parliament, darling,' she told him. 'You've the potential to get right to the top. But it would be more their loss than yours. You would be all right. Father would give us a house and some land on the estate and you could relax and be happy there. It would be wonderful for us both.'

He could not help smiling as well as sighing. 'I've worked hard all my life. I cannot imagine myself being happy for long doing nothing, even with you by my side in such beautiful surroundings.'

'It would simply be a change in the direction of your career, darling,' Caroline insisted. 'You could write books about politics. I've seen you write in your journal. You enjoy writing. You've told me so. Why not express your beliefs and influence people through the printed word?'

150

It was an intriguing idea that had never occurred to him before. The more he thought of it the more seductive it became. He had always been an inward kind of person, preferring isolation in the thoughtful world of books even as a child. Not that he had been the delicate studious type of youngster that was the constant butt of more extrovert or bullying types. He held his own at sports and doggedly exercised in private to strengthen his muscles. He had a temper and when it was roused he could be wildly vicious. The school bully had picked on him only once and had been beaten nearly senseless as a result. The savagery of that one occasion was enough to deter other potential tormentors. As a thin vulnerable-looking lad on the railway it had been much the same routine. By that time he had taught himself ju-jitsu. It was not the physical side of life that had ever daunted him. That was not where he had found himself out of his depth. The problem was simple normal, everyday socializing. The kind of thing that most people took for granted.

Looking back, he supposed he had just been excruciatingly shy. Yet he had, at an early age, mastered the art of public speaking. If he was speaking on a public platform, or taking part in a political discussion or debate anywhere at all, he was confident and in control of himself. Even now, the same applied. Years of practice had helped him to perfect a smooth technique of social intercourse when it was unavoidable. But he still opted out of social contact as often as he could.

To him, a quiet retreat in the depths of the beautiful border countryside, where he could commune with himself on paper to his heart's content, was a balm to his very soul. He kept stealing glimpses at this utopia with his mind's eye, then, each time, hastily dousing his excitement. So much did he long for this dream to come true, he was afraid to believe in it. Facts had to be faced. Victoria had to be faced.

'I dread going back home now,' he confided in Caroline. 'I don't mean I dread telling Victoria about us. Although admittedly I'm not looking forward to that either. No, I was thinking of the whole milieu. I never realized how much it

151

was destroying me until I had been away from it for a while. I feel physically ill now when I'm there. I get blinding headaches and pains in my chest until I can hardly breathe.'

'Oh darling!' Caroline alerted with anxiety, her eyes filling with tears. 'You're making me frightened. You must see a doctor and have a check-up right away. You should have told me this before. . . .'

He laughed and took her comfortingly into his arms. 'It's tension, that's all. I feel so frustrated and claustrophobic and angry. All the worst side of me comes out and I'm angry at myself as much as anyone or anything else, because I can't control it. Or if I do manage some semblance of control I feel this tension building up.'

'Go to have a check-up. Oh darling, please, for my sake?'

'All right, I will one of these days, when I get time.'

'Soon, oh please! Promise me.'

He kissed her into silence and with whispers of 'Don't worry, my dearest love. The only cure I'll ever need is to be with you.'

It was true. He had never felt so relaxed in his life as he did with Caroline. Whether it was while he was working in his office, or they were together in her flat, or on a visit to Innerleithen House. Never, in his wildest dreams had he imagined he could be so at ease, feel so attached, so *at home* in such a place. Nevertheless it was a fact that as soon as Caroline's car neared the Peebleshire area with its backcloth of hills and the peaceful winding River Tweed, he felt sweetly happy. He unwound. His soul opened up to take in the beauty of it all. They approached the tall wrought-iron gates and there it was – Innerleithen House, sheltered among the trees with the hills a protective wall behind it. It slept quietly, peacefully, with a soothing calmness that had lasted for centuries. The peacefulness, the tranquillity, the permanence of it had a stabilizing affect on him. No doctor's pills or potions could ever make him feel so good.

Even in the winter he loved it. He could smell the rain and it was quite different from the rain in the city. In the city it fell like a dingy grey veil that covered everything with dullness and depression. Here it sparkled the land and made the trees, the shrubs, the plants, the very air, sweet and fresh and fragrant.

It was a terrible wrench and deeply disturbing to go from there to the crowded streets of Glasgow with its jungle of tenements in which people lived in such squalid overcrowding, often eight or nine or even more in one room and all sharing the same outside lavatory with several other families. The sight of these grim conditions plummeted him back into the tensions of the political arena and the difficulties of his socialist commitment.

Now that he was Minister for Education of course, his main interest was concentrated in that field. Education, he believed, was of vital importance to the whole community. Everyone, no matter what their job or environment, was entitled to and needed to have a good education. Education was not just a firm stepping stone on the road to success in the practical side of life, it was a door that opened onto life's true riches, the world of books. He had come to appreciate keenly the true worth of teachers, a dedicated, much maligned and disgracefully taken-for-granted breed. The trouble with teachers was that they had no clout. Unlike the powerful Miners Union, for instance.

The danger, as he saw it, in the future was that the capitalist 'Every man for himself', and the survival of the strongest and most ruthless mentality, would come to apply to the unions. It would be every union for itself and the strongest and most ruthless would win over others like the teachers' representatives. Everyone would be fighting his own corner and what good was that in a socialist society where, as he believed, it should be, 'From each according to their ability and to each according to their needs.' The selfishness in human nature was something common to all political creeds. It was, he believed, the socialist commitment more than any other to fight it.

He was dedicated to the cause of education and the ancillary area of libraries. He was devoted to the cause of the teacher. Thinking of his work in these fields he felt the keen pull of duty. On these occasions the idea of retiring to

153

the country to write books seemed no more than an unforgivable piece of self indulgence.

Yet, oh, how his heart longed for it.

23

Dear Veronica.

You can't imagine how *awful* it is here. It's worse than my worst nightmares. You ask to be told every detail from the moment I arrived in Moscow, but it's all so *dead boring*! Moscow airport was dark and gloomy with a low roof and too few light bulbs. There were some pillars in the central area with kind of table shelves around them, but what they were for I don't know. I didn't see any câfés or restaurants. There weren't even enough luggage trolleys and I had to stagger along carrying two heavy suitcases. Dad carried his one and another of mine. I got no sympathy from him, of course. He just said I shouldn't have brought so much stuff.

After absolute *ages* we got to our hotel. Veronica, I kid you not, it is the absolute *dregs*. It was like a better-lit Moscow airport (but not much better). There were no carpets on the floor in the foyer and the most awful jostle of people, and nobody bothers to say sorry if they bump into you. They were mostly men with briefcases. Trust dad to book us in some sort of commercial traveller's dump. We had to queue for our room number, then for a key at another counter. Nobody, absolutely nobody could speak English and they have a sort of detached expression when they look at you almost as if you weren't there. Or didn't want you to be there.

We were absolutely starving, so after dumping our cases in our bedrooms we went to the restaurant which was on the third floor. I was slightly cheered by the sight and sound of beautifully costumed Russian balalaika players. I was soon depressed again by the meal. The starter of sardines and salad was OK, but the steak (God knows what it came from), apple and rice (yes, baked apple and rice with steak!) was cold. Unlike my bedroom which was boiling hot. That was after I found it! They are so mean with electricity, you have to grope your way along endless badly lit corridors.

After dinner, despite torrents of rain, dad dragged me out for a walk to see Red Square and the Changing of the Guard at Lenin's tomb. I suppose it's all part of my punishment. He's even trying to rope me in to help him with his work! Honestly, Veronica, it's going too far. I was absolutely soaked. Red Square was miles from the hotel. I had to admit (to myself not to dad) that Red Square and the Changing of the Guard was impressive. In fact, I don't mind telling you it makes the Changing of the Guard in London look silly. Anyway, dad relented (by this time it was well after midnight). Instead of walking back we took the metro. It too was impressive, all marble and chandeliers, but it reeked of vodka or some sort of spirits and there were one or two drunk men quietly propping each other up.

Not like in the hotel basement bar, which was packed with men and so noisy with shouting and singing you couldn't hear yourself think. I was glad to escape up to bed. Dad, of course, stayed and, I learned next day, he palled up with some Yugoslavs and went to another hotel where the bar was open all night. Honestly, Veronica, it makes me mad. He dragged me all the way over here to teach me how to behave myself, by his way of it, and he's the one that's having all the wild carry-on. I bet mum doesn't know half of what he gets up to.

He had a hang-over next day. He made me type an article for him which he dictated from bed where he was lying nursing his head like a Victorian poet. I must admit the article was witty despite dad's awful condition. Don't miss it when it reaches the Glasgow papers. It's all about the trauma of making friends with Russian men. They kiss each other on the lips, you know. Big rugged men like bears hug and kiss each other in greeting. It's absolutely hilarious!

Anyway, I escaped from dad as quickly as I could. After posting his article I went for a wander round the shops. There was absolutely nothing else to do. I've never seen such awful shops in all my life, not even in Glasgow during the war. There's nothing in the windows, Veronica, absolutely nothing and every window is hung with, you'll never believe this, dingy net curtains! Yes, *in shops*, even department stores. Right up against the glass too and not even nicely gathered. Just clinging flat and limp against the glass.

And the people in the streets! Honestly, Veronica, if you think Glasgow streets look dull and dead boring with people dressed in made-up black-out curtains and army blankets, you should see here! The streets of Moscow make Glasgow look like a colourful fashion parade. No, honestly, I'm not kidding. The women don't seem to have heard of corsets or roll-ons, they're so shapeless and frumpy, and everybody, *absolutely everybody*, wears head squares. And they all look so serious and self-absorbed. It's beginning to affect me already. Veronica, you wouldn't know me, I'm getting so morose.

We're supposed to be going to Leningrad next and I've been pleading with dad to leave here as soon as possible. Although what Leningrad will be like, I daren't think. Surely though, it couldn't be any worse than Moscow?

I'm thoroughly sick of Russia already and in more ways than one. I dread going into the dining room for meals. You know how I always enjoy my food? You remember what a good appetite I had? Well, not any more. And no wonder! The food here is disgusting. I'm beginning to get really angry; it's an absolute disgrace. We're paying good money for this hotel and we're not getting value for it. If dad doesn't say something I will, although it's maybe not worthwhile making a fuss now that we are about to leave. (At last!) It's so difficult anyway when no one understands a word I'm saying. If this sort of bad food and service continues in Leningrad, I certainly will make a fuss. I'm working myself into such a state over the food in particular, I'm ready to throw a plate of it at one of those gloomy Russian faces.

Yours, fed up and far from home,

Helena

Dear Veronica,

It was dark when we arrived in Leningrad and I was half asleep. (More from boredom than anything else.) The hotel seemed much more civilized (I noticed some shapely and rather attractive women), but when we arrived in the dining room it was to find the food was even worse than in Moscow. There wasn't even enough of it. (I viewed this, of course, as a mixed blessing!) I was too tired to complain on that first evening but next day at breakfast on my own I certainly did. (Dad was working. Or trying to. This assignment is turning out a lot more difficult than he expected and I'm not surprised.) I was given a hunk of the most unappetizing-looking grey bread and a portion of cheese, and that was it. I rebelled. I disdainfully tossed the bread and cheese from my plate across the table and told the waitress in no uncertain terms what I thought of her rubbish of a breakfast. I knew she understood because I heard her speak some English the night before. There's a receptionist here who also speaks English, thank God.

Anyway, the waitress understood all right because she burst into tears. Serves her right, I thought. I mean honestly, Veronica, fancy a slice of bread and cheese for breakfast. It wasn't good enough for an in-between meal snack, not that I'd want to eat anything so dead boring at any time. Then I was *absolutely shattered*! A man suddenly shot across like a bullet from a gun and shouted at me, Veronica. Yes, he actually shouted in my face. Swore at me. Verbally abused me. Called me for everything. I was stunned. Absolutely speechless with shock. Well, you can imagine.

He was in his early thirties, with blue-black hair and wild, dark eyes. He spoke half in English, half in Russian which was most confusing. He was absolutely livid with rage. Honestly, Veronica, he nearly frightened me to death. His eyes weren't just dark. They were black and really wicked-looking. It was awful, the woman sobbing and crying as if she'd never stop and this fierce man raging on at me. Eventually I picked up something about how thousands of people had died of starvation in Leningrad and how this waitress's son had starved to death. This bread and cheese was precious, he said, and I was damned lucky to be offered it.

I must admit once I heard this I felt awful, Veronica. But I mean, how was I to have known. I tried to protest, 'I know nothing about Leningrad. I knew nothing about all this.' Not that I believe he had any excuse to shout such abuse at me, Veronica. However I managed to apologize to the waitress and make amends to her as best I could by rescuing the bread and cheese from where I'd flung it and putting it back on my plate. I then forced myself to take a bite of it and after making a brave attempt at appearing to enjoy it (it really was disgusting!), I said to the woman '*Spasiba!*' which dad had told me meant 'Thank you'.

The man sat down opposite me at my table, *my* table, and had the cheek to ask my name. At first I ignored him. The waitress, who was now swollen-faced and trembling but at least dry-eyed, asked if I would like tea. Again I managed '*Spasiba.*' She poured a cup of horrible tarry stuff and then went away. There was no milk, of course. There never is. Not a drop. And you know how I absolutely *hate* tea without milk. Still, on this occasion I was glad of any kind of drink to help steady me.

'What is your name?' he demanded. He seemed to have suddenly calmed down but his voice was deep and husky and, as I say, demanding. I thought he had the most awful nerve. I mean just calmly sitting there after what he'd done. I still felt shaken and the way he was staring at me didn't help. I don't know why I answered him.

'Helena.'

'What is your father's name?' he asked then, and I said, 'Donovan.'

'Helena Donovanovna. I am Ivan Burgeyev or Ivan Mikhailovitch.'

Honestly, Veronica, these people are so difficult to understand. They all seem to have more than one name for a start.

'I don't understand,' I said irritably. 'Why the different names?'

' "*Ovna*" means "daughter of". "*Ovitch*" means "son

of". Most Russians had no surnames until comparatively recent times. My surname is Burgeyev, but I am the son of Mikhail.'

'Oh.'

'You are English, of course.'

'No, I am not,' I told him. 'I am Scottish. From Glasgow.'

'Ah,' he said, 'Robert Burns!'

Then he started quoting one of Burns's poems. Honestly, it was so odd to hear it delivered in such a strange accent. He looked so foreign too. Yet I can't exactly fathom why. I mean, you could just say he was tall, dark and handsome. I don't know whether it was something about his eyes or his mouth that gave him his foreign look, but he certainly could never have been mistaken for an open-faced Englishman or even a dour Scotsman. It was very strange. I didn't know where I was. I am beginning to understand dad's difficulty. Dad and I had a long and interesting conversation next day about Russia and Russians in general.

But back to what I was telling you about Burgeyev. Suddenly he said, 'Ah, there is the man I have to meet. I must go, but I will see you again.'

'No, you will not,' I told him.

'I am going to teach you about Leningrad,' he said, his dark look daring me to contradict him. 'You have obviously much need to learn.'

'And you have much need to learn how to treat a lady,' I flung back at him.

'You were not behaving like a lady,' he said. 'I will return here tomorrow.'

I was all churned up and upset by the whole incident, Veronica. I felt so guilty about the waitress. It was absolutely *awful*. You know me, I wouldn't hurt a fly normally. I mean, all I want is to enjoy life and have a bit of fun. There's no harm in that. The thing was, I couldn't *do* anything to make it up to her. They don't allow tipping here. Dad say's that, since the revolution, it's viewed as an insult. I don't know if he's right or not, but I was afraid to offer her money just in case. How I *suffered*, Veronica.

160

I decided to take my mind off the whole terrible incident by studying that book dad gave me before coming here. You know, the one about how to speak Russian. I thought I might as well try and learn the language. It is so frustrating when you don't know half what people are saying.

That's all for now, Veronica.

Yours,

Helena

24

'I'm worried about Matthew,' Bridget Dunbar said. 'Aren't you, Victoria?'

'Worried?' Victoria looked puzzled. 'In what way exactly?'

They had bumped into one another in Springburn Road and stopped for a chat. The street was busy and they had to move closer to the black wall of the tenements to avoid being jostled. They still had difficulty in making themselves heard above the clang of the tramcars and the rhythmic echo from a nearby close of a ball banging against the wall and chants of:

> 'One, two, three, aleery; four, five, six, aleery;
> Seven, eight, nine, aleery; ten aleery postmen.'

'He's changing, don't you think?' Bridget said.

Victoria stared at the neatly dressed spinster in the maroon velvet hat and fur tippet. It had been fortunate that Bridget had the same build as her late mother and so had fallen heir to all her clothes. Good stuff too. Velour hats and tweed suits and coats. Even a fur coat that had been so well preserved it reeked of moth-balls. Victoria always felt it a feather in her cap to be seen with someone so obviously a lady, and she was proud that she had been instrumental in getting such a superior person to work on Matthew's behalf. (Bridget was a member of the same church and women's guild as herself.) She also enjoyed Bridget's visits, regarding them as a challenge to her own gentility. She made special fairy cakes and cut the crusts off the sand-wiches when Bridget came to tea. At the same time, she felt superior to Bridget because she had a man and Bridget had not.

'In what way do you mean exactly?' she asked.

Bridget hesitated. 'Well now, it's difficult to pinpoint, it's so subtle. But I can assure you it's there all the same.'

'What is?' Victoria asked somewhat testily. She was beginning to feel the draught whistling round the corner from Wellfield Street despite wearing two pairs of long-legged knickers. A spring sun was struggling to penetrate through the smoke of the tenement chimneys but, like most people, she had not recovered from the ravages of the 1946–47 winter. She and Amelia had taken turns to queue at the coal yard in Atlas Street with Harry's pram, hoping, not always successfully, to get it filled with coal. Harry, now nearly a year old, had fallen heir to a go-chair from one of the neighbours whose family was now at school.

'Well now,' said Bridget, 'what I think is, he's losing touch with his roots. It's understandable, of course, being so far away in London and mixing with so many foreigners. Socialists, especially,' Bridget's voice lowered confidentially, 'have to be so careful.'

'Right enough,' Victoria agreed, not quite sure what she was agreeing with.

'To be perfectly honest,' Bridget kept her voice low and leaned closer to Victoria. 'I just wonder what this new secretary's like. Secretaries, especially full-time secretaries, can be a very strong influence, you know.'

Victoria was beginning to see the light. Bridget was jealous of Matthew's London secretary. She'd always known, of course, that poor Bridget had a soft spot for Matthew. 'Dear knows,' she said, 'I've never met her nor have I any desire to. English women can be so gabby, can't they? Remember that woman who spoke at the Church Guild last month? What an awful blether she was. And what a terrible accent! I couldn't make out half what she was saying.'

'Well now, I'll maybe meet her.'

'Who?'

'Matthew's secretary.'

'Don't tell me he's bringing her up here?'

'No, no. But next month I'm going to visit my cousin Jessie in London. Her husband's firm moved him down there after the war. I thought I might call in to say hello to Matthew while I'm there.'

'To the House of Commons?' Victoria was impressed. It was, to her, like announcing a visit to Mars.

'And why not?' A defensive note stiffened Bridget's voice.

Victoria could not think of any reason she would care to admit to. 'Better you than me.' She laughed. 'I'd no more want to go away down there than fly in the air.'

'I bet you anything,' she confided later to Agnes McDade, 'Bridget will come back with a long tale of how awful and inefficient and all things bad Matthew's secretary is. It's pathetic, isn't it? She'll never get a man now at her age.'

In actual fact Victoria felt she had more important things to worry her than Bridget Dunbar's imaginings. Amelia had always been moody and a bit queer like her daddy but recently she had been getting worse. There was something very odd and strangely disturbing about the way she sat every chance she could, cradling wee Harry in her arms and rocking backwards and forwards with him while all the time chanting, 'Mummy's wee darling boy . . . mummy's wee darling boy . . . mummy's wee darling boy. . . ,' over and over and over again. At night it rocked Harry to sleep or hypnotized him more like. During the day he stared up at Amelia and she stared down at him. They just stared and stared at each other. It was all very worrying and unnatural.

Of course she snatched the child away from Amelia as often as she could. What black looks the girl could give! Often she suspected that Amelia 'wasn't all there'. She had been complaining so much about headaches, she had eventually sent for the doctor. Unfortunately she had been along at the shops when the doctor had arrived and she had never yet found out what Amelia had said to him or what he had said to her. The upshot of it all was that Amelia had to attend Stobhill Hospital as an out-patient to see a psychiatrist. *A psychiatrist*! The shame of it was too much. Victoria had not been able to bring herself to tell even Mrs McDade. Never once had any of her family ever been to a psychiatrist. Indeed she had never in her life either known of anyone or heard of anyone who had ever been to a psychiatrist. She had tried of course to persuade Amelia not to go but the girl could be so stubborn when she set her mind to anything.

'It's time you pulled yourself together and snapped out of it,' Victoria kept telling her. The only response would be for Amelia to disappear into her bedroom and shut and snib the door.

'I know what you're doing in there,' she would call against the door. 'You're scribbling again. You're worse than your daddy the way you keep scribbling in jotters. It's time you pulled yourself together and did something useful for a change like scrubbing a few floors.'

Then suddenly Amelia had announced that she was moving into digs.

'Moving into digs?' She had not been able to believe her ears. 'Don't be daft!'

'I've got a place. It's only a couple of streets away. I'll visit you, mummy. You'll still be able to see Harry.'

'Visit me? Visit me? Don't be daft. You've a perfectly good home here. What will people think?'

'I don't care what people think.'

'Oh, isn't that typical,' Victoria said bitterly. 'I'm left to get a showing-up. No wonder you've to see a psychiatrist. You're not right in the head. Why should you leave your good home? That's what people will want to know. It doesn't make sense.'

'I've got a place of my own to be with Harry.'

'Oh, that poor wee lamb,' Victoria cried out. 'What's going to happen to him?'

'I'm going tomorrow.'

'Going where? You've gone off your head.'

'I've got a room at Miss Niven's in Chapel Street.'

'What? With that eccentric old spinster? She's off her head as well. Everyone knows that. Talk about birds of a feather! You're not going there and that's final.'

'It's all settled.'

'I'll soon unsettle it.'

But even as she spoke Amelia was packing Harry's clothes and his teddy in the pram. Victoria tried everything including the fact that God would punish her and that one day He would take away someone she loved. That at least made Amelia tremble but it did not stop her. She made several trips round to Chapel Street, trundling the pram heaped with clothes and blankets and bottles and baths, and with brown paper parcels clutched under each arm. The whole thing was so ridiculous Victoria could not believe it was happening. Yet, at the same time, she was deeply upset and acutely anxious about Harry.

Up until the last minute she held protectively on to the little boy while keeping up her warnings to Amelia of God's wrath for her wickedness. At the last minute there was an actual physical struggle as she still tried to hold on to her grandson and Amelia cruelly wrenched him away. In the struggle poor Harry began to scream and she shouted brokenly at Amelia, 'You see what you've done already, you cruel wicked girl!'

But Amelia had gone. Gone, no doubt, to sit chanting all the time in that queer way of hers to the poor wee chap.

Victoria had gone round to Miss Niven's that very night. The old spinster lived in a four-in-a-block type of house and her door was at the side and led right in to a steep flight of stairs. The room Amelia had was at the top of the stairs. It was not as big as the front room in Hilltop Road and it was crammed with Harry's pram and cot and bath and dear knows what else. It was a wonder Amelia had managed to get the bed-settee opened down. There literally was not room to move.

'This is ridiculous,' Victoria told her. 'The quicker you come back home the better. You'll never manage here. How will you get the pram up and down these stairs, for a start? You're liable to fall with it and be the death of that poor child.'

'He was sleeping,' Amelia said, 'and you wakened him with banging on the door.'

'Are you listening to what I'm saying?' Victoria demanded, but Amelia lowered her head and made no

166

reply. She was getting queerer every day, that girl. It was a terrible worry. That much she did confide in Mrs McDade.

She did not know in fact what she would do without Mrs McDade. It was a great comfort to be able to run into the next close, just as she was, in apron and slippers, and sit by Mrs McDade's fire while Mrs McDade administered tea and digestive biscuits. They had sat opposite each other, toasting their legs at the fire until they were strawberry-marked. Mr McDade would be out at his Highlanders Institute or his Scottish country dancing. He was a terribly energetic man and could not stay in or keep quiet or still for a minute. He exhausted Mrs McDade and, when he did stay in, perhaps to listen to the football results on the wireless turned up far too loud, Mrs McDade escaped round to Victoria's to be settled safely at Victoria's fireside and comforted with tea and home-baked scones. Mrs McDade always put her coat on over her apron before putting her foot over her threshold because she was so 'cold-rifed' and she always wore her close-fitting brown felt hat with the turned-up brim indoors or out, winter or summer.

'You poor soul.' Tears of sympathy welled up to Mrs McDade's eyes and she had to remove her spectacles to wipe them dry. 'After all you've done for Amelia. You don't deserve all this worry, Mrs Drummond. I don't understand why you are being made to suffer like this.'

Victoria sighed. 'It's life, Mrs McDade. Life's just one long struggle.'

And Mrs McDade wholeheartedly agreed.

25

Although Amelia worried about the earthy fusty smell in the house, she did not mind the crush in the room. When the bed-settee was down there was not an inch of floor space. She had to clamber over the bed to reach either Harry's cot or pram or go-chair, or the small table at the lace-curtained window at which she sat to eat or drink a cup of tea. She did not do much of either because it meant going through Miss Niven's living room to reach the tiny kitchenette. Each time, no matter how silently and un-obtrusively she slipped through, Miss Niven would look up from the bible she was reading, or from her *Christian Herald*, and tut with irritation at being disturbed.

Amelia felt guilty and afraid. For Harry's sake, nothing must be allowed to happen to cause her to lose this place. As a result, she only ventured through to the kitchenette to prepare Harry's food. She ate when she could, mostly things that did not need cooking, like bread and jam or biscuits. She did not have the money for anything else by the time she paid for the room. She could not even afford to get her hair cut and had to twist it each morning into a corn-coloured chignon at the nape of her neck. Untidy wisps kept straggling out over her face or were pulled out by a mischievous Harry.

For what little money she had, ironically enough, she had her mother to thank. Her mother had forced Douglas to, as she put it, 'stump up'.

'She's your wife,' Victoria had insisted, 'and you're legally bound to keep her. Now, we can go to a lawyer if you like and bring the whole sorry business out in the open. Or you can arrange privately for Amelia to be paid something every week.'

Amelia had never seen such hatred in anyone's eyes as she did when Douglas looked at her. If it had not been for Harry she would have refused to accept a penny. She had to swallow her pride, however, and agree to the arrangement of a few pounds being paid weekly into a bank account in her name. Once she had to buy Harry a coat and became overdrawn by two shillings. She had received a summons from the bank manager, a nasty-eyed ferret of a man, who had lectured her on the merits of thrift and warned her that a repeat of such extravagance and bad management would not be tolerated. She had the feeling that Douglas and his mother, who both had bank accounts in this bank, had given this little Hitler carte blanche to bully her. She felt powerless to defend herself, hemmed in as she was by desperate necessity.

There were so many things she had to be excruciatingly careful about. Miss Niven had been used to living by herself with her own strict routines until the need arose to supplement her pension with a lodger's rent. Lodger or no, Miss Niven's routines and preferences could not be interfered with, as Miss Niven would be quick to point out. Miss Niven had to have kitchen and bathroom towels folded in a particular way and no other, and hung exactly in the centre of each towel rail. Each bar of soap, kitchen sink, bathroom sink and bath, had to be dried and set down after use in exactly the right position on the right-hand side of each place. Face cloths had to be kept in sponge bags and sponge bags out of sight. No splashes of water were allowed anywhere at all. This made the filling of Harry's bath and the carrying of it through to the room and then bathing him an absolute agony. Although she tried very hard not to reveal her anxiety to Harry. She even tried to make his bath time fun but as quietly as possible. She talked to him in whispers and laughed with him without making a sound. Miss Niven could not abide noise.

Every night Amelia prayed that Harry would not cry. She slept lightly, all the time anxiously tuned to pick up the slightest sound. She was forever tensed, ready to jump up, grab him from his cot and burrow deep under the blankets of the bed-settee clutching him in her arms while desperately shushing him. Sometimes he refused to be muffled or

169

shushed, and they would huddle together under the blankets, hot cheeks wet with each other's tears. Next day Miss Niven would summons her through to the living room and inform her that she had not slept a wink the whole night and people who did not know how to look after children properly should not have any.

During most days Amelia took Harry out in his go-chair, walking quickly about the streets to keep warm, the bottle-green bell-tent coat that she had worn during her pregnancy, and now the only one she had, flapping loosely against her body. Harry was well wrapped-up in woolly hat, scarf, coat, leggings and blanket. She had got his coat two sizes too big to make sure it would last him as long as possible. She would sing to him, as they hurried along, or recite nursery rhymes or make up stories for him until she got so breathless she was forced to stop. Harry liked stories best and she enjoyed how they gave free rein to her imagination. His favourites were the ones made up about Bowf the dog and Dinky the cat. It was an especial joy to hear him laugh at her sound effects. She did not care what people thought of her as she trekked the streets, nose and ears tingling with the cold, talking dramatically all the time and making funny animal noises. Nobody mattered except Harry. It was her and Harry against the world.

After Harry went to sleep at night she would sit at the table and write other kinds of stories, stories for herself. Not that she found this as easy to do as telling stories to Harry. In fact it was not easy at all. Sometimes she sat for hours staring helplessly at a blank page of her notebook trying to squeeze something out of her equally blank mind. It had been all right penning descriptions of places and people, but to construct action to form a plot was a very different matter. It never occurred to her to give up. It was something she had to do. She knew it without thinking about it. It was a certainty in her. Like her love for Harry.

She had not even thought to mention it to the psychia-trist. The reason she had gone to the psychiatrist was because she had blurted out to the doctor that she wanted to kill her mother. He had taken her outburst very calmly. He

had just said, 'Would you like to see a psychiatrist, Amelia?'
Glad to clutch at any straw of help she had readily agreed.

The visit to the psychiatrist had been a harrowing
experience in one way. In another it had been quite
astonishing. She had spent hours, or so it had seemed, with
a fair-haired man in a white coat who had sat at his desk,
head down, penning her answers to his questions. It was the
deep probing of her relationship with her mother that had
proved harrowing. Then, suddenly, to her complete
astonishment, the man had looked up and she had seen that
he was flushed with anger.

'Why didn't you slap her face?' he said.

For a few seconds she stared at him uncomprehendingly.
Her whole world had been knocked off its pivot by his
unexpected attitude. He was actually thinking her mother
was in the wrong and she, Amelia, was not the guilty,
reprehensible person. It was inconceivable and far too big a
switch to grasp in a few seconds. It was like someone
suddenly asking her to believe the world was flat, or that she
was not a girl, after all, but a boy. The psychiatrist had
stared back at her in a silence that she was too stunned to
break.

Eventually he had led her to another bigger room where
an older man was sitting behind a desk. The young man and
herself sat in front of this desk, one at either end. The senior
psychiatrist leafed through the papers on which his young
colleague had written her answers and began asking her
some of the same questions over again. She had been
slouched helplessly in her chair, exhausted and apathetic,
when suddenly every nerve in her body was alerted. He had
slipped in the comment, 'So you want your mother to look
after your baby.'

'I'm perfectly capable of looking after my own child,' she
had immediately flashed back at him.

He looked down, trying to hide his smile. Then he said,
'There's nothing wrong with you that getting away from
your mother can't cure. Get away from her and from then
on your life will start to improve. We'll help you all we can.'

Only she was not far enough away from her. Sometimes

171

she wondered if she ever could be. If she had money to get away from the district, away even to a strange town, would her mother not follow her and torment her as she was doing now? Banging at the door several times a day, talking loudly not only in the room but coming up the stairs, marching through to the kitchenette as if she owned the place. She had made Miss Niven flush with anger by telling her that there was an unhealthy damp smell about the house. Before Miss Niven could say a word in protest, Victoria had lifted one of Miss Niven's books in the book-case and cried out triumphantly, 'Look at that! That proves it. That book's green mouldy. You'll all get your death of cold.'

Miss Niven had said nothing to Victoria but later she had said to Amelia, 'This won't do. Either you stop your mother coming here or you'll have to go. I can't allow my life, and the peace and quiet of my home to be disrupted by such insensitive and selfish people.'

Her mother had to be stopped. Then, as if in answer to her prayers, Victoria took a bad dose of flu and could not come round. It afforded at least a temporary respite. Not that she enjoyed it. Guilt and anxiety about her mother refused to go away; except when Harry was asleep in his cot and she sat with stubborn concentration trying to write stories. The trouble was she had no idea how to tackle the problems of her writing.

Then one day, while she was preparing Harry's lunch, she heard a programme on Miss Niven's wireless. A man was being interviewed about his first novel. It had won an award and he was explaining how he had based one of the main characters in his book on his mother and one of the most poignant scenes in the book had encapsulated his feelings about her death.

'One should write about what one knows,' he said, 'but the art of being a writer is to create something new from one's experience.'

This came as a revelation to Amelia. She had not been relating her need to write, to any *feelings* she had, either about her own or anyone else's experience. She had been thinking in terms of plot, of somehow drawing action from the air and pinning it down on paper. She felt an enormous rush of gratitude to the man. He was called Andrew Summers and the titel of his novel was *Hannah*, the name of the main character. Amelia hurried straight down to the library in Springburn that very afternoon to borrow the book. And a nice picture book for Harry while she was at it.

Hannah completely absorbed her. It made her laugh. It made her cry. Most of all it deeply affected her by its compassion and insight into the mind and heart of a woman. It was a shattering experience for her to realize that anyone, far less a man, could have such sympathetic understanding of another human being. She had to read the book again to grasp the truth of it, and once it had really sunk in she trembled with gratitude, as if Andrew Summers had been tender and compassionate and understanding to her personally. She felt inspired. She wanted to write like that. One day she *would* write like that. There had always been steel in her soul, hiding deep down, surfacing only in the form of a stubbornness to hang on, to survive. Now she knew why the steel was there. She drew it up, hardened it and pointed it in one direction. No matter what happened, no matter what anyone said to the contrary, she was going to become a writer.

26

'I told you mother and father approved of you,' Caroline said happily, hugging his arm as they strolled through the lush perfumed countryside.

'I doubt if "approve" is the most accurate word to use,' Drummond observed. 'I'm sure your parents would have preferred, for their only daughter, a man who did not need to become involved in a divorce case. I feel too that they had hoped you would choose a man from your own class.'

'Nonsense!' Caroline protested indignantly. 'Mother and father aren't snobs.'

'That's not what I meant. They naturally want what's best for your happiness and the more you have in common with a prospective husband the better chance you'd have of happiness.'

'I have everything that matters in common with you and, what's even more important, I love you.'

'I know, darling,' he said gently. 'But . . .'

'Mother and father know it as well. They know that all I need to make me happy is you.'

'It's extremely generous of your father to offer me this cottage.'

'It means you could move in any time, you see,' Caroline's voice quickened with eagerness. 'You wouldn't need to wait for the divorce to go through.'

He hesitated, still hedged around with doubts, not the least of which was the question of whether he was competent enough to write publishable books. More important than his doubts about his writing ability was his belief that his practical role in politics was of more help to ordinary working people. What help would a book on politics have been for instance for the old man and wife who came to his surgery, both of them near to tears, the other week-end? It was not the mix-up over the man's pension

174

from a monetary point of view that upset the old couple. It was the fact that some faceless bureaucrat had written saying that he was not entitled to a married man's pension because there was no record that he had ever been married.

It was the shame and disgrace that was distressing the couple, and the fact that they could not produce their copy of the wedding certificate as it had been destroyed with their house in the Clydebank blitz. The husband had done some detective work and discovered that the place where the original records had been kept had also been bombed but some files had previously been moved to a local church for safety. A bit of extra leg-work and persistent searching had eventually tracked down the old man's records. At the next surgery he had sent for the couple and presented them with their wedding certificate. He could still see the joy and gratitude that lit up their eyes.

There were hundreds of other cases. A constant stream of people queued patiently to see him at every surgery – people with housing problems, legal difficulties, deportation emergencies, health problems, even mental difficulties. They all came to him with their troubles, large or small, depending on him to help and advise them. He had built up a reputation for being an earnest and conscientious worker, who always did his best for his constituents. People trusted him. He did not find it easy to think of abandoning them and continued to be unhappy about making any definite decision. He had a lifetime of practice pouring out his innermost thoughts and feelings in the yearly diary he kept in his inside jacket pocket with his wallet, and he always wrote, in more detail, in the large hard-backed notebook he called his journal, about special events like his wedding-day, the birth of his children, his first day in Cabinet. These writings, however, were of a completely different format and far too sensitive in content to be in any way helpful in the writing of books on politics.

He had not committed himself either to the cottage or to giving up his career. He felt Lord Ridgeway understood and appreciated his worried hesitancy. After all, Lord Ridgeway had been faced with a similar decision. He had been forced to decide whether or not to give up his career. The situation was being treated by Lord and Lady Ridgeway with great delicacy. Nothing was said directly about the relationship between himself and Caroline, or about his personal dilemma. There had only been oblique remarks when some kind of reference could not be avoided or when it was brought into the open by the more direct Caroline. Lord and Lady Ridgeway would catch each other's eye in faintly unhappy embarrassment and Lady Ridgeway would murmur, 'I'm sure you know what you're doing, Caroline darling. You've always been such a capable person.'

One day after breakfast, while sitting in the panelled dining room reading *The Times*, Lord Ridgeway had suddenly announced, without looking up, 'Cottage in the grounds you might be interested in, Drummond. Caroline has the keys if you care to have a look.'

He and Caroline had followed the river through fields and alongside a wood and through a turnstile leading into a lane. At the end of the lane, Caroline cried out, 'Here it is. What do you think of it, darling?'

He had vaguely expected a small dwelling like the low-roofed, two-apartment farm-workers' cottages he had noticed dotted around the countryside. Here, however, was what he would have termed a substantial red-roofed villa of two storeys, plus attics, with its doorway sheltered by a porch. Its latticed windows blinked sleepily in the sun and a breeze like a sigh of contentment rustled through the ivy that clung to its walls. Its front garden was wild with roses and fuchsias and sweet peas and sweet-scented honeysuckle. There were larch trees with pink flower tassels on their drooping sprays and under a shady canopy of older trees there was a rustic seat.

'I've never, even in my dreams,' he said, 'ever imagined anything so beautiful.'

'You sound more sad than happy. What's wrong?'

'If only I was faced with a simple choice. If only I could just say, "Yes, I will give up everything and start a new life in that beautiful place tomorrow." '

'But you can, darling, you can! It *is* perfectly simple.'

'Caroline, we've never even discussed money.'

'Oh that!' Caroline said dismissively.

He gave her a quizzical smile, 'It's well seen you have never needed to worry about it.' She lived in a different world from Victoria and had never had to grapple with the problems of poverty. It had never occurred to her, it seemed, that he would have to continue with the upkeep of Victoria and the house in Glasgow. It was his legal obligation, but he would not have it otherwise.

'We don't need to worry about it,' Caroline said. 'You'll make plenty of money with your books.'

'We don't know that.'

'Darling, you will, you will! You're just feeling over-tired after so many all-night sittings. It's ridiculous the long hours MPs work. No one else in the land would put up with it,' said Caroline. 'There's no need to worry about money, darling. I've got what grandfather left me, so we'll have plenty. We'll be rent-free here and there's a huge vegetable garden at the back. Apple and pear trees, too.' She laughed happily. 'Don't worry, we won't starve. Oh, darling, it could be so idyllic. Can't you see?'

He could. 'It seems too good to be true.'

'Matthew, it's time you thought of yourself and put your own wishes and your own needs first. You *deserve* happiness. You've been putting other people first for far too long. Let's have a look inside.'

The garden gate creaked and he became aware of water tinkling into a trough. He was enfolded in a glorious riot of colour on either side of a winding path and the heady nosegay of perfumes created by the flowers and trees cut him off from any other world he had ever known. He would have been too embarrassed to say so but he felt that he was alone with Caroline in Paradise. He was harrowed with happiness as he entered the porch, with its smothering of purple clematis, and strolled silently through the house. Caroline earnestly drew his attention to its various attributes, but eventually she sighed, 'Darling do say *something*!'

177

'I've already given you my opinion of the place.'

She made to speak again, then checked herself and kissed him instead. He held her close. What use were words after all? How could they convey what he felt for her? His gaze, tenderly moving over her vulnerable, bespectacled face, his fingers gently tracing every contour, was a far more voluble language of love.

'Darling Matthew,' she whispered, as if afraid to break the unspoken bond between them. 'We could be so happy here.'

He nodded and, arm-in-arm and in silence, they returned outside. The lane was embroidered with the white lace of wild parsley and everywhere there was the heavy scent of hawthorn blossom, now fading and shedding its petals over the grass. White dog-daisies were sprinkling the fields with stars and above them the larks were singing. He was thankful this was not his fortnightly week-end for going to Glasgow. He could relax and be at peace before plunging back into work in London. He had no premonition at that point of exactly what was going to go wrong. It was not until he was in his office and Caroline, in her role of earnestly efficient secretary, announced that there was a Miss Bridget Dunbar to see him, that he felt the first chill. His dark eyes glanced up from the paper he was signing and held Caroline's worried stare before saying, 'Show her in.'

Bridget looked her usual genteel self in her maroon velour hat and suit of the same colour, and a fur tippet wound high round her throat.

Drummond rose with hand out-stretched, 'Bridget! This is a surprise. What brings you here?'

'I've been visiting my cousin. Her husband works in London now.'

'Ah yes. Caroline, perhaps you could organize some tea and biscuits? Do have a seat, Bridget.'

Bridget accepted his invitation, then carefully smoothed down her skirt with a leather-gloved hand and said, 'Your secretary's younger than I thought.'

He raised an eyebrow but made no comment.

'I tried to contact you on Friday,' Bridget went on. 'I was told you'd gone away early. So had your secretary.'

Again he made no comment and in the silence that followed raised a cool, enquiring brow.

Bridget shifted somewhat resentfully in her seat. 'I naturally thought you'd be here when it wasn't your weekend for going home.'

'Why didn't you let me know, Bridget? All it needed was a 'phone call. I could have perhaps taken you out for a meal and showed you around. Unfortunately . . .' he slid his watch from his waistcoat pocket – it had once belonged to John Drummond and was dented and discoloured, but as precious to him as it had been to his father – '. . . I'm rather pushed for time today. Ah, here's your tea! Just leave the tray on the desk, Caroline. I'll attend to Miss Dunbar.' His voice sounded cool and perfectly controlled. It seemed to him disembodied, as if it was coming from an unseen stranger. He hid behind the calm sound, his feelings in disarray. Razor-sharp apprehension tumbled about with sadness and bitterness and resentful anger.

Bridget meant trouble. Of that he had no doubt. She had always been of a somewhat malicious and gossipy nature and she had never forgiven him for dispensing with her services. Also, he suspected, she bore him an even greater grudge for not responding to her 'come on' signals. Bridget would have been only too willing to have had an affair with him.

As she sipped her tea, her eyes made a survey of his office. 'You've done very well for yourself,' she commented.

'I'm fortunate that, as a minister, I'm entitled to an office of my own.'

'The extra money's obviously a help too,' Bridget said, 'when you can afford to go for week-ends to the country.'

He blessed the telephone that rang at that moment. He picked it up and made a determined effort to concentrate all his attention on the caller. After he replaced the receiver he made a few notes on some paper in front of him, taking his time, before looking up. 'Sorry about that. More tea, Bridget?'

'No, thanks.'

'Are you returning today?'

'Yes, later this afternoon.'

'Well, have a good journey and no doubt I'll be seeing you again on one of my visits to Glasgow.'

'I went to your digs when I didn't get you here. I mean, I didn't really believe you'd go away a week-end to the country instead of going home. Especially when poor Mrs Drummond is having all that worry with Amelia. And, of course, as you no doubt know – Jamie is a different boy since that girl got her clutches into him. Hardly ever comes to see his mother. She's not good enough, it seems, since he and his little gold-digger of a wife have been kowtowing with Sir Alexander Forbes-Cunningham. Thick as thieves they are with him.'

He took out his watch again. 'I'm sorry, Bridget, I have someone else coming to see me in five minutes, but it was nice of you to drop in.' He pressed the call button on his desk and Caroline appeared almost immediately. 'Will you show Miss Dunbar out, please?'

Afterwards Caroline shivered, 'I got an awful feeling about that woman.'

'Yes,' he said. 'I know exactly what you mean.'

27

What little self-confidence Amelia had came crashing down like a castle of cards with her first rejection. For a time she was disorientated by the rejection slip. She could not make up her mind about simple things like what clothes she would put on in the morning or what she had to do for Harry. The cluttered room closed in on her, making her trip over and bump into things, and go round and round in hopeless circles. Until after Harry was sleeping in his cot and she was sitting at the card-table by the window, and she suddenly thought, 'Damn it, I don't care what the editor of that magazine thinks. One day I'll show her. One day I'll show everyone. I *will* become a writer!'

Her mother was an avid reader of women's magazines. They were stuffed under cushions and in drawers. Amelia collected them and studied them. She decided to get herself organised and attack the smaller pieces first. She would master them before working her way up to book-length material. She read the short stories, summarized them, analyzed them, counted each and every word. She also studied the articles and even the adverts to see exactly who the magazine was aimed at, what age group, what social class and whether it was aimed mainly at single or married readers. She asked herself questions about the stories. They were simple enough little tales. Why then was it not a simple task to write one? As indeed it was not. What was the secret, the trick, the method, the technique? Whatever it was she meant to find it. She came to the conclusion that there was always a story problem and some aspect of the story problem was more often than not stated in the first paragraph. That caught the reader's interest. Once caught, little bits of information could then be fed in, sometimes in flashback. This constituted the suspense element. There was always a climax and then, quickly after that, a resolution of the heroine's story problem.

Amelia carefully recorded all this in her notebook while sitting jammed against the window with Harry's pram not allowing her much elbow room. In his cot, a few feet away, his breathing sounded worryingly adenoidal. Part of her mind stayed tuned to the crackly breathing, praying that he was not going to take another cold. His nose always seemed to be either stuffed up or running. She could not bear it if he was suffering in any way. She was in anguish every time he looked flushed and had difficulty with his breathing. She would have gladly suffered anything to save him the slightest distress.

She spent hours trying to decide if she was being selfish to keep refusing to return to live with her mother. She tried to disassociate her own feelings and think only of what would be best for Harry. At her mother's, Harry would be coddled with too many clothes and overheated in front of the gas fire every night. His stomach would be upset by being fed titbits of chocolate or chips or whatever her mother happened to be eating. He would be lifted from his cot and dandled and showed off to whatever visitor her mother happened to have, at no matter what hour.

Here though, Harry was in a house that had an unhealthy smell of damp. The steam rose off his cot blankets when she heated them in front of the gas fire at night. And was she not putting him at risk of catching pneumonia by being so worried about gas leaks that she kept the window open wide every night? Often when he cried and she lifted him into her bed his little face and hands and feet felt icy-cold.

If she had more money, she might have found an alternative in other lodgings (Miss Niven's was at least very cheap), although few people, she had discovered, welcomed a baby. Her dream was to have a place of her own. Not one room. A flat. A whole place of her very own where she could shut the door and be safe and private. Harry and her. It was a dream so obviously unobtainable that it always left her weighed down by sadness as well as longing. If she could just establish some sort of income with writing she could perhaps find a room that was not damp.

Then, – oh, joyous unforgettable day – she received an

acceptance for one of her stories and a cheque for seven pounds. Self-confidence soaring, she thought, 'If I can do it once, I can do it again!' The trouble was she had borrowed Bridget Dunbar's typewriter to type the accepted story and she had practically to go down on her knees to plead with Bridget to allow her to use it again. Every waking minute she either planned stories in her head or typed them out. She bombarded the magazine which had accepted her story with other stories. All she received in reply were rejection slips. The cost of postage (return postage had always to be enclosed) was now an added worry.

Then she saw, in her mother's evening paper, an advert for a housekeeper. She wondered with tremors of ecstasy if this might be the solution to all her problems. Housework she could do. She had become well-practised from a young age in dusting and tidying and beating rugs over the rope in the back green and scrubbing floors for her mother. She was as obsessive in this work as she was in her writing. She tidied and cleaned everything in the house until there was not a biscuit crumb left under any cushions or blankets (her mother enjoyed having a cup of cocoa, a few biscuits and a read in her bed every night), or any old newspapers or tram tickets lying about, and you could see your face in the brown linoleum. Her mother always complained that she could not find anything afterwards and never seemed happy or completely at ease until the place was in chaos again.

The advert said to write in the first instance giving particulars and she typed out a neat letter which included a plea on Harry's behalf. He was an exceptionally good baby, she said, and absolutely no trouble. She made it clear, without saying so in so many words, that wherever she went, Harry had to go too. Despite doing her best with the letter, she thought having a baby would prevent her from being considered. To her surprise and delight she received a letter in reply asking her to come to an address in Bearsden for an interview. Bearsden was the poshest area for miles around Glasgow. It consisted mostly of small and large villas and some solid-looking terrace houses.

Amelia had spent most of her life without ever setting

foot in the area although it was only a few miles from the centre of the city. She had been there for the first time not long ago when she had accompanied her father who was chairing a meeting in the Town Hall. It had been like being allowed a brief glimpse of heaven. There were trees in the streets. There were meadows behind houses. There were meandering streams. There were parks and playgrounds. What a dream of a place to bring up a child!

She did without lunch to help scrape up enough money for the bus fare and set out for the interview carrying Harry in her arms. For most of the way she spoke to him with quiet urgency, 'This is our big chance, Harry. Please be good, darling. You will be a good quiet boy for mummy, won't you? It is *so* important. This could solve all our problems, you see. If I get this job, maybe it would mean you'd have a garden for your pram to sit in. You could watch the trees rustling and listen to the birds singing. Then when you get older you could run about and play in safety there. Mummy would be able to buy you big toys, like a wheelbarrow perhaps.'

Harry gave her one of his rabbit-toothed grins, as if he understood and appreciated every word she was saying. But his nose kept running and he did not know how to blow it. She had to keep rubbing at it, and he began to get annoyed and fought to punch the offending handkerchief away. She decided eventually that it was better to let it run than risk arriving with Harry howling in protest.

'It's all right, darling. It's all right,' she soothed desperately, and began nursing him from side to side. 'Mummy's wee darling boy. Mummy's wee darling boy. Mummy's wee darling boy.' At the same time she carried on a harassed conversation with God in her mind, 'Please let me get this job. Please, please, for Harry's sake. I don't care what happens to me but please, please, for Harry's sake. . . .'

The house turned out to be a sooty-looking villa with not much garden at the front. Amelia hoisted Harry into a more comfortable position, then rang the bell. For what seemed an age nothing happened and she could hear no sound from inside. Trying to ignore flutterings of panic she tried the bell again, this time pressing as hard as she could. Again she waited. This time she thought she heard something and was so busy straining to listen, she did not pay any attention to Harry tugging her hair and straggling it from her chignon. When the door did open, it was to reveal a bent, grey-haired woman in a wheelchair.

'Mrs Donovan?' the woman said, with a ghost of a smile, 'Do come in.'

The wheelchair backed away and turned. Amelia followed it along a gloomy hall and into a dusty sitting room.

'As you can see,' the woman's eyes clung to Amelia's in a kind of dumb pleading that did not seem to have any connection with what she was saying, 'the place is shamefully neglected. It's as much as I can manage to do a bit of cooking.' The eyes shied away. 'My husband eats out during the day so I've only myself to see to until evening. I'm Mrs Robertson. Sit down, dear. Your little boy looks heavy. What's his name?'

'Harry.' It was certainly a relief to take her own and Harry's weight off her feet.

'What age is he?'

'Nearly fifteen months.'

'Goodness! He's big for his age. What a lovely boy!'

Harry jumped up and down on Amelia's lap, juddering her. Then he grabbed a handful of fair hair and tugged it gleefully about.

'He's very good. Never any trouble,' she managed breathlessly, hanging on to the energetic Harry as best she could.

'Put him down, dear, and let him crawl around.'

Amelia flicked an anxious glance around the room to see if there was anything he could destroy, before reluctantly complying. Harry shot off as soon as his knees touched the carpet. He had never set eyes on such an expanse of floor space in his life and was obviously not going to waste a second in his exploration of it.

'You're separated from your husband, you said in your letter,' Mrs Robertson leaned forward. 'Is your separation permanent or do you think that perhaps. . . ?'

'Oh, permanent,' Amelia interrupted, 'there's no doubt about that.'

'Your minister gave you an excellent reference. He said you'd been a regular church attender and you came from a good family background.'

'I haven't been to church since Harry's christening. It's a bit difficult to get out anywhere now. There aren't very many places where you're allowed to take a baby.'

Mrs Robertson sighed. 'I suppose you're right. It's like having a wheelchair in a way. There aren't many places where you can take this either. Do you think you could manage a housekeeper's job?'

'Oh yes,' Amelia hastily assured her, 'and I'm a very conscientious worker.'

'It's a case of keeping the house clean and doing the shopping. The washing and ironing too, of course.'

'I could manage all that – no bother.'

'I'm afraid I can't get up the stairs, so I don't know what it's like up there. It must be an absolute disgrace.'

'I'd soon have it perfect – no bother.'

'I have one of the downstairs rooms as a bedroom now.' Mrs Robertson's eyes wandered over to the window where the sunshine was spotlighting a million dancing motes. 'It saves my husband carrying me up and down the stairs and gives him peace in his room at night. He's in the building trade and he had a bathroom installed en suite to my room. It saves such a lot of trouble.'

'I could do the cooking, too, if you like,' Amelia said. 'It would be no bother.'

Mrs Robertson hesitated. To Amelia's desperately alert and eager eye, she thought she detected a look not only of unhappiness but guilt. 'It would be no bother,' she repeated. 'I'm much stronger than I look.'

'Well, if you're sure, dear. . . . When can you start?'

'Oh!' Amelia was too overcome to speak for a minute. 'Right away. I could start bringing our things over tomorrow. Harry's cot folds down. I could balance it on top of the pram and walk with it. . . .'

'Walk? All the way from Balornock? Nonsense!'

'I don't mind walking. I'm used to it. It would be no bother.'

'My husband will arrange for one of his lorries to collect your things. Just have everything ready for tomorrow afternoon.'

'Could Harry and I get a lift in the van too, please?' Amelia ventured.

'Yes, don't worry. I'm sure that will be all right. I'll speak to my husband when he comes in tonight.' Her eyes wandered away for a few seconds again. 'I hope you'll be happy here, Amelia. It'll be a good home for you in many ways.'

Amelia experienced a surge of gratitude and relief. It was as much as she could do not to burst into tears. 'I'll have everything packed and ready by lunch-time,' she said. 'There isn't much really.'

'The salary mentioned in the advert doesn't sound much, I know, but it includes your room and board. It's an attic room but it's a good size and it's carpeted.'

Amelia could not get away quick enough to start packing. Hurrying, almost skipping down the garden path, she sang to Harry and bounced him in her arms, making him screech with laughter. She was laughing along with him when she bumped into a man at the garden gate. He was tipped back by an enormous fat belly and a bushy moustache straggled wetly over his face.

'Oops!' he bellowed, catching her against his belly and doing a little dance that turned her out through the gate. 'D'ye come here often, hen?'

She lowered her eyes and shrank away from him.

'You'll be the lass about the job?' He gave a spluttering laugh that puffed out whisky fumes like poison gas. 'Did the wife manage to fix you up all right?'

'Yes, thank you.'

'You're a bonny wee thing.' He winked. 'You and I'll get on fine, eh?'

She managed a wisp of a smile before escaping. But she did not feel like singing any more.

28

'Come,' Burgeyev's voice startled her. 'I will give you a tour.'

She had been sitting in the lounge, writing a letter to her mother, when he suddenly appeared at her elbow. She experienced a shock at the sight of him, almost as if he had shouted abuse at her again. He was a tall man with perfectly sculptured features and an energy that seemed to simmer under a calm surface. His movements, especially when he walked, looked measured and unhurried. He had the dignity and grace of a sinewy dancer or a cat.

'Come,' he insisted, 'Leningrad is waiting.'

Her first thought was to refuse. A man as handsome as that was bound to be unbearably conceited. But, as she wrote to Veronica later, 'It was dead boring with dad so engrossed in his work and with nothing for me to do most of the time, so I thought – why not?'

Gone was the flashing-eyed rage of the day before, but she resented Burgeyev's calm detachment even more. It irritated her. She wondered if she dared to give him a tip at the end of the day in order to take him down a peg or two.

'Is this your first sight of Leningrad?' he asked, in his deep, thick accent, as he guided her outside. She shook off the hand that was firmly cupping her elbow.

'Yes, it was dark when I arrived last night.'

'Dark?' he echoed, with what she judged as such exaggerated incredulity she was sure he was making a fool of her. 'We have white nights in Leningrad.'

She shrugged, intrigued despite herself at the 'white nights'. 'I was half-asleep.'

'Here it is!' he said. 'My Leningrad.'

She meant to smile patronizingly at what she regarded as a piece of conceit, but was suddenly diverted by the beauty of what met her eyes. All was cool, balanced and spacious.

Quiet dwellings lined the river and canals. Elegant street lamps with embossed bases and dangling brackets graced every street. Single-spanned bridges of handsomely wrought iron, decorated with winged heads and ancient coats-of-arms, reached over canals. Even the quays and pavements were a joy to the eye in a delicate shade of pink-grey granite.

'The style here,' Burgeyev told her, as they strolled along, 'is stucco, colour-washed in bright hues.'

She had never seen such elegant architecture or such colourful buildings, mint green, rose pink, honey, ochre, mustard, sky blue, sparkling white, glittering gold. They made her want to cry out like an excited child, 'Look! Look!'

'It is mostly eighteenth-century,' Burgeyev went on with pride in his voice, 'stylishly laid out, as you can see, with wide roads and squares. It was founded by Peter the Great, called St Petersburg at first, then Petrograd and finally Leningrad. The city sprawls over more than one hundred islands in the Neva delta and there are ninety-five rivers and canals and innumerable buildings within its boundaries. Some people call it the Venice of the North others say there is no other city like it in the world.'

The day gradually took on a dream-like quality. The lovely river Neva, shimmering in the sun, blended with the breathtaking splendour of the Winter Palace on its banks and dissolved into the wide Nevsky Prospekt with its elegant buildings and statues.

'It's all too much to take in on one day,' she admitted eventually.

'You are right,' he agreed. 'You shall accompany me home now where we will rest and have tea with my family. But you like what you have seen of my Leningrad, yes?'

She understood now why he used the personal pronoun. She would be proud to lay claim to such beauty herself. 'I can honestly say,' she told him, 'I have never seen any place so absolutely enchanting in my life.'

'Ah, but you come from Scotland. I have heard there is much beauty there too.'

'Not like this. I mean, there is natural beauty – in the Highlands, for instance – mountains and glens. There's some glorious colour there, especially in the autumn. But this. . . ,' she hesitated, dazedly shaking her head. 'This has man-made beauty to rival anything from nature. This demonstrates what civilized man is capable of.'

'Lenin used to have Beethoven's *Appassionata Sonata* played to him on every possible occasion and, on hearing it, he always used to observe, "Of what is man *not* capable." '

'The funny thing is,' she said, 'I never thought it was like this. I don't think anybody at home thinks of Russia as anything but . . .' She stopped in embarrassment.

'The enemy?' he said.

She had actually been going to say grey, dreary and repressive, but she refrained from correcting him.

'It is very strange to us,' he went on, 'that you in the West, the inheritors of European power, – especially you from Britain with its far-flung Empire – regard us as aggressors. It is we who have been invaded time and again by other European powers. Who are you to tell us to forget Napoleon, or the British and French in the Crimea, or Hitler?'

'In don't think of you as the enemy, honestly!' she said. 'I mean, you were our allies in the war.'

'Ah yes, you cry out for our help against Napoleon, against the Kaiser, against Hitler, and in so many cases ours was the sacrifice that assured victory – in the snow on the road from Moscow, among the ruins of Stalingrad, or here in starving Leningrad. Then once victory is achieved,' he gave a shuddering sigh, 'and at what cost, *at what cost*, you regard Mother Russia as the enemy once more. Yes, it is very strange to us!'

A wave of deep emotion lapped around him in the silence that followed and she became aware that, although his eyes could be black and frightening, or distant and expressionless, they could also hold compassionate regret.

'Did you and your family suffer much during the war?' she asked.

'I was a soldier on the Leningrad Front.'

'Wasn't it the Leningrad Front that prevented the Germans getting into the city?'

'Long-range guns were brought to destroy Leningrad and murder hundreds of thousands of civilians. The guns were silenced. Every man, woman and child fought to protect the city. One of my sisters was in the Women's Detachment. She died bravely, but quickly. Others, like my grandfather, my young brother, my cousin, and his wife and children died a much slower death during the blockade.'

Again she felt sick with shame at having been so ignorant and thoughtless in her treatment of the hotel waitress. 'Starved, you mean?' she asked faintly.

'The daily ration of bread,' he said, 'was the size of two matchboxes and thirty per cent of that was wood pulp. Soup made with glucose and laurel leaves was the only other food. Eight thousand people were killed by enemy gunfire, but two million died of starvation.'

'How dreadful!'

As she wrote to Veronica afterwards, 'It's difficult to make you understand when you haven't been here. There's been so much suffering, Veronica. Honestly, it's overwhelming. You can almost see it in the air like ghosts hovering around the people. You see, no one has been forgotten. Nothing has been forgotten. And I have a feeling no one or nothing ever will.

'I know this must all sound dead boring to you, Veronica, but honestly I can't help it. This place and the people here are affecting me more than I can say. . . .'

What had affected her most was her visit to Burgeyev's home. He lived with his mother and his grandmother in the bottom flat of an old building in a cobbled side street. The powder-blue walls had faded almost to white and large flakes of stucco were peeling off. The small deep recesses of the double windows were hung with skimpy lace curtains, their shutters hanging slightly askew. Inside the house, along a dark corridor, she was shown into a cell-like room which was overcrowded with furniture. Aspidistra plants sat on window-sills and on the plush tablecloth that covered the table. A high bed had lace-covered pillows and the chairs had antimacassar-like trimmings. The room, the whole building, it seemed, was permeated with a stale, damp smell.

'This is my *babouchka*,' Bergeyev led her immediately to a corner where an ancient-looking woman was sitting. Helena had not noticed her at first because she blended so completely into the shadows, with her long black dress and black headscarf that almost hid her sallow hook-nosed face. She remembered from her Russian language book that '*babouchka*' meant 'grandmother' and she was able, also from her study of the book, to greet the woman with 'Good afternoon' in Russian. The wrinkled face showed little if any response.

Burgeyev said something to the woman in Russian and she replied in a surprisingly strong voice which Burgeyev translated, '*Babouchka* says my mother is out with Nikolai and Sasha, my sister Vera's children, but she will return shortly. Meantime, *babouchka* will give you a glass of tea.'

The samovar was steaming in the corner and soon glasses of tea were poured and handed round. The old woman drank hers in the old Russian way, holding the sugar between pursed lips and sucking the tea from the saucer through the sugar.

'How did you learn English?' Helena asked Burgeyev.

'At school and at university. I also have done translating work which has given me practice in conversing with people.'

'Do you enjoy doing that kind of work?'

He shrugged, 'It is interesting to see the differences in character of Western people from us.'

'What do you think are the differences?'

'Ah, they are too many and too subtle to tell you in a few minutes. I would need a few weeks or months or even a year to explain. Even then I doubt if you would understand. I remember one of the first things I noticed was that English people and all foreigners smile very much. It is a custom, no? When we Russians meet a new person we do not smile,

192

unless, of course, we think we like the person at once. It is not necessary to smile unless we feel like it. Among Russian tourist guides there is a saying, "Remember, many smiles!" '

'I must remember to tell my father that,' she said. 'He's working on the Russian character at the moment.'

'Really?' Burgeyev said without smiling and again she felt a ripple of irritation, wondering if he was expressing interest or derision. 'I work only occasionally, to supplement my income from writing, but it is very good as I have said for learning about people. I regard it as my research.'

Interest overcame irritation, 'What do you write?'

'I have had two books of short stories published and at present I am writing a novel.'

'I was at art school before I came over here,' she said. 'It seems a million years ago now.'

'You are being affected perhaps by the size of Russia. Time cannot have the same meaning.'

'I suppose that could be part of what I feel,' she said thoughtfully.

'And yet you have seen so little.'

'My father has to travel a great deal more before he finishes his assignment and I shall be going with him.'

'It will be interesting to hear what you and your father think you have discovered about the Russian character.'

His tone made her feel defensive. 'My father is very well thought of at home. He's a first-class investigative journalist.'

'Ah, first-class!' he echoed in a voice polite with derision.

She thought him the most insufferable man she had ever met.

29

'I've no secrets from Mrs McDade,' Victoria assured Bridget Dunbar. 'You can talk freely in front of her.'

Mrs McDade and Victoria had just been settling down for a happy discussion about when they would have the next whist drive for Labour Party funds. They had raised quite a sizeable sum of money so far. Victoria enjoyed organizing these social occasions and catering for the cups of tea, sandwiches, scones and cakes that were enjoyed after the whist was over. Rows of three-tier cake-stands were made ready on one of the long trestle tables in the ante-room of the Labour Party hall, a plate of sandwiches, a plate of scones and a plate of cakes were set on every stand, and one stand was to be allocated to each green-baize-topped table.

Victoria supervised all the arrangements and issued directions to her small band of helpers. Mrs McDade was next in charge. Everyone knew she had this special status and, being Victoria's best friend, Mrs McDade was also privileged to be in at the beginning when decisions were made on what kind of sandwich fillings, scones and cakes to have.

It had been a nuisance to have the unexpected intrusion of Bridget Dunbar but Victoria had never turned anyone away from her door in her life. 'Come in, come in, Bridget.' She had welcomed her with such warmth that Mrs McDade later assured her that she deserved an Oscar. 'Mrs McDade and I were just having a cup of tea. I'll put out another cup.'

'Now look,' Bridget said, 'I don't want to be any bother. . . .'

'Sit down,' Victoria said, 'and don't be daft!'

It was once the tea was poured and Bridget was daintily nibbling an Empire biscuit that she said, 'In actual fact, what I came to talk to you about, Mrs Drummond, is rather delicate and confidential.'

'Oh dear,' Mrs McDade looked anxious, 'maybe I'd better go, Mrs Drummond.'

'You'll do no such thing, Mrs McDade. Say what you have to say, Bridget, and less of your nonsense.'

'Well now,' Bridget's face assumed a dignified but huffy expression. 'I hardly think my concern for your feelings and welfare should be classed as nonsense, Mrs Drummond.'

'Have another cream cookie, Mrs McDade,' Victoria urged, helping herself to another. She enjoyed her food despite, as she put it, suffering purgatory with her stomach at times.

'Now, as you know,' Bridget pressed on, 'I've recently returned from London. And while I was in the capital city I paid a courtesy call on Mr Drummond.'

'How about a cream cookie for you, Bridget? It's not *real* cream right enough. I've forgotten what that tastes like, haven't you? But they're lovely. Go on, try one.'

'No, thank you, Mrs Drummond,' Bridget said, somewhat testily. 'I met Mr Drummond's new secretary.'

'Hardly new any more,' Victoria laughed through a mouthful of cream cake. 'What was she like?'

'Well now, she's nothing to look at. Not even smartly dressed.'

'Fancy!' Victoria wiped her mouth with a corner of her apron. In the mornings she wore a floral wraparound. But in the afternoons or evenings, if she was having visitors, she wore what she called her Dutch apron – a short scarlet one that tied round her waist.

'She has straight mousy hair – that hair has never seen a perm or a marcel wave – and heavy horn-rimmed glasses.'

'Fancy!' Victoria absently repeated. Her mind had drifted on to the question of meat or fish paste for the whist drive sandwiches.

'As long as she's a help to Mr Drummond,' Mrs McDade said. 'I mean, is she good at shorthand and typing, that sort of thing?'

'Well now, I'd say she must be good at a lot more than that.'

In the pause that followed Victoria's attention wandered back, 'How do you mean?'

'Well,' Bridget sniffed, 'there's something going on there if you ask me. He wasn't there when I called in on the Friday. He'd gone to the country for the week-end.'

'Good gracious!' Victoria rolled her eyes. 'Don't tell me the Tories have persuaded him to join them for the Glorious Twelfth, as they call it. A lot of nonsense, of course. There's nothing glorious about killing poor defenceless birds.'

'No, it was before the twelfth.'

'He usually comes home by then,' Victoria explained. 'But this time he's staying down south for a few weeks extra. He's some research to do in the British Library.'

'I don't think so, Mrs Drummond.'

'What do you mean, you don't think so?'

'Well now, my guess is he's spending those few weeks in the country.'

'For the grouse shooting?' Victoria was incredulous.

'I hardly think so.'

'What then?'

'His secretary lives in the country. I've got her address here.' She opened her handbag, extracted a piece of paper and handed it to Victoria.

'Innerleithen?' Victoria read. 'Where's that?'

Mrs McDade nervously cleared her throat. 'I think it's down near the borders, Mrs Drummond. Over the other side of Edinburgh.'

'It's farming country, I believe,' said Bridget. 'Her people probably work on one of the farms there.'

'Innerleithen House,' Victoria said. 'It sounds like a farmhouse right enough.' Her ruddy cheeks had gone a bit pale and her dark eyes held a mixture of puzzlement and worry. 'All that extra work he had to do; he probably had to go with her to get it all sorted out. That is if he *did* go with her. He could have gone somewhere else entirely.'

'No, he left a forwarding address with his landlady. It was the very same as "plain Jane" Ridgeway's. That's her name, Caroline Ridgeway.'

Victoria's whole being stiffened. Her chin tipped her head back. 'What are you suggesting, Bridget?'

Bridget paused uncertainly, then an expression of malice twisted her face and made her blurt out, 'I believe he's being unfaithful to you, Mrs Drummond. I felt it my duty to tell you.'

'Don't be daft,' Victoria said.

'Oh dear,' Mrs McDade wrung her hands, 'is this not terrible!'

'I swear there's something between them,' Bridget insisted. 'They've got that look.'

'What look?' Victoria scoffed, but even her lips were tinged with pallor now.

'You'll know it when you see it,' Bridget prophesied with a wise nodding of her head.

'And you'll know my door when you see it, too,' Victoria retorted. 'I'll not have you coming here slandering my man.'

'Oh, if that's how you feel,' Bridget rose, her cheeks flushed with indignation.

'Yes, that's how I feel, Bridget. You'll be welcome to come back here any time but only on the condition that you watch your wicked gossiping tongue.'

'Oh!' Bridget nearly fell over her chair in her fury and desperation to get out. 'I've never been so insulted in my life!'

'You'll see yourself out, then?' Victoria took a nonchalant mouthful of tea. She later confessed to Mrs McDade, however, that she felt so shaken she couldn't have seen Bridget to the door. Her legs would not have carried her.

'Oh dear,' Mrs McDade pressed her hanky to her cheek, once Bridget had stalked out. 'What do you think, Mrs Drummond?'

'I hardly know what to think. But I'm a great believer in action, Mrs McDade. With God's help I always *do* something.'

'But what can you do about this? Oh dear, you mean confront him when he comes home?'

'No. I'm not going to be made to suffer the worry of this for weeks on end. I'll never sleep a wink. I've a bad enough time with my weak bladder. I'm going to confront him right now.'

'But he's not here and you said . . .'

'Tomorrow then. Will you chum me there, Mrs McDade? I'd do the same for you.'

It was Mrs McDade's turn to blanch. She was wearing a black felt hat, underneath which her anxious face had turned positively sickly. 'You mean away down to Innerleithen?'

'I'd do the same for you,' Victoria repeated. 'It's just to chum me. But if you'd rather not, I'll just go by myself.'

'No, no,' Mrs McDade made a brave attempt to rally. 'I'll stick by you, Mrs Drummond. All the way.'

'We could take sandwiches,' Victoria said brightly, 'make an outing of it. I'm sure there's nothing in what that Bridget Dunbar said. I know my man, Mrs McDade. He would no more think of carrying on with another woman than fly in the air. We've never had a holiday for years, you and I, have we? Never been out of Glasgow. Yes, we'll make a right day of it. Everything will be fine. Just you wait and see.'

30

Victoria and Mrs McDade had to set out, as Victoria said, 'at the crack of dawn'. They had discovered that it was necessary to take a train to Edinburgh and then a bus from there. The journey alone was an enormous adventure. Neither of them had been further than a trip down the Clyde to Rothesay at the Glasgow Fair. Victoria had only been once to Edinburgh. That was a lifetime ago when she had been friendly with Rory Donovan and Rory had taken her there for a treat. The enormity of the situation and what she was about to do had receded to comfortable proportions. Victoria had always possessed the happy art of shutting out most of what she did not want, or could not bear, to think about. She had a romantic turn of mind and also a highly developed sense of drama. She acted out situations which, although having some basis in reality, soon became lost in the more romantic scenario she made up as she went along.

She had not had much time to think about the journey to Innerleithen because, after Bridget and then Mrs McDade left the day before, Jeannie Burns had arrived. Jeannie was the latest lodger. She was a waitress in Miss Cranston's Restaurant and 'run off her feet'.

'And you're no chicken as well,' Victoria sympathized. 'You're as white as a sheet. You don't look fit for all that running about all day and carrying heavy trays.'

It was agreed with a grateful Jeannie that she would have one of the bedrooms to herself and share everything else.

'I'm going to make you a good strong cup of tea,' Victoria said, 'and with the rest of the water out the kettle I'll melt some epsom salts in the basin. You can steep your feet in that while you're drinking your tea.'

Administering to the footsore Jeannie and getting her settled in had taken Victoria's mind off the journey next

199

day. Jeannie had been glad to help with travelling instruc-
tions. She seemed to have been the original wandering
waitress. She had worked everywhere. Not exactly in
Innerleithen but while working in Edinburgh she had been
sent as part of a private catering job to Peebles, the nearest
market town to Innerleithen.

'It's like a picture postcard down there, so it is,' she had
assured Victoria. 'All grass and trees and sheep. You'll love
it.'

Victoria was less than convinced by this. Grass and trees
had never been of the slightest interest to her and sheep
even less. She had an equally dismissive regard for country
people. She had come across a few farm workers in her day
(mostly big Teuchters, as Highlanders were disrespectfully
nicknamed) and regarded them as being very coarse and
ignorant. 'Give me the city and city folk any time,' she
always said. She belonged to Glasgow and she was proud of
it.

'Still,' as she said to Mrs McDade, 'a wee breath of
country air won't do us any harm. You're looking very pale,
Mrs McDade. A wee trip to the country will do you good.'

Indeed, if Jeannie could have managed the day off, she
would have taken her as well. 'The more the merrier' was
one of Victoria's favourite sayings.

Only when she was alone did cracks appear in her cheery
scenarios. Only then were doubts and realities briefly
revealed. Alone in the living room, adjusting her scarlet
straw boater (she had lacquered it herself) and pinning her
Woolworth's ruby and diamond brooch to the lapel of her
air force blanket coat, a lightning flash of fear illuminated
her mind and made her heart palpitate. Matthew and
another woman? No. No. It was unthinkable! Matthew was
her man. He was hopeless in any social situation and no
doubt he had got himself, in all innocence, into a situation
that could be easily misinterpreted by people like Bridget
Dunbar. 'Honestly,' she thought, 'he's an awful man!' It
was not the first time that she had had to extricate him from
an embarrassing misunderstanding. He was always putting
his foot in it by saying or doing something silly or awkward

at parties or social occasions. She had thought he had got a bit better since he had gone to London but – here he was again! He really was an awful man. She saw herself acting out scene after scene of her goodhumoured rescues of Matthew over the years. In the early days, she and Matthew used to laugh over what he, in his usual flowery way, called his 'gaffes and social peccadilloes'. He never laughed at the time. On the contrary he could fly into the most shocking tempers and call her for everything as if she was to blame. But, to give him his due, he always apologized afterwards and eventually they were able to laugh about it. Indeed it was one of her favourite 'turns' at gatherings of friends to tell stories about Matthew's 'gaffes and social peccadilloes'. Many a time at parties people would say, 'Come on, Victoria, tell us about the time when Matthew . . .' This Innerleithen episode would be no more than a hilarious addition to her repertoire.

The palpitations moved to the pit of her stomach and became sickening as she and Mrs McDade set off. Soon, however, Victoria was fully taken up by looking after her friend. Mrs McDade's nervous short-sightedness had always been a problem, but now she seemed nervous all over. Victoria had practically to lift her on to the train in Glasgow, and then the bus in Edinburgh. Even sitting in the bus, Mrs McDade, in her black hat and black-out material coat, remained clinging like a starving leech to Victoria's plump arm.

'Oh dear,' she absently repeated, and then, 'Mrs Drummond, what are you going to say?'

'The Lord is on my side, Mrs McDade. "I shall not fear, What can man do to me?" Psalm twenty-seven, verse one. Or woman for that matter,' she added.

'I've always admired your courage, Mrs Drummond, but never more than I admire it today.'

'Tuts,' Victoria said. 'Have a toffee ball, Mrs McDade.' Victoria had a weakness for sweet things and she particularly enjoyed toffee balls. The size of this confectionary, however, made it well-nigh impossible to speak. It took a few minutes of energetic sucking and chewing before she could continue the conversation. 'I always say my prayers every night, do you?'

The anxiety on Mrs McDade's little pixie face became more acute. 'I try but I find it terribly difficult.'

'It's just speaking to God,' Victoria said. 'I chat away quite the thing. My mother use to say grace before every meal. Or make my father say it.'

'Fancy!'

'She wouldn't hurt a fly, my mother.'

'A good Christian woman.'

'The salt of the earth.'

'It was her heart, wasn't it?'

'Matthew was very good at the end. He used to hold her in his arms and try to soothe her when she was gasping for breath. She died in his arms, in fact. He was terribly upset. He was fond of my mother.'

'A good Christian woman,' Mrs McDade repeated.

'My Matthew's been a hard cross to bear, Mrs McDade, but he's my man and he's got his good points.'

'So has my Hector,' Mrs McDade agreed, but without much conviction.

They indulged in another chew at their toffee balls, then Victoria said, 'Her folks will probably be black affronted.'

Confusion crinkled Mrs McDade's face. 'Whose folks?'

'This secretary, what's her name?'

'Oh, Caroline Ridgeway, wasn't it? You had it written down. You haven't lost it, have you?'

'No need to panic, Mrs McDade. I'll have it somewhere. But I think you're right. Ridgeway, that was it. Sounds more like an English name, doesn't it? That would be just like the thing!'

Mrs McDade and Victoria shared a distrust of the English which, had they not both been good Christian women, could have hardened into downright dislike.

Between chatting and chewing, the journey passed quite quickly. In no time, it seemed, they had reached Peebles.

'We must be nearly there,' Victoria said. 'Jeannie told me it wasn't far from Peebles.'

They both stared with varying degrees of anxiety out of

202

the window after that. As Victoria said, 'We don't want to miss it after coming all this way.'

Jeannie had been right about the trees and the grass, but she had forgotten to mention the hills.

'I'd hate to be stuck away out here, wouldn't you?' Victoria said. 'There's not a soul in sight.'

'Not a soul,' echoed Mrs McDade.

'Give me civilization any time, Mrs McDade. They can keep their sheep. I like decent, God-fearing folk around me.'

'Indeed. Indeed.'

Suddenly the bus conductor shouted, 'Innerleithen!' They had asked him to give them a shout but had not really trusted him to do so. Now, they both started with surprise. Victoria was the first to recover. 'Just keep a hold of my arm, Mrs McDade. You'll be all right.'

It took them a few minutes to essay the narrow aisle stuck together like this, but eventually they managed it. They stepped off the bus like two alien beings from another planet. Victoria had never seen any place so pristine clean. The line of buildings on either side of the street and the street itself sparkled a bright silvery grey in the sunshine.

'They never get any fog here,' Victoria said, taking it for granted that Mrs McDade was thinking along the same lines as herself.

'Fancy!' Mrs McDade's voice had dropped to a reverent whisper.

'I wonder where this cottage or farmhouse or whatever they call it is?'

'Innerleithen House,' Mrs McDade whispered. 'I expect it's further out. In a field or something.'

'This is going to be absolute purgatory on my varicose veins,' Victoria said. 'Just you wait until I get my tongue on that man. He's gone too far this time, dragging me away out here to the back of beyond!'

'Oh dear,' said Mrs McDade, 'there's nothing but fields for miles.'

'We'll have to ask somebody,' Victoria said, looking

around. But the bus had gone and not a soul was to be seen. 'There's a wee shop. We'll try there.'

The shop-door tinged and they found themselves in a brown shadowy interior. For a few seconds Victoria could hardly see a thing, so great was the contrast to the dazzle outside. Nobody came even after Victoria loudly cleared her throat several times, then trilled out, 'Anybody at home?'

'This is ridiculous,' she told Mrs McDade. 'I'm going round the back to see what's what.'

'Oh dear,' Mrs McDade was still whispering, 'what if someone sees you?'

'That's the whole idea!'

With a trembling Mrs McDade still clutching her arm, Victoria went behind the counter to peep round a door that lay slightly ajar. 'Yoohoo!' she sang.

'What do you want, eh?' Both friends jerked with fright as the voice unexpectedly issued from behind them. An old woman in a long black dress and black lacing shoes stood with a basket over her arm containing lettuce and tomatoes.

Victoria said, 'Good gracious, I nearly jumped out of my shoes! We're looking for Innerleithen House.'

'What do you want, eh?' the old woman repeated. She had wispy white hair on her face as well as her head and the more Victoria looked at her the more ancient she seemed.

'She must be stone-deaf,' she remarked to Mrs McDade. 'That's all we need.'

'Oh dear!'

Victoria pushed her face close to the woman's left ear. 'Innerleithen House,' she bawled.

'Yes,' the old woman said.

'Where is it?' Victoria yelled again.

'It's a long walk.' The old woman regarded them with satisfaction as if to say, 'and you two'll never manage it.'

'What way?' Victoria shouted, then in a normal voice to Mrs McDade, 'I'll be exhausted before I start.'

'Is this not terrible,' Mrs McDade commiserated.

The old woman gave an impatient wave of her hand before pushing past them. 'Cross the road there and take the first turn on the right. Follow the road. You can't miss it.'

There was still not a living soul to be seen when the two friends emerged on to the street again.

'This gives me the creeps,' Victoria said. 'It's as silent as the grave.'

'Oh, Mrs Drummond, I wish we hadn't come!'

'On the contrary, Mrs McDade. My man's somehow, for some reason, been persuaded to come to this place, and it's my duty as his wife to get him safely home where he belongs.'

31

The attic, despite the ceiling that sloped steeply down at either side, was huge compared with the room at Miss Niven's. It ran practically the whole width of the house and was partitioned off into bedroom and sitting room accommodation. It had a square somewhat threadbare but still good-looking Axminster carpet in the sitting area, two sagging moquette armchairs, a gate-legged table ringed with glass marks and a shoulder-high chest of drawers. The sleeping area held Harry's cot (the pram and go-chair were kept in an all-purpose room off the kitchen down-stairs), an old brass-framed double bed with a locker beside it on which sat a bedside lamp, another chest of drawers with a cracked mirror above it and one spar-backed wooden chair with a spar missing.

The attic had obviously been a dumping place for furniture that was no longer good enough for downstairs. To Amelia, however, it was luxurious, it made of the attic a Shangri-La. She was in heaven. The garden at the back had the dreamed-of trees and a fence all round that kept Harry safe. He sat in his pram (firmly secured by reins) for hours, happily gazing around him. He was especially fascinated by the birds. This gave her peace and freedom to attack the cleaning of the house, although she did keep popping out from time to time to ask him, 'Are you all right, darling,' or to confide to him, 'Isn't this wonderful, Harry? Aren't we lucky?' Mrs Robertson had to insist that she stopped working first of all for a cup of tea and a biscuit at eleven o'clock and then for lunch. On each occasion Harry was brought in and given a drink and something to eat too, allowed to crawl about the kitchen floor and even have a noisy game of banging pot-lids. Amelia's heart sang with happiness to see him so happy. The attic, Mr Robertson's bedroom, the spare room, the upstairs bathroom and the upstairs landing were all spotless by lunch-time.

'You mustn't overdo things and knock yourself up, Amelia,' Mrs Robertson said. 'You look so flushed, dear. Are you sure you're all right?'

'Oh, I feel great, Mrs Robertson, just great!' she assured the older woman and, despite her red knees shining through the holes in her stockings, her crimson, sweating face, her wild ruffle of hair, it was true.

She had not been able to believe her luck since she had seen the attic. It was *almost* a flat. Had it had a kitchen and a bathroom, it *would* have been a flat. It was a pity that she would need to go downstairs for both facilities, but the thought only caused a momentary shrinking. Nothing could spoil the happiness and the gratitude she felt. She would have done anything for Mrs Robertson. She regarded her with reverence as her fairy godmother and at the same time loved her almost as passionately as she loved Harry.

The attic was reached by a permanent staircase that Mr Robertson had long ago built on the top landing. He had also had the loft opening in the centre widened so that there was plenty of room to get up and down. Once up, a hinged wooden flap could be lowered over the opening. This was very necessary to prevent Harry from falling through when crawling over the attic floor.

By the time four o'clock came and Mrs Robertson had made afternoon tea, Amelia was nearly dropping with exhaustion, but still hysterically happy.

'I forbid you to do another thing for me, Amelia,' Mrs Robertson said. 'You just see to Harry and yourself for the rest of the day.'

'But what about the evening meal and the dishes, and don't you need help to wash and get into your bed?'

'No, dear. Roller's very good and he'll be home about seven. That's my husband's nickname. Everyone calls him Roller. Partly because he started by driving a steam-road-roller and partly, I believe, because of the way he rolls along,' she laughed, but Amelia thought talking about her husband must in some way embarrass her. Her eyes always became vague, even furtive, at the mention of his name. 'He carries everything before him and it gives him a rolling kind of a gait.'

'Does he make the dinner?'

'No, I manage, thanks to the way Roller's had this kitchen converted. As you can see, even the sinks are lower than normal to suit the height of my wheelchair. And of course I can drag myself around for short spells on crutches. I keep them handy beside my bed. If I get stuck with anything, Roller helps me.' Her eyes flicked away from Amelia's. 'I know he's not perfect, but then who is? He's very good in lots of ways and he's fond of children. He'll be good to Harry.'

This news brought a sweet surge of relief. Yet trailing the relief were uncertain thoughts of the hungry eyes, the wet moustache and the huge protruding belly. She fervently wished it could be just Harry, Mrs Robertson and herself all the time.

By seven o'clock Harry was tucked in his cot and sound asleep. She left the flap open so that she would hear him downstairs if he wakened and started to cry. She would have preferred if she could have stayed in the attic and eaten by herself, but Mrs Robertson would not hear of it. 'Roller and I enjoy a bit of company,' she said, 'and anyway I don't like the idea of you sitting up there by yourself like orphan Annie.'

Amelia nearly confessed that she valued every moment on her own so that she could write. She checked herself just in time. Nobody understood about writing. There seemed to be a kind of mystique about it, almost as if it smacked of witchcraft. At first her mother had been irritated by her 'constant scribbling' and accused her of being 'just like your daddy, blethering to yourself all the time in diaries and notebooks.' When she had discovered it was stories she was writing, her mother's attitude had seesawed between ridicule, 'Don't be daft! You could no more tell a story than fly in the air!' and serious concern, 'Sometimes I think you're not right in the head!'

The day she had sold her first story her mother was having one of her tea-parties and the front room was full of friends happily chatting. She had rushed in excitedly to announce her stupendous news. Her mother's reaction and that of everyone in the room was one of silent embarrassment. It stopped Amelia in her tracks and made her blush and miserably lower her eyes as if she had done something to be ashamed of.

Then her mother said, 'Try these Empire biscuits, Mrs Henderson. They're delicious. . . .' It was the signal for the happy chattering to resume again. Amelia escaped, vowing to herself that she would never embarrass anyone or shame herself like that again.

'I love reading,' she told Mrs Robertson. 'If it will please you, I'll come down for dinner but, if you don't mind, I'd rather sit upstairs afterwards and read one of my books.'

What joy it was when the time came to escape upstairs. Once there, she first of all stood gazing admiringly at Harry's peacefully sleeping face. Lovingly she traced with her fingers his soft downy head and tiny pink sea-shells of hands. Then she undressed, brushed her hair and donned her nightgown. With a sigh of pleasure she settled herself cosily in bed, propped up with pillows, and balanced her notebook on her knees. The lamp bathed her in an amber circle as she bent earnestly over her embryo words. She was continuing to bombard with short stories, not only the editor who had bought her first short story, but every editor she could find. The novel on which she was also working, however, gave her the truest and deepest satisfaction. To be a novelist had become her one and only personal ambition in life. She felt inspired to concentrate only on her novel notebook that first night in her new home. Words flowed so freely from her pencil, she had to sharpen it twice. Every now and again she stopped to gaze incredulously around. She and Harry were safe at last. It was true what Mrs Robertson had said. Mr Robertson had been good with Harry. He had arrived home early and presented the delighted baby with a cuddly teddy. He had tickled him, flung him up in the air and caught him, making Amelia anxious but Harry squeal with hilarity.

Eventually Mrs Robertson had to say, 'Stop it, Roller! You're making him far too excited. It's time the wee chap was settled down to sleep.'

At first she thought the noise that broke the silence in the attic was Harry beginning to cry. But Harry lay still and quiet in his cot beside the bed. As her senses alerted she realized it was the squeaky creaking sounds that she had heard when opening the trap door. Her heart pounded like a big drum until it seemed to shake the whole bed. Clutching the bedclothes up in front of her, she managed to whimper, 'Who is it?'

From behind the partition appeared the giant form of Mr Robertson dressed only in pyjama trousers tied under his enormous hairy belly. He had more hair on his body than he had on his head. 'It's only me, hen,' he said, in a voice that trembled slightly. 'I've just come up to give you a wee goodnight cuddle.'

He looked pathetic, revolting, terrifying. She could not speak, her heart was choking her, thundering in her ears, convulsing her body. He was padding, bare-footed, towards her, his thick protruding lips hanging open.

'Go away!' Her words were an incredulous moan and all she could think was, 'Don't open your eyes, Harry. Don't open your eyes.'

'No, you'll have to go away, hen, if you can't be nice to me.'

As he climbed heavily into bed beside her she panicked and struggled out from underneath the blankets. 'Go away,' she repeated. 'I'll tell Mrs Robertson. I'll scream and scream.' She was shaking so much she had to clutch on to the baby's cot for support.

'Come on, hen, there's no need to be like that.'

'Oh yes, there is.' Bitterness iced her voice. 'Get out and don't you dare come up here again or everybody in Bearsden will hear me screaming.'

'I didn't mean any harm.' He heaved himself out of the bed and shuffled dejectedly across the room.

'Get out,' she repeated.

'All right, all right, I'm going.'

She waited until she heard the creak of the trap door shutting. Then she slumped over the cot. She was still weakly trembling, and she was broken-hearted.

32

'Christ!' Donovan exploded. 'This place is enough to drive anybody mad!' He and Helena had returned to the Moscow area to do more work from there. They had travelled to Moscow's water port at Khimki, intending to explore as far as the local transport would take them on the lakes of the Moscow-Volga canal. They had not known at this point that thirty miles from Moscow or much less than that in some directions was far enough to reach the wild. Nor had they realized exactly what the Russian *wild* meant. They had associated wild Russian countryside with the Highlands of Scotland. The first difference they found from their travels in the Highlands was that here in Russia travel was not a matter of maps and time-tables. It was a matter of argument, in this instance between the crowd on the landing-stage and the captains of the waiting boats.

Between Donovan's and Helena's sketchy knowledge of the language and a couple of men who had a smattering of English, they learned a mixture of conflicting pieces of information. There were no boats. The boats were reserved for special excursions. No boat could take everyone. To mention but a few. At long last, in typical Russian manner, the knot of conflicting requests and incompatible rules and regulations issuing from a dozen different authorities and organizations was cut through by a sudden common-sense decision. Everyone was squeezed on to a single white bateaumouche. The skipper made extravagant gestures to convey that this was a calamity and he was breaking all the rules. Nevertheless he conveyed everyone as far as Tishkovo.

Helena did not think she would ever forget the terror of the journey as long as she lived. To start with, the diesel engine, she was sure, was a hundred times too powerful for the flimsy vessel. The noise was ear-splitting and it seemed as if at any moment it was going to tear away from the boat and go pell-mell through the water on its own. The engineer must have feared this might happen, too, because for most of the journey he sat hard on the most violently bouncing part of the engine-mounting. The vessel screamed across dead waters and past silent forest shores until Helena's head was in a jangling turmoil with the noise and vibration. The only thing that kept her sane was the hope that at Tishkovo there would be some peace and quiet. Anything with '*tish*' in Russian, she had read, was supposed to mean 'peace and quiet'. People were cast off at shaky little piers along the way and, by the time they reached the end of the longest lake, there were only five or six people left to struggle ashore at Tishkovo. And it was a struggle, because there was only a single insecure plank between them and the water. Helena's nerves were shattered but at least, once they reached Tishkovo, the maniacal engine stopped. There was only the fluting sound of birds.

Tishkovo turned out to be a tiny forest settlement of a few brown huts with giant fir trees towering all around. There was an avenue leading from it, however, and before the other passengers disappeared into the village to bargain for country food, Donovan asked the one with the few words of English where the road went. He was told to the 'railway line'. Donovan and Helena dreaded facing another journey in the boat and Donovan decided they should start walking towards the safer and less noisy train.

'You didn't ask him how far it was,' Helena pointed out.

'I had a hard enough job trying to make him understand what I did ask. But it can't be that far. If you're worried about that now, you should have asked him yourself.'

'I don't know any more Russian than you.'

'Well, stop complaining then.'

At first, walking by her father's side in the silent summer forest was pleasant enough. Especially after the trauma of the boat journey. She did not feel nervous at the lack of habitation or of any other person. As they went deeper and deeper into the forest, however, she began to feel a tinge of unease. A squirrel darted across the path, a jay croaked a couple of times, then all was quiet again. The silence continued all the way up towards the cupful of light balanced on top of the infinitely far-off pines. The avenue gradually closed in, the gloom deepened, the track became faint. Then there was no track at all.

Suddenly Helena burst out, 'I've just remembered something I read.'

'A fine time to start a literary discussion!'

'There are bears in this area. Wolves too, I think!'

'Now she tells me!' Donovan said.

'Dad, what are we going to do?'

'We keep on going in this direction.'

'I'm frightened.' She was ashamed of the tears that came before she could stop them.

'Snivelling won't help. Your mother never snivels and, if it's of any comfort to you, this is going to make hell of a good copy.'

'That's all you care about. Your copy!'

The sun was completely shut out now and, despite her anger at him, she clung to her father's arm and jerked nervously at every crackle in the dark under-forest of spikes. They stumbled through this dead forest, snapping off branches in their desperation to reach the source of the ghostly light they occasionally had glimpses of ahead. They passed several rocky clearances, the strangely threatening shape of the rocks haunting them long after the gloom of the forest closed in again. Helena began to understand some of the power and fear of the Russian folk legends that grew from these ugly aberrations of nature. The silence of the fir trees towering around them was powerful, too, and deeply more disturbing than the cries of the strange birds or the lumbering of animals would have been.

'This is all your fault,' Helena burst out. 'Dragging me out to this God-forsaken country. I'll never forgive you. Never, as long as I live.'

'Aw, shut up!' Donovan was carrying his jacket slung over one shoulder and now he tugged his tie loose.

'You're unnatural. Do you know that? You're an unnatural father. You don't care what happens to me.'

214

'Damn you, I'm trying to concentrate on where we're going.'

They had stumbled on a path no more promising than any of the other tracks they thought they had made out. Until this one's silence became laced with the faint tinkling of bells and the reedy piping of a flute. Then goats came stepping daintily through the pine needles. A sallow-faced goatherd followed, piping thin notes on his flute. His inexpressive Russian face showed not the slightest surprise at the unexpected sight of two strangers.

'What do you bet he doesn't speak English?' Donovan observed, then mouthed slowly to the man, 'Where is your village?'

The goatherd seemed to have no inclination for conversation. Helena propped herself against a tree for support. All she had the strength left to do was pray that, somehow, by some miracle, they would get back to Moscow. Donovan's persistence, or perhaps it was Helena's distress, eventually resulted in the man pointing in the direction they were walking and saying a few Russian words they could only guess at.

The trail he had directed them to did lead to a village.

'Look at it!' Helena felt like weeping again but was far too exhausted. 'I never thought anything so primitive still existed anywhere in the world!'

'Yes,' Donovan said. 'I can see we're going to get a lot of help here!'

It was like something out of an old Russian engraving, with its plots of bluish stunted rye and huts scattered around a shallow ravine. At a wooden well-head, barefoot women, their heads covered with white kerchiefs, were drawing water. They, like the goatherd, displayed no interest in them. Donovan persevered with his questioning, illustrated by gesticulation and such ridiculous steam-engine impersonations that in any other circumstances Helena would have laughed. At last one of the women pointed across to a muddy track that plunged into the forest again.

'Oh dad, we're never going to get out of this,' Helena's voice was weak with exhaustion and fear.

215

'Cheer up! I've never been lost in a forest yet,' said Donovan.

'How you can joke about this, I don't know. It's an absolute nightmare. I mean, we must still be in the Moscow Province. Who would have thought it could be like this?'

'Yeah, I realize now we shouldn't have moved from the city without a guide or translator. And don't worry, we never will again. How about that chap you've got friendly with?'

'I haven't got friendly with anybody.'

'Yes, you have. The guy that bawled you out for slagging the waitress.'

'What about him?'

'He's a translator and you said he'd bummed about the country a lot to get experience for his writing. Ask him to travel around with us for a few months. He might be glad of some extra roubles into the bargain.'

'I'm not asking him!'

'Why not? He sounds exactly what we need.'

'I don't know. I just don't like him, I suppose.'

'I'm not asking you to marry the guy. Just ask him if he'd like a temporary job.'

'Anyway, he's in Leningrad.'

'It's only a plane journey away. I'll ask him, if you won't. Give me his address when we get back to the hotel.'

'If we get back,' she said. The thought of Burgeyev joining them on any future travels did nothing to help her anxious frame of mind.

'Of course we'll get back. We're going in the right direction. And look – see – over there – logs! Not long cut by the look of them. That means roads and lorries and trains.'

The path had broadened into a road bearing marks of lorry wheels. Soon the road became a wide sandy avenue in the dusty twilight between the fir trees. It stretched dimly into the distance, still and silent. Helena, although so exhausted she hardly knew how she was keeping her feet, no longer felt so afraid, even when it got so intensely dark that they could only go on by feeling their feet along the ruts. At last the firs began to roll back to reveal a copper-coloured moon and the warm air became scented with hayfields. The avenue opened into a crossroads and from there they could see, deep in dust and sleep, the wooden shacks of a settlement. There also shone a single light above the rickety planks that served as a railway station. It was then that Helena's legs gave way and she sank, weeping, on to the sandy ground.

33

'This is getting worse,' Victoria said. 'Just you wait until I get my hands on Matthew.' She and Mrs McDade seemed to have been walking for miles and were thoroughly footsore and weary. 'Why couldn't he just have stayed on the railway like any other sensible man? Instead of stravaiging so far away from home and getting mixed up with all sorts of queer company. I'll have a sharp word or two to say to this secretary of his, I can tell you.'

'He could have had a good job in the railway offices,' Mrs McDade agreed, 'and still been a collar-and-tie man.'

'Oh, but not him!' Victoria said bitterly. She was remembering the only other collar-and-tie man she had known. Archie, her boy-friend before Matthew, had worked in a bank and was a good singer. Many a duet they had sung at church socials and temperance meetings. Or if she had been giving a piano solo, he always stood adoringly by her side, waiting to turn over the pages of her music. She had taken it for granted that once they were married, Matthew would be like that. She couldn't see why not.

'Between you and me, Mrs McDade,' she said, 'Matthew Drummond is the most awkward, irritating man alive. I've come through the mill with him, I can tell you. This isn't the first time he's nearly been the death of me. All this walking and on such a terrible rough road is playing havoc with my piles. How're your corns, Mrs McDade?'

'Agony, Mrs Drummond. Sheer agony!'

'Just wait until I get my tongue on him. I'll not let him forget this in a hurry. What did he need to come away out here for? Any extra work he had to do he could have done at home.'

Mrs McDade, her hat slightly askew, blinked up at her friend. 'Do you think he might be having a wee holiday on the quiet?'

218

'I'll holiday him,' Victoria said, beginning to get breath-less. The words were hardly out of her mouth when she stumbled and made Mrs McDade cry out in panic, 'Oh, Mrs Drummond, are you all right?'

'I've just gone down on my heel; I'm going to lose this heel any minute. My good shoes are getting ruined.' It was then she discovered that both she and Mrs McDade had walked through cowpats. A pungent smell was following mercilessly in their footsteps.

'They can keep their countryside as far as I'm concerned,' Victoria said, now even more breathless and dishevelled than Mrs McDade in her efforts to clean the muck off her shoes with handfuls of grass.

'Surely it can't be far now,' Mrs McDade wailed. 'I don't think I can last much longer.'

'And to think,' Victoria said, 'we've all this way to go back!'

'Oh dear!'

Then suddenly Victoria cried out, 'Look! Let's hope that's a sign of civilization.'

Mrs McDade blinked anxiously, 'What?'

'Those big iron gates over there. Oh here, would you look at that place!' she added, as they drew nearer and saw the castle in the distance. 'And see, there's another gate and railing away at the end of this avenue.'

'I wonder why there should be two sets of gates?' Mrs McDade clung to the railings for extra support. 'It's queer, isn't it?'

'I know. And you could put the whole of our street in between them. Here, could you beat this?' Victoria was now doing her best to shake the gates much to Mrs McDade's agitation. 'These have got overgrown and stuck in the earth, so they've just left them and had these new ones put away at the other end.'

'Oh please, Mrs Drummond, don't shake them like that in case anyone comes.'

'I wish someone *would* come so that we could ask the way. I wouldn't put it past that awful old woman to have put us on the wrong road. Either that or we've got lost.'

'Oh dear! But they might give us a ticking-off.'

'Fancy anyone living in a place like that. Can you beat it?' Mrs McDade could not.

'One half of the world doesn't know how the other half lives,' Victoria sighed. 'If we don't find Matthew soon we're going to collapse, Mrs McDade. I'm going to ask the way.'

'Oh, you wouldn't dare. You couldn't!' Mrs McDade's voice rose an octave with incredulity and horror.

This was as good as a challenge to Victoria even in her exhausted and dishevelled state. She drew herself up with dignity, 'And why not? I'm as good as the next man, Mrs McDade. We're all Jock Tamson's bairns.' Then she added in a more relaxed manner, 'It'll be a maid that comes to the door, anyway. These kinds of folk don't open doors themselves.'

'I don't see how we could reach the place anyway, Mrs Drummond.'

'Tuts, don't you worry. Just hang on to me. There's a road at the side there. We'll manage.'

But they only managed with much dangerous wobbling of heels and great difficulty. The narrow earthen road was rutted with car or cart wheels and it seemed to them that no other human foot had ever trodden it.

'If I ever get out of this,' Victoria vowed, 'I'll never set foot on a country road again, never as long as I live.'

'Oh Mrs Drummond!' Mrs McDade wailed.

'*When* I mean,' Victoria soothed, '*when* I get out of this.'

'Oh, me too, Mrs Drummond. This place looks awful creepy. I don't like it.'

'Nor do I, Mrs McDade. Nor do I. It looks as if it goes back to the year dot. Give me my nice wee council house any day. I wouldn't live in that place, Mrs McDade, for all the tea in China!'

They lapsed into silence for a few minutes, the image of unlimited and much-needed cups of tea adding to their agony.

'Maybe there's a back door we should go to,' Mrs McDade's voice shrank to a reverent whisper now that they were physically dwarfed by the enormous size of the building.

Even Victoria looked somewhat uncertain and her voice, although retaining its challenging tone, dropped considerably in volume, 'I don't know about you, but I haven't another ounce of energy to waste wandering about. There's a door here and I'm going to knock on it.'

She discovered, however, that her clenched fist made hardly a whisper on the massive door. She tried the iron knocker and it had the opposite effect. Both she and Mrs McDade jerked with fright at the explosive clanging that reverberated all round them. Victoria was surprised too at the energy Mrs McDade had left, her friend's grip on her arm tightened so forcibly. They stood, clinging together, paralysed into silence and immobility until, before their wide, apprehensive eyes, the door creaked open. A tall, thin man stood gazing at them enquiringly. Victoria wondered if he was the butler. As she said much later, she had never seen anyone so toffee-nosed in her life but she believed butlers did have this superior, looking-down-the-nose look. She had seen a butler like that only the other day in the main feature at the Wellfield Picture House. Admittedly that butler had been wearing a uniform.

'Good afternoon,' the man broke the silence.

'Eh . . . good afternoon,' Victoria said, in as polite a voice as she could muster, 'I wonder if you could help us?'

'What is your problem?'

'I think we're lost.'

'Lost?' the man echoed in a slightly incredulous, slightly amused tone.

Victoria felt irritated by it. 'Yes, and it's not surprising. Where we come from there's a name on every street and lane so you know where you are. How's anyone supposed to know where they are in this wilderness?'

She was aware of Mrs McDade twitching and squeezing at her arm, but chose to ignore these desperate pleas for caution and diplomacy. No man was going to be allowed to look down his nose at her in such patronizing amusement. What was a butler, anyway? Nothing but a trumped-up servant. A servant putting on airs. She tipped up her head and did her best to look down her nose at him.

'We're looking for Innerleithen House,' she said. 'I'd be obliged if you'd tell us where it is.'

The amusement in his eyes changed to surprise. 'This is Innerleithen House.'

A silence followed in which Victoria struggled valiantly to get her bearings again. Caroline Ridgeway's parents must work here. They must be servants, not farmers.

'Then would you please tell Miss Caroline Ridgeway that Mrs Matthew Drummond would like a word with her.'

The surprise in the man's eyes now merged into realization tinged with horror. Eventually, with an obvious effort, he said, 'Perhaps you'd better come in.'

Victoria managed to keep her head held high but she felt far from happy. She wished now she had taken Mrs McDade's advice and sought a back door that might have led into a more homely and familiar surrounding, like a kitchen. In the gloomy hall she noticed a collection of ancient-looking servants' bells and, on the wall below the bells, an equally ancient-looking display of swords. The man hesitated at the front of a curving stone stairway. ('Fancy! Not a scrap of carpet on it!' she had told Amelia later.)

'I was going to take you to the lower drawing room but I think it would be better if we went upstairs.'

Mrs McDade gave her arm a violent shake as they puffed as best they could after the man who seemed to have unnatural energy for someone of his age. He was obviously no chicken. Victoria was far too out of breath to speak at that juncture but she managed to squeeze Mrs McDade's arm in reply, indicating that she too thought that what was happening was very odd.

They turned left on the first landing and found themselves in a room the like of which they had never set eyes on in their lives, not even at the pictures.

'Do take a seat,' the man said. 'I'll go and see if my wife is downstairs.'

Victoria wanted to say, 'It's not your wife we want to see. It's Miss Caroline Ridgeway,' but, by the time she had recovered enough breath, he had gone. 'When the cat's away, the mice play,' she managed eventually.

'Eh?' Mrs McDade looked quite distracted.

'Obviously the folk that own this place are away somewhere. He would get what-for if they knew he'd brought us up here. I've read about this sort of thing, you know. Servants having a rare old time living like lords while the toffs are away. Och, well, what's the harm in it, I suppose. Why shouldn't they get a turn? Here, I hope his wife brings us a cup of tea.'

'I need the toilet,' Mrs McDade whimpered.

'I'll ask her when she comes. Here, look at that,' she indicated the seventeenth-century Ruckers harpsichord.

'Oh, Mrs Drummond, please don't touch it.' Mrs McDade still clung to Victoria's arm, and was dragged protesting in terrified whispers over to the instrument where Victoria defiantly struck a few chords.

'What a disgrace!' Victoria gasped. 'That piano sounds as if it's never been tuned for years!' She sighed. 'I'm so exhausted I don't think I could give them a tune if they asked me. I don't know about you, Mrs McDade, but I'll have to take the weight off my feet. Let go of my arm and sit yourself down on the settee beside me.' The settee was not very comfortable and they perched on the edge of it, shoulder to shoulder and hip to hip, clutching their handbags on their knees.

A few minutes later the door opened and the man entered with a brown-haired woman wearing an expensive-looking tweed suit in soft heather colours. The woman looked calm and dignified. The man said, 'I'm sorry, I didn't introduce myself. I'm Lord Ridgeway. This is my wife, Lady Ridgeway. I'm afraid my daughter, Lady Caroline, is not at home at the moment.'

34

Harry was happy. Amelia fed off his happiness. Hungrily she watched him laugh and play and enjoy his food. Harry was happy. That was all that mattered. Anything she suffered, she suffered for that.

Physical exertion no longer alleviated her bitter thoughts. So this was life? This constant betrayal? There was clever Douglas, the talented artist and charmer who had recently written to her saying he was divorcing her for desertion. He had obviously met somebody else and was desperate to be legally rid of her. He had also stopped paying her the monthly allowance. She had not mentioned this to her mother. She had never wanted to take anything from him in the first place. Nevertheless she felt betrayed. There was the genial Roller Robertson, the good-natured employer who did not think twice about mucking in with the lads and who often stood them a pint at the pub. She had thought he was being kind and generous to her in giving her a job and a home, despite having a baby. Employers would not normally countenance the 'emcumbrance' of a child. She had actually thought he was being kind and, fool that she was, she had felt grateful. As it was, he did not pay her a living wage. If she did not get her room and board she certainly could not have lived on the pittance she was paid. He had taken her for the fool that she was, and used her in every way he could. She had managed to continue fighting off his most intimate advances thanks partly to a conversation she had overheard between Mr and Mrs Robertson in which Mrs Robertson was more or less warning her husband to be careful because Amelia was such a good worker that they couldn't afford to lose her as they had lost so many other girls. But she had still to suffer his lascivious looks and his furtive touches and groping every time he passed her and came near her.

She had managed to get another appointment with the psychiatrist and told him about the situation. The psychiatrist had said, 'Well, look, you've got to decide what you're going to do about this, Amelia. You either walk away from the situation, or you confront this man and tell him you're not going to put up with his behaviour. You're not going to allow him to get away with it. You're going to go to the police or take whatever steps are necessary.'

Her hatred had given her strength to do this and since then Mr Robertson's behaviour had become more circumspect, although still revolting and very hard to bear.

There was the considerate, pathetic cripple, Mrs Robertson. She knew what was going on. Of that Amelia was certain. Unable to satisfy her husband's sexual needs, Mrs Robertson was glad of somebody who could be used for this purpose. Now Amelia understood the ingratiating attitude the older woman had towards her, almost as if the roles were reversed and Mrs Robertson, with her grey wispy hair and rounded shoulders, was the one who was the employee and Amelia was the boss. To think, Amelia raged bitterly to herself, to think she had been so intensely grateful to the woman for what she had thought was kindness. She had been ready to pour out a lifetime of devotion at her feet. She would have not only willingly kept the house like a palace, but cooked for her, run errands for her, nursed her, pandered to her every whim. Bitterness stuck in Amelia's throat, choking her. She had been used, it seemed, all her life. She wanted to rage and kick against life, against Mr Robertson, against Mrs Robertson, against Douglas, against her mother, against her father.

But Harry was happy. That was all that mattered. Harry had to have a stable, secure and loving childhood as a firm basis for a strong, healthy and happy manhood. She had to efface herself, and suffer slowly passing, tortuous time as best she could. She set herself a goal: 'When Harry starts school, I'll leave this place. That gives me nearly three years to make enough money with my writing to get a home of my own and furnish it.' She did not care where it was or what size it was, as long as she and Harry could be safe and on their own. Then she thought, yes, it did matter where it was and what size it was. Harry must not be brought up in a slum in a bad area which could adversely affect the direction and quality of his life. She would have to be able to afford a decent place.

Every spare moment, she sat at the table in the attic, head bent over her notebook. Well on into the night and often until the early hours of the morning she struggled with her literary inadequacies, determined somehow to overcome them.

Her father had shaken his head when she had confided in him her ambition to write books.

'I can't see how you can achieve that, Amelia,' he murmured in genuine puzzlement. 'Without a grounding in Shakespeare. You never showed the slightest inclination to go to university.'

She could not see that going to university had anything to do with it. She had never mentioned the subject to her father again.

Meantime she sold two more stories to the pulp magazine market. She had meant to put the money straight into a bank account but the temptation to enjoy a treat with Harry overcame her. On her day off she took him to the zoo, bought sweets, ice cream, lunch and tea for Harry and herself. It was wonderful to be away from the house and the people who made her feel sick with hatred. The money from the next story she sold she would put in the bank but, when the next cheque came, Harry was desperately needing a jersey and trousers, a pair of pyjamas and a warm dressing-gown. She had discovered comfort from the habit of smoking cigarettes, a habit which proved expensive.

The book was progressing slowly and painfully. It exhausted her far more than all the hours she slaved at housework. It also strained her eyes and she had to go to an optician and get fitted for reading glasses. She had finished the first draft of the novel and was now in the process of laboriously re-writing the whole thing. She no longer had dinner with the Robertsons but took a tray upstairs to the attic, writing while she ate. Mrs Robertson kept making feeble attempts to be friendly. Amelia was polite and restrained, speaking only when she was spoken to and agreeing monotonously and meaninglessly with everything that was said.

The only time that any sign of emotion escaped her in the presence of Mrs Robertson was when they were having coffee in the kitchen one morning. Harry was toddling around playing with one of his push-toys. Amelia was pretending to read the local paper to avoid talking to the older woman who sat poised as usual like an eager sparrow hoping to catch any crumbs of friendship. Suddenly an article caught Amelia's eye. It was about Andrew Summers, the novelist who had so inspired her before. He was a local school teacher. He had written another novel and a collection of his poems had just been published. He was to be giving a lecture that evening in the Town Hall.

'Oh!' Amelia cried out, before she could stop herself, 'How I'd love to hear him!'

'Who, dear?' Mrs Robertson brightened hopefully and leaned her hunched shoulders forward.

Amelia tried to douse the enthusiasm in her voice but failed. 'Andrew Summers. He's a marvellous writer. I enjoyed reading his book so much! He's speaking tonight in the Town Hall.'

'Well, what's to stop you?' Mrs Robertson cried eagerly. 'Harry'll be all right. Both Roller and I will listen for him, but you know what a good sleeper he is and you'd only be away for a couple of hours. A night out will do you so much good.'

Amelia struggled with guilt about leaving Harry even if only for a couple of hours. Since the moment of his birth she had scrupulously put him first and studiously ignored her own interests or needs. Anything to do with writing, however, and especially someone from whom she could get help for her writing was a powerful temptation.

'Oh, go on, dear,' Mrs Robertson urged. 'Why not? You deserve it!'

'Well . . .,' Amelia's face creased with anxiety, 'I'll see how I feel later on. . . .'

Later on she felt even more desperate to go but was still worried and anxious. It was Mr Robertson who decided her.

'You're going to be one of them possessive mothers,' he accused. 'You're going to suffocate that boy.'

'Roller's got a point, dear,' Mrs Robertson ventured. 'It's not good for a child to fuss so much, dear, especially a boy.'

'All right,' Amelia said stiffly, 'I'll go.' She churned inside with hatred of them for telling her what she should or should not do for Harry. Who were they to tell her what was the right or wrong way to behave?

The Town Hall was less than ten minutes from the Robertsons' house and, as she hurried towards it, she thought how strange it felt, a kind of nakedness not to be pushing a go-chair with Harry in it, or struggling along with Harry clutched in her arms. She could not remember a time now when Harry had not existed. Nor did she wish to. He was the only good and successful thing she had ever done. Even if she wrote a hundred successful books, the joy of them would never match her love for him.

She was disconcerted to find the Town Hall already packed when she arrived and she stood for a moment in confusion, not knowing what to do, until someone indicated a seat still vacant in the back row. She had just got settled into it when a burst of clapping indicated the arrival of the Chairman and the guest speaker. They came in by the same door through which she had entered. They had to walk all the way down the passage between the seats, then climb the three steps up to the platform.

Amelia's eyes followed Andrew Summer's back. He was a tall man with a self-conscious and shy hitch to his shoulders and a loping kind of gait. She had the strange feeling of immediately tuning into his character even before she saw his face. Then he turned and she thought she had never in her life seen such handsome features. There was compassion as well as a twinkle in his eyes, and a humorous quirk about the wide well-shaped mouth. Just the sight of him melted her heart, her mind, every bone in her body. She was so overcome with emotion at the sight of him she

228

was afraid to close her eyes in case she would slither off her seat like a rubber ball. Every word he uttered was hungrily devoured. Then at the end of his talk questions from the audience were requested and her desperation for help with her writing was so intense she rose and stammered out, 'I've been working on a novel but can't seem to get the beginning right and the ending is worrying me.'

'I bet you're not too sure about the middle either!' he said with a smile. The audience burst into a roar of laughter and she hastily sat down with lowered eyes and burning cheeks. He proceeded to give a serious and helpful explanation about the difficulties of beginnings and endings of books. He understood her problem, he assured her, because he had suffered the very same.

Later, when the meeting was over and she was slipping away, she suddenly felt a gentle inquisitive touch on her back, an enquiring caress, the merest feather of fingertips. She could not understand how, despite the crush of people, he had reached the back of the hall so quickly, but she knew before turning round that it was him.

'I'm sorry if I sounded insensitive. I know it's no laughing matter when one is struggling with the difficulties of writing a novel.'

'Oh, it's all right,' she said. 'You weren't insensitive. You've been nothing but helpful. I've learned so much tonight. Thank you.'

Just then the Chairman interrupted, 'Right, Andy, the car's outside and the wife will have the supper ready and waiting.'

The crowd closed in and, before she could say goodbye, he was gone.

35

The touch still tingled the exact spot on her back, on her spine, just between her shoulder-blades, for hours afterwards. She concentrated on it, relived the precious seconds of contact with each minutest nuance of sensation, savoured it, was grateful for it, did not want to let it go. She began to day-dream about him touching her again. Not primarily in a sexual way. Only in loving variations of that first gentle communication. She dreamed about him gazing down at her with those smiling eyes. He was a kind man. He had been worried in case he had hurt or upset her. She basked in the warmth of that kindness. It melted, for frequent if short spells of time, the hatred and bitterness that was freezing her soul. She borrowed his book of poems from the library. There was a photograph of him on the cover which she stole. She cut it out before returning the book, then locked it away with her notebooks in the dresser drawer. She had an obsession about keeping her writing safe and locked away where no one could see it, which, when she thought of it, was illogical. After all, she hoped one day to get everything she wrote into print. Then everyone and anyone could see it. Nevertheless she felt sure that if, for instance, Mr Robertson's bleary eyes fastened on it, or his pudgy fingers touched her notebooks she would kill him. Her real, her free, her only self was in her writing. She guarded her notebooks from prying eyes as zealously as she guarded Harry from harm.

Every afternoon, rain, hail or shine, she took Harry for a walk and, after the evening in the Town Hall, she began walking past Bearsden Academy where Andrew Summers still worked as a teacher. It was not that she wanted him to see her. Apart from anything else she had not been able to afford any decent clothes for herself. Her wardrobe was an eccentric mixture of garments picked up at local jumble sales. Their only purpose was to cover her and protect her from the cold. She had never even thought of beautifying luxuries like hair-dos and make-up. No, she only wanted to catch a glimpse of him. Once she saw him laughing and talking to some gangly youths in the playground. On another occasion she had watched from a safe distance as he left the school in the company of two of his colleagues.

His latest novel, like his first, had won a literary award. She saw pictures of him quite frequently in the newspapers now, sometimes photographed with beautiful women. She could imagine how women would regard him as quite a catch. He was being acclaimed as brilliant, as indeed she believed he was. Quite apart from the humanity in his writing and his depths of understanding, particularly of women, there was a lyrical quality in his prose that made the reading of it not only an intellectual but a sensuous experience. She knew in her heart she would never be able to use words as he did but she determined to write to the best of her ability. One day she would get a book published, that was for sure. She posted her first novel to a London publisher, whose address she had taken from the cover of a book in the library. She had begun to get her short stories published at a ratio of about ten rejections to two accept-ances. It meant she had to spend most of what she earned on stamps because return postage had always to be enclosed and each of the ten stories rejected had usually been rejected by dozens of magazines.

It did not make financial sense but by now she had recognized that her impetus to write was not just a financial one. It was a matter of communication. It was a need to reach out to someone, somewhere. It was a cry of 'I exist. This is me!' Nor was it only that. It was a need to make sense out of confusion, to try to understand her world and what motivated the people in it, especially herself.

A strange phenomenon happened regularly now. It was as if she had become two completely different, quite separate, people in the same skin. There was the ordinary self, helpless, anxious, fearful, panicky, confused with the constant batterings that a cruel fate kept meting out to her.

At the same time there was her detached writing self, watching with cool interest every emotion of her ordinary self, every event and reaction to it. Her writing self was ruthless and calculating, someone who could view the most anguished experience and calmly think, 'How interesting! I must remember that and use it!'

Shortly after her novel had been posted to London (at frightening expense), she unexpectedly bumped into Andrew Summers at the shops, or in 'the village' as the shopping centre of Bearsden was called. She did not see him. She was constantly obsessed now not only with a loathing of Mr Robertson, she also felt sick with ambition. The drive to succeed and escape from her situation possessed her like a madness. She was hysterical with impatience to succeed. Her writing became all she thought about from morning till night. Not a moment could be wasted. She was feverishly searching her mind for another idea for a short story, hardly even aware of pushing Harry in his go-chair, when a voice penetrated through the chaos of her thoughts.

'Hallo. Is this your little boy?'

She gazed blankly up at him for a second or two, unable to switch speedily enough from her short story permutations to reality. Then she said in surprise, 'Oh, it's you!'

He was bending over Harry now, speaking to him, tickling him and making him laugh. Harry was as eccentrically dressed as she was in his too big trousers and jacket, the hood of which kept drooping over his face and covering his eyes. She had to keep plucking it back so that he could see. She never had the nerve to buy anything that fitted him neatly because of her nightmare of him growing out of his clothes before she had enough money to buy him any new ones.

'What's his name?' Summers asked.

'Harry.'

'Hello, Harry,' he said, then straightened up and smiled down at her, 'And what's yours?'

'Amelia Donovan.'

He put out his hand. 'I'm pleased to meet you, Amelia. May I call you that?'

She nodded.

'You can call me Andy. OK?'

She nodded again.

'How's your novel doing, Amelia?'

'It's finished. I sent it away.'

'Well, you know what to do now.'

'What?'

'Start another. Never hang around waiting for publishers. Forget about that book. Get on with the next.'

'Yes, I will.'

'It can't be easy to concentrate on your writing when you've a young child.'

'No, but I'm determined.'

'Yes,' he said. 'I'm sure you are. And that's the way to succeed.'

'Is it?' She gazed anxiously up at him really wanting to know.

'Of course. If you're determined to make it, you will!'

It was exactly what she needed. A perfect jewel in the counterfeit of her day. Now she had to get on with it. 'Thank you,' she averted her eyes. 'I'd better go now.'

'We'll probably bump into each other again,' he called after her.

After that, each journey to the shops or anywhere she went with Harry in Bearsden, became something to be looked forward to with a mixture of apprehension and awe. It was like meeting God in the street every time she saw his tall figure approaching. His hands were dug deep into the pockets and he had a self-conscious twitch of his shoulders as he walked and he was usually hunched deep inside the turned-up collar of his anorak. Even the thought of him brought a surge of affection and admiration. At the same time she had become beset with a host of extra worries that she had no energy to cope with. Her own appearance had never been given priority in her scheme of things. Now she felt she must try to look presentable before setting foot out of doors. Just in case he saw her. This meant taking time to wash her hair more often and trying to do something with it. It meant rummaging through her clothes and experimenting with different bits and pieces to try to look respectable. It meant tensing herself to be ready to try and sound intelligent in conversation. Sometimes she would not see him for days or weeks. Then suddenly he would be there and they would stand and talk about writing. She was fervently glad she met him on the day she had her book returned from the publisher. It had been a far more devastating blow than having any of her short stories rejected. The novel, quite apart from the enormous amount of hard work it had entailed, was much more an intimate part of herself.

'I know how you feel,' he said. 'But don't despair. Most books are rejected several times before being accepted. It's a matter of finding the right publishing house. My first novel was rejected by three publishers, but I know of others who were turned down as many as seventy times before going on to become bestsellers.'

Each meeting was a straw to cling on to. Each meeting was a drop of opium to soothe away her pain. They never spoke for long. Afraid she would keep him back or be a nuisance, she was always the one to bring the conversation to an end.

One day he said, 'What does your husband do, Amelia?'

She averted her eyes and wanted to be away. Outside of the writing world or context there was nothing she had any desire to talk about. 'He's a painter.'

'Really? What's his name?'

'Douglas Donovan.'

'Not the chap who did the experimental stuff that all the fuss was about? I didn't see the exhibition but I read about it in the *Herald*.'

'Yes. I'd better go now,' she said, and even forgot to smile before leaving.

She tried to blank the reference to Douglas out of her mind. He had no place in the dreams she wove around Andrew Summers. Dreams that made going to bed something to look forward to. Dreams that she could settle down and enjoy, and in which the comfort of friendship was intensified. Nor were they diminished by catching a glimpse of him through the window of a restaurant sitting laughing and talking in a relaxed manner to an attractive girl. Her own meetings with him, although still brief, became more numerous. The number of times she heard him lecture at public meetings increased. She always sat hidden at the back. Perfectly content and happy to be an observer. The more she got to know him through his work, the more her feelings of friendship and admiration deepened into what she concluded must be love, because she cared about him as truly and as intensely as she cared about Harry. She wanted him to succeed, to keep well and to be happy, just as she wished these good things for Harry. Every night now she included him with Harry in her prayers.

36

'With what language do you wish to become familiar?' Burgeyev asked. They had retreated from the busy hotel lounge to the privacy of Donovan's bedroom and Donovan was flicking through his notebook.

'Russian, of course,' Helena said.

Burgeyev raised an eyebrow, 'Why the *of course*? There are over a hundred different nationalities and ethnic groups in the Soviet Union.'

Donovan said, 'That must make it hell-of-a-difficult to govern.'

'Yes. Most foreigners do not realize this. And there are such great differences in stages of development as well as language. For instance, the Russian working class and intellectuals have achieved a great deal in social and technological fields, but at the same time people of Chikotka in the north end of our vast country are still sewing garments made of animal skins with bone needles, and lighting their dwellings with a moss wick dipped in seal fat.'

'Fascinating!' Donovan lolled back in his chair with one knee propped up to hold his notebook.

'I can teach you Russian,' Burgeyev went on, 'although you will not find it easy. And even so, if you go into GUM, the large department store in Red Square, and speak Russian to other shoppers, you will find at least every third person speaking a different language.'

Helena lit up a cigarette and tried to sort out her feelings while Donovan and Burgeyev continued this conversation. She was disturbed by his presence and decided it was because she still held a grudge against him for verbally abusing her and for making her feel so guilty. All right, she had behaved badly but she could not accept that there was any excuse for his behaviour. Not even the fact that he had a volatile temper. She was not even convinced that this was a fact. Since their first abrasive meeting he had seemed exceptionally calm and detached. At the moment, conversing with her father, he had a cool, watchful look. She sensed in it too the hint of distrust and disapproval of the foreigner she had seen in other Russian eyes. She had observed disapproval of herself being registered several times on the street. It had happened when she had been wearing a sleeveless and strapless sun-top and several middle-aged and elderly women had not only sent sad disapproving glances in her direction but they had sorrowfully shaken their heads at each other. They were obviously observing that she was a typical example of the decadent West. She had discovered disapproval too when she had not taken her coat off and put it in the cloakroom when she had visited the Opera. Later she had learned that, because traditionally winter clothes were so dusty, it had become the custom, the polite thing to do, always to remove outer clothing indoors.

In many ways, too, the people she had come across so far were quite Victorian in their attitudes and there was a surprising shyness and modesty, especially among educated people, about sex, nudity and the private parts. Her father had responded with others to a plea for blood donors. He told her afterwards that the middle-aged doctor in attendance had given him an examination and asked questions about every ordinary disease. When he had come to ask if he had ever suffered from piles, however, the doctor, who must have examined hundreds of donors by this time, blushed and stammered like any young probationer nurse.

'Yet everyone, including doctors, lives in such crowded conditions,' Helena said. 'You'd think shyness and modesty would have disappeared long ago.'

'Community living,' Donovan said, 'has always been a very strong part of their tradition. I was reading about a sugar factory where the government inspector was so shocked at the crowded barrack-like living accommodation, he ordered partitions to be erected to give each man some privacy. This was bitterly resented. The workers said, "Are we cattle that we should be thus cooped up in stalls?" Even today, the universities report that single rooms for students are not popular. They prefer more communal life.'

'There're so many contradictions, too,' Helena said. 'The lavatories in the hotel, for instance, are perfectly civilized. But the public lavatories! Apart from the disgusting unhygienic conditions, I'll never forget the first time I went into one and saw women squatting over holes in full view of one another.'

Donovan had laughed, 'I suppose togetherness can go too far. Yet you know, this lack of partitions seems to have the surprising result of making private life among Russians *intensely* private. They've perfected a privacy of the spirit. Haven't you noticed?'

She had. Was that what she saw in Burgeyev's eyes, she wondered now. To her surprise she heard her father bring up the subject of the lavatories with Burgeyev.

'Well, I admire much that your country has achieved,' Donovan said, 'but your public lavatories are hellish!'

Burgeyev shrugged, 'I agree! But with a vast country of the size and complexity that we have been discussing there must be priorities. Many more important tasks have to be accomplished before such things as public lavatories can be even thought of.'

A glint of – was it annoyance or embarrassment? – showed in Burgeyev's eyes for a moment. She almost wished her father would pursue the subject so that she could capture Burgeyev's reaction more clearly, but instead he flicked shut his notebook and said, 'I don't know what you young folk plan to do, but I'm going to the bar for a drink, then I'm having an early night. We've got to be up at the crack of dawn tomorrow, remember.'

They all rose and filed out to the corridor. In the ill-lit hall, sitting at a desk peering at a newspaper was the inevitable solid middle-aged woman who supervized the maids on each floor and dealt with any problems or emergencies. Burgeyev greeted her with a nod and a 'Good evening' in Russian in passing. She replied with an unsmiling 'Good evening' in reply.

Then Burgeyev said to Donovan, 'There is music and dancing in the basement bar. Would you both care to join me there?'

Donovan said, 'No. You and Helena go ahead. I'm going to my usual one on the first floor.'

Before she could protest she found herself guided to a 'Down' lift, the doors of which had just opened. In a couple of minutes Donovan had alighted at the first floor and a few seconds after he had bid them goodnight, she and Burgeyev had reached the basement. A small group of musicians over at right angles to the bar were playing a fox-trot and several couples were up dancing, including a small boy circling in solemn dignity with his mother.

'What would you like to drink?' Burgeyev indicated an empty table. She sat down, trying to remember what she usually ordered. Her mind had lost its ability to function. In desperation she said, 'Vodka.' She remembered too late that she never drank anything but gin and tonic, beer or white wine at home. The vodka was definitely a mistake. She tried to copy the way Burgeyev tossed his down in one quick action and nearly choked herself in the process. The innocent-looking liquid had the kick of a mule. It snatched her breath away and made her cling to the table to steady herself.

'Russian vodka is stronger than Scottish vodka. Yes?' Burgeyev said.

'Yes,' she managed eventually.

'You would like another one?'

'No.'

'Then we shall dance.' He rose. His hand cupping her elbow forced her to rise too. Still stunned by the strength of the vodka she allowed herself to be led on to the floor, then held in his arms. The band was playing a slower, sadder tune now, something with a very Russian flavour. Not for the first time she had the impression of moving in a dream. The nerve-plucking music of the violin and balalaika intensified the strange sensation. Then she became more acutely aware of the presence of Burgeyev. Even wearing her high heels, her eyes were just level with his shoulder. He was formally dressed in a dark blue suit and light blue shirt instead of the fawn linen jacket and open-neck shirt she had seen him wearing on previous occasions. She gazed up at the firm tanned line of his neck and, as if suspecting her of intimate thoughts, he gazed down at her face, his dark eyes searching deep into hers. For the first time in her life she found herself blushing. Her annoyance and resentment returned.

'It was my father's idea, not mine, you know, to ask you to come along.'

'Ah, yes.'

'You don't sound as if you believe me.'

'Why should I not believe you?'

Avoiding his eyes, she watched his mouth as he spoke, a mouth that he often pursed thoughtfully. Another thing she began to notice was that a lock of his straight black hair sometimes fell down over his forehead. Every now and again he slid his hand up over his brow to push it back. While they danced, however, his hands held her firmly. She became acutely aware of them, the heat of them, the strength of them, and she felt as if she had known the touch of these hands all her life. Returning to the table after the music finished, she dismissed her feeling of intimacy with him as a temporary aberration caused by the vodka. She asked for a gin and tonic and was still carefully sipping it after Burgeyev had tossed back another vodka. It did not seem to have the slighest effect on him.

'I used to go dancing back home in Glasgow,' she told him, 'but it is very different from this.'

'In what way?' Interest sharpened his voice and stare.

She did not know where to start, the gulf was so great. Could she tell him that here it was how she imagined dancing in her mother's day must have been? She decided not to risk it in case he would feel hurt or insulted. Yet why should she care? Eventually she laughed and said, 'Obviously you haven't had the numbers of Americans over here that we've had in Britain.'

'There is a strong American influence in your country? Yes?'

'I believe you could say that.'

His sorrowful shake of the head triggered more laughter. 'There're plenty of good things come from Ameria.'

'Give me examples, please.'

All she could think of at that moment was the sex she had had with some of Uncle Sam's representatives. It occurred to her then that it had been a long time since she had had sex with anybody. And she began to wonder, with quickening heartbeat at her own daring, what it would be like with a representative of the Russian Bear.

37

Burgeyev had not warned them about the Russian winter. Helena had read something of it, of course. She knew it had defeated Napoleon's troops and Hitler's. She had vaguely imagined, however, that it was because the troops had been caught out in the open for too long without enough food and proper clothing.

The Russian winter, she discovered, was the great educator. She learned more about Russia and the Russians from it than anything else. Winter in this huge land, as the peasants used to say, 'has a belly on him like a priest'. The priest produced nothing for the land but he came to the peasants' table and ate his fill. Winter came as the great waster and consumer. It ate away the hard-won hoards of grain and cabbage, of cucumbers salted in the pickling pond and firewood stacked in frozen passages. It made wolves lean and hungry enough to pull down the horses and cattle. It wasted the fat of the hibernating bear. It destroyed the energies, the imaginations, the very breath of human beings in the stale air of the huts and houses where they huddled round stoves. Or as they shuffled through the city streets to and from work. The crows on the Kremlin were the first sign. The grey-headed Russian crows flocked in from the countryside to roost among the spires and gilded bulbs.

There was no longer any green except the dark fir trees. Everything seemed to crystallize into ice overnight. It was bearable at first and she had been fooled into thinking this was how it would be until the spring. She thought she looked very fetching in her fur hat and leather coat with its smart fur collar and cuffs. The outfit had been supplied by her mother before she had left Glasgow and she had been eager to wear it.

'How do I look?' she had asked Burgeyev with coquettish, provocative movements to show off herself and her outfit.

'Leather is no use,' he said.

'How do you mean?' she gasped in frustration. He really was a most irritating man.

'It will freeze.'

'Oh nonsense,' she said, 'it's meant for cold weather. It's a winter coat.' She had begun to give him little come-on signals but either he had not recognized them, or he was choosing to ignore them. She found the latter explanation impossible to accept. No man had ever chosen to ignore her before. It must, she decided, be yet another difficulty in communication between people of different cultures. She would have to be more direct.

However, they were on their way with Donovan to sample village life at a friend of Burgeyev's. The challenge of how to make more direct communication with the Russian would have to wait. The train was packed, the closeness of many breathing bodies creating a stifling heat. Sitting on the bare slats of the wooden seat next to Burgeyev, she could feel the warmth of his body even through the sheepskin coat that he wore with the fleece inside. Her first kindling of sexual awareness of him was becoming stoked to fever heat by every physical contact now. She wanted him. She had no longer any doubts about this. Nor did she see any reason why she should not have him. She passed the time on the long journey by looking forward with pleasurable anticipation to the moment when she would see him naked, when the soft light of a bedside lamp would reflect off the smooth expanse of rippling deltoids, triceps and biceps. One day she would sketch him in the nude, but first she would trace delicate lines with her tongue, leaving a shiny trail along the tanned neck that curved gracefully into a collarbone and down the small of the back swelling subtly into a rounded buttock.

Every now and again during the journey Burgeyev responded to opening gambits of conversation by her father. Donovan was obviously pumping him for information of one kind or another each time, not simply being companionable. Burgeyev answered him easily and politely enough but soon lapsed back into his distant silence again. She was interested to read much later in one of Donovan's newspaper stories: '. . . The Russian is an unself-conscious human being, living in a society of unself-conscious human beings. It seems to me, from what I've observed so far, that this detachment is the result of the way the Russian was treated as a child. Children here are not disciplined or fussed over. Nor are they sentimentalized. There is an interesting balance of affection and detachment. The Russian man, never having been fussed over at home, is therefore perfectly composed among his fellows who have been equally unfussed over. It is expected by no one that he needs to assert himself merely for the sake of establishing his identity. It is because of this that Russians are ill at ease with Western people brought up in a convention of self-assertion . . .'

'This is good,' she told Donovan.

'Of course,' he grinned at her. 'Didn't you know your father is *the* best journalist ever to come out of Scotland?'

'No one could mistake you for a Russian, anyway,' she said, with off-hand good humour. 'You're far too self-assertive and insensitive. You must have been fussed over like mad as a child.'

'That's an interesting thought,' mused Donovan. 'I don't think I was spoiled, if that's what you mean, and yet I haven't any of the detachment of, say, a Burgeyev. I wonder why not?' He dragged at his cigarette and watched the smoke for a minute. 'The weight of a whole different culture is behind him, I suppose. Mostly suffering. Not that the peasants were cowed, any more than they are cowed by dictatorship. You only need a slight experience of Russians to find out that they have no natural tendency to do as they're ordered, far less have any feeling, like a lot of Germans confess to, of actually preferring to receive orders. You only need to read about the robust peasants who fled from their masters and became partisans and Cossacks, and the revolts and myriad other more subtle ways they subverted discipline and authority, to find out their attitude to these things.'

' "Subtle" is the operative word,' Helena said. 'So subtle I can't put my finger on anything concrete most of the time. It's frustrating!'

'I'm beginning to understand it. At least I think I am. All I can say is, the few times so far that I've been accepted as a friend by Russians or temporarily included in a crowd of Russian peasants, I've felt admitted into a taut conspiracy against all external authority. I think it must stem from an old silent spontaneous conspiracy of peasant cunning against landlords and masters and representatives of the law.'

'Burgeyev's no peasant,' she said. 'He strikes me as being a very cultured and sophisticated man.' She hesitated, '. . . And yet . . .'

'And yet,' her father said. 'Exactly!'

It was all very intriguing but, as far as she was concerned, too difficult to put into words. She seldom wrote to Veronica now and, when she received a letter from her friend, its contents seemed so trivial, shallow and un-interesting, she could hardly be bothered reading it. On the few occasions when she did bring herself to write now she no longer mentioned Burgeyev. It was strange. At one time, men, and their intimate relationships with them, was the mainstay of every conversation she and Veronica had. There was nothing they enjoyed more than, after meeting a new man, swapping blow-by-blow accounts of their experiences with him and their feelings for him. How they both used to whisper and giggle over it all! Somehow it did not seem a laughing matter any more. Nor one she could bring herself to share with Veronica.

Burgeyev's friend, Igor, was of peasant origin, a lean and hardy hunter of wolves, but he, like millions of other country dwellers, spent a lot of the winter in bed trying to keep warm, and shifting his couch every time he felt water dripping from the ceiling. He was in bed when they arrived but struggled up immediately to welcome them, hugging Burgeyev and kissing him warmly. Donovan's welcome was given with more reticence, a slight bow and a hand-shake when Burgeyev introduced them. Helena was given a

245

polite kiss on the hand. Then Burgeyev introduced them to Igor's *babouchka* and his young sister, Natasha. She was a pretty girl with shy eyes and a long plait of black hair. Helena experienced an immediate stab of jealousy, especially later when she noticed how Natasha could make Burgeyev smile. The smile melted Helena's heart until it pained her. Such a smile it was: a softening of the almost prim mouth, the revealing of strong white teeth, the folding of flesh on either side to create a charming, dimpled effect. The warm sexual glow from dark eyes.

As honoured guests they were plied with everything Igor and his family had. First they were given a meal of a bowl of soup which was mostly cabbage but tasted very strong and rich. There were also pickled ridged cucumbers and tomatoes, fried potatoes, *kasha* of large-grained buckwheat also fried, and hunks of good brown bread. Then Igor, talking all the time (how he could talk!), plied them with Armenian brandy while the *babouchka* and Natasha served them with glasses of Russian tea that came steaming from the samovar. It felt as if they were being swept along on a great sea of generous Russian nature, yet still the reticence and even diffidence appropriate to a new acquaintance was preserved.

As Donovan said later, it seemed to typify so well the pervading atmosphere of the Russian people. But it had almost blotted out the poverty of the surroundings for him, had even inhibited him from asking about them. The poverty and the cold was brought home to Helena when she had to dash out to the lavatory hut with its throne of yellow ice.

What had upset her most, however, was Burgeyev's relationship with Natasha. The question of whether they were friends or lovers tormented her all the time they were there. She still had not made up her mind, she still could not be sure, even on the day they said their goodbyes. She thought she detected love in Natasha's expression but Burgeyev's eyes had become veiled and private again.

Once more the conversation was between her father and Burgeyev. This time mostly about the effects of the Russian climate, how it played havoc with bricks and mortar, how no one could keep up with the constant pointing and repairs needed by the blocks of rusty concrete flats and brick dwellings. Although in Leningrad, Burgeyev said, the nights were warm and short and nothing could spoil the beauty of many miles of streets which were cream and pink with low-pitched roofs of Italian red. The red was actually rusty iron sheeting used to resist the snow but it looked like southern tiling. Armies of workers were needed to keep roads usable, to stack up banks of snow until, by the end of winter, there was barely room for a car to pass. Then there was the ice to be tackled. After that the *rasputitsa* began, the roadlessness caused by mud and icy slush and floods. In summer the opposite extreme of weather could crack roads, open up great holes and send clouds of dust to veil clothes, windows and buildings.

Helena listened to Burgeyev and watched him in rising desperation. She longed to be alone with him to talk about what was going to happen between them. To hell with the weather!

Yet ironically it was the weather that brought them, to her mind at least, a stage further in their relationship. Her smart leather coat and boots she soon discovered were no match for the Russian winter. The cold burned. Every time they launched themselves out of doors they gasped. They narrowed their nostrils to give their lungs a chance to get acclimatized but had to go on gasping nevertheless. She, and indeed her father too, would have died of frostbite had Burgeyev not come to the rescue.

'There is no use trying to look neat,' he said. 'First of all I will show you how to wrap your feet and legs.'

She watched him and longed to touch his dark head as he knelt in front of her and began wrapping her feet with strips of cloth like puttees. He worked slowly as if performing a religious ritual. Every touch of his hand sent exquisite sensations travelling up each nerve of her body. After carefully binding her feet and legs he produced what he called *valenki*. These were clumsy right-angled tubes of felt closed at one end.

247

'I look ridiculous shuffling along in these things,' she protested.

Shuffling was all you could do in them, but Burgeyev assured her, 'Nothing will keep frostbite from your toes except *valenki.*'

He was right, of course, just as he was right about getting her father and herself wrapped up in padded clothes until they each looked like a bundle on two bundled legs. The cold became so severe and so painful, she knew that neither she nor her father could have survived as they had been dressed before. Even so, Burgeyev warned them to watch for white, bloodless patches. Every illusion she had had about enduring Russian cold had gone.

Now she understood the shuffling masses. Now she understood the ravaged peasant faces and why so many of them had immobile flattened appearances all the year. Now she understood and recognized the wounds of winter when she saw them: the zig-zag ears and nibbled noses that healed in clean new skin and looked like deformities. Now she understood the stifling, smoky stove-heated one-roomed cells. She appreciated the tiny double windows and double-doored and curtained corridors, every chink stuffed with rags. To come through so many thicknesses of doors and curtains into such a fog, to live crammed into such a choking, stifling room and still be cold made her understand the impotence and despair generated through centuries of Russian winters.

Her heart went out to the Russian people and to Burgeyev in particular. Through the miseries of travelling in the open country, through icy desolation, through a swirling white world where the air gnawed and bit her cheeks until it gripped like an iron mask, here, strangely, love warmed her heart.

38

Victoria had had to go to bed as soon as she got home from Innerleithen House. Months after the incident she still had not recovered from the shock or the humiliations of that day. She had been stunned into silence by the discovery of who Caroline Ridgeway was. She was totally confused by the idea that such a woman could be Matthew's secretary, or anyone else's secretary for that matter. The world had suddenly turned upside down. She could not make head or tail of it.

Lady Ridgeway had ordered tea, and a maid in a black dress and white apron and cap floated in with a tray. She placed it on a table near the settee on which she and Mrs McDade were perched. Lady Ridgeway dismissed the very superior young woman and poured tea from a silver pot into cups so delicate-looking it was an agony for Victoria and Mrs McDade to hold them. Victoria, in her anxiety not to drop or in any way damage her cup, used two hands to hold it. As a result she had lost control of her handbag and it had fallen to the floor. The catch had been broken for ages and it allowed all the contents of the bag to spill out. There was the buttoned purse that Jamie had given her many years ago. It was shabby and the word *Mother* printed on the front was faded but she treasured it as a memory of her son and the love he had once shown her in the happier days before his marriage. There were hundreds, it seemed, of old bus and tram tickets. There was a dirty hanky, a broken suspender, and some sticky-looking toffee balls. Worst of all there were the crusts left over from the sandwiches she and Mrs McDade had eaten on the journey. The navy-blue handbag, lying there so cracked that the fawn canvas underneath was showing, was a humiliation in itself. Victoria, still hanging on to her cup with both hands, stared down at it and its contents in undisguised horror. She did not know what to do.

'Allow me to put your cup down on the table,' Lady Ridgeway said kindly.

Somehow even that felt like a humiliation. Victoria managed to say 'Thank you' with dignity.

While she was stuffing everything back into the bag, Lord Ridgeway was attempting, unsuccessfully, to make polite conversation with Mrs McDade.

'It was a long and very tiring walk from Innerleithen.' Victoria, breathless from her exertions, answered his question of how they had come. 'But where there's a will, there's a way.'

'I'm not surprised you're exhausted,' he said. 'You should have taken a taxi. There's a private hire firm there, I believe.'

Both Victoria and Mrs McDade stared at him as if he had gone stark raving mad. Victoria in fact nearly gasped out 'Don't be daft!' She only stopped herself in the nick of time. As she said to Mrs McDade later, 'It just shows you! These kind of folk have no idea about money.'

After a few mouthfuls of tea she felt strengthened enough to ask, 'When will your daughter be back?'

'I'm sorry I can't tell you that.'

She was not quite sure if that meant he knew but was not going to tell her or he did not know.

'Is my husband with her?'

'Caroline is Matthew's secretary,' Lady Ridgeway said.

'So I believe,' Victoria was beginning to get into her stride. 'But how is it that my husband's work takes him down here?'

'I think you had better ask your husband that,' Lord Ridgeway said.

'Don't worry,' Victoria replied grimly, 'I intend to!'

'As soon as you finish your tea,' Lord Ridgeway informed her, 'I'll give you a lift down to Innerleithen.'

The relief was incredible.

On the bus to Edinburgh, then on the train to Glasgow, neither she nor Mrs McDade uttered more than a few words to each other and these were in the form of unanswered questions: 'What do you make of it?', 'Can you credit it?',

'Wasn't that terrible?', 'I can't take it in, can you?' They had automatically murmured 'Cheerio' at the close mouth and disappeared thankfully into their respective homes without another sound.

Victoria did not have the strength to open down the bed-settee. She collapsed on it as it was and covered herself with her coat. She was still huddled in a foetal position under her coat when Matthew arrived. It was late but the curtains were not drawn and neither the light nor the fire was lit.

'Oh, Victoria,' he said. 'I'm so sorry!'

She did not move, 'Don't come near me!'

'You must be frozen,' he said. Hurriedly he drew the curtains and switched on the light. Then he set about getting a good blaze going in the grate. After that he went through to the kitchenette and made a pot of tea. 'Here, drink this, Victoria. It'll make you feel better.'

'Nothing will ever make me feel better,' she said but she struggled to sit up and accept the cup he held out.

He waited until she had finished drinking, then he said, 'I wanted to tell you before but something always came in the way. All that worry about Amelia and . . .' he shrugged and helplessly spread out his hands. 'I don't know . . .'

'I know,' she said. 'You've betrayed me.'

'Oh, Victoria, I'm sorry, but our marriage wasn't working out. We haven't lived as man and wife for years.'

'Whose fault is that?' Victoria cried out indignantly. 'You were the one who left home and went to live in London, not me.'

'I didn't mean that.'

'Well, what do you mean?'

'We haven't made love.'

'Oh that!' Victoria said dismissively. 'You never think of anything else.'

'That is not true.' He was trying hard to remain calm. 'I have natural instincts in that respect.'

Victoria's lip curled in disgust. 'You're like an animal!'

'There's something far wrong with you,' he said, suddenly losing the battle with his temper. 'It's you who ought to have seen the psychiatrist, not Amelia!'

'How dare you!' she shouted back at him. 'How dare you suggest I'm in the wrong when it's you who have betrayed your marriage vows. And not only that, you've betrayed your class.'

'It's not a question of class.'

'And you've betrayed all the folk that voted for you and put you where you are in Parliament.'

'Oh, be quiet, woman!'

'Yes, we'd all better be quiet, hadn't we? Very quiet! If anyone in Glasgow hears about this, you're finished.'

'You can go around broadcasting it with a loud-speaker for all I care,' he said bitterly.

'That's so like you. You've never cared about anybody but yourself. What do you care about all the people who worked hard to get you where you are? What do you care about the shame and disgrace? What do you care about your wife and family?'

'I can't talk to you.' He shook his head. 'I've never been able to talk to you. You're incapable of discussing anything in a reasonable manner.'

'Oh, you want me to be reasonable, do you?' Victoria gave a burst of sarcastic laughter. 'That's rich. That really takes the biscuit. After a lifetime of doing my best for you, after sticking by you through thick and thin, good times and bad, what do I get? Lied to, deceived, betrayed and humiliated. And you expect me to be reasonable?'

'I never meant you to be humiliated, Victoria. You should not have gone there today.'

'That's rich,' she repeated incredulously. 'That's really taken the biscuit. You're the last one to tell me what I should or should not do. What should you have done, that's more to the point.'

'I fell in love with Caroline, Victoria. One can't help one's feelings.'

'Oh, can't one?' Victoria sneered. 'Well, I think it's about time one learned.'

'This is getting us nowhere,' he said. 'We can't go on like this. I'll have to leave.'

'Don't be daft! You'll get neither bus, tram nor train at this time of night!'

'I mean leave you for good.'

'But you can't,' she said, and he could not bear to look at the unexpected bewilderment in her eyes. 'You're my man!'

'I'm sorry, Victoria, but everything is finished between us.'

'But everything can't be finished between us until we're dead.'

'I love Caroline,' he repeated helplessly.

'You can't have anything to do with her and her kind,' Victoria, with equal helplessness, shook her head. 'They're not our kind of folk.'

'Victoria, you don't understand . . .'

'No, I don't.'

Suddenly she burst into tears. It was the first time, as far as he could remember, that he had ever seen his wife weep, or show any sign of weakness at all. He was appalled, 'Oh, Victoria!'

'That was awful for me today,' she sobbed. 'Just awful. It was the most awful day of my whole life.' She was making no attempt to mop her tears or control the contortions of her face. She was just standing, trembling, before him, weeping in helpless abandon like a defenceless child.

'Oh, Victoria,' he said and gathered her into his arms.

39

Amelia was shattered when her mother told her about her
father and Caroline Ridgeway. It was as if the last piece of
secure earth had crumbled away beneath her feet. With it
went any hope of ever seeing her parents in any harmony.
At least before, there could at times be the illusion of
pleasant normality, the kind of thing she once imagined
that other people enjoyed. She did not even have faith in
that any more.

Her mother's bitter talk against her father was constant
now and it invariably ended with '. . . And you're not
much better. A lot you care about me. You only come here
when it suits you, the very same as him. You'd no need to
take Harry away from here. I could have looked after Harry
while you went out to work. It's sheer badness of you to
leave me alone here and take Harry away to live with
strangers. God will punish you, Amelia. One day He'll take
somebody you love away from you.'

She dreaded going home at any time but especially when
it was her father's week-end for coming to attend his
'surgeries'. Her parents' bickering and her mother's knife-
edged, nagging tongue whittled away at her nervous system
until Amelia thought her nerve was going to fail completely.
She seemed, when she was at home, to be teetering on the
verge of nervous chaos, of weeping, of ghoulish laughter, of
violent trembling. And to go back to be at the mercy of the
Robertsons was not much better. She had been swept
struggling along on a nightmare wave for so long she almost
wished she could drown. If it had not been for Harry she
would have gladly gone under. The fact that Harry needed
her, kept her stubbornly hanging on.

There was also her writing. Her book had now been
returned from four London publishers. Each time the
postman delivered the all-too-familiar parcel she felt

painfully disappointed. Each time it came back she read it again to see if there was still some way she could improve it. She had the book practically off by heart. By the time it was rejected by the fifth publisher she was thoroughly sick of it and wondered how on earth she could ever have written such rubbish.

She believed the second novel she was half-way through writing, however, was different. It rekindled all her hopes and dreams. *This* would be the one that would be successful and make her enough money to get a flat of her own. Thinking of her second novel she soared to the dizzy heights of optimism again. She indulged in it secretly at night in the attic while Harry slept. She hugged her notebooks and gave quiet, excited little laughs to herself and jigged a few steps around with them.

Andrew Summers said she would be getting better all the time. She was serving her apprenticeship as a writer. She was learning and everything she learned was of value. He told her of some books to get from the library that he thought might be of interest and help to her. He also confided some of his own writing difficulties and disappointments and how he coped with them. She felt writing was a unique bond between them. It not only, she felt, gave them authorship in common but also a shared outlook on life. She was beginning to see through the mirror of his philosophy, mostly through his books. They met in passing only briefly, but she was with him for much longer and on a much deeper level in his writing. She bought a copy of each of his novels and his slim volume of poems. They were her islands in her sea of despair. She had her dreams about him too. She hoarded them in her mind like sweets to treat herself to every now and again and enjoy with secret, childish pleasure.

Then one day he stopped her and instead of asking about her writing, he said, 'I met your husband the other day.' It was like a slap in the face. She felt so shocked she could make no reply.

'It was at a party,' Summers went on. Then after a moment's hesitation, 'I didn't realize you were separated.'

What had Douglas said to him, she wondered? Nothing good, of that she could be sure. Douglas would have jumped at this opportunity of being vicious and spiteful about her. She felt sad that this delicate flower of friendship had been trampled on and destroyed. She had not fully realized what the good opinion of Andrew Summers meant to her until she had lost it.

'You'll have to excuse me,' she said. 'I'm in an awful hurry today.'

She was surprised to find the incident affected her more than the rejection of her book. Tears fell down her face as she walked rapidly through the streets oblivious even to Harry's noisy indignation at being bumped so roughly and rapidly along.

Nothing is ever lost on a novelist, he had once told her. Eventually this gave her comfort. But even that day as she hurried broken-heartedly through the streets of Bearsden, the writer part of her was all the time floating calmly by her side, observing her distress, filing each nuance of it away in case it might be of use in her novel. The distress also kindled in her a furnace of emotional energy. She had a very productive evening of writing and collapsed into bed utterly exhausted. Head aching with tension, heart palpitating through her whole body with overstrain, she nevertheless lay in bed, happily floating on a euphoric cloud of achievement.

It was over a week before she saw him again and in her excitement about how well the book was going, she forgot about her previous distress. She could hardly wait to tell him she had written three whole chapters. He told her to be careful, to remember quality was more important than quantity and to read and re-read what she had written with an objective and critical eye.

'I can do that afterwards,' she said impatiently, 'once I've finished the book. It's getting it finished. It's *doing* it that's important to me at this stage. Not having any blocks or blank pages. The actual *achieving*.' Her eyes stretched huge and burned with joy. 'The achieving against all odds. That's what matters to me.'

'Amelia,' he said, 'we've snatched bits of conversation at street corners and beneath lamp posts and in rain, shine and force ten gales. Why don't you come to my flat one evening and we can talk at more length and in more comfortable surroundings?' He smiled. 'Will you?'

The furnace of joy in her eyes immediately went out. She shrugged, 'Oh, I don't know. I'll see.' She had in her dreams, enjoyed many visits to his flat. They had not only talked there. They had made passionate love. Why, she kept asking herself, did she not feel overjoyed that here was a chance to make at least part of her dreams come true. She did not have the self-confidence to believe he would want to make love to her – at least not in the loving way of her imaginings.

But was it true that he just wanted to talk? She had no experience of friendship with any man except the brief encounters with him, and those were safely in the public domain where no harm could come to her. She had no reference point, no criteria for relationships with anyone, male or female, except rejection, betrayal and abuse. All the variations and vibrations of feeling she had for him deadened into sulky resentment. She tried to analyse her sudden change of mood. She tried to be fair. But all her energy had dribbled away. She could not feel excited. She could not feel interested. She could not even be bothered thinking.

He had called after her, '7, Park View.' She knew where it was. She had seen the small block of flats in the quiet cul-de-sac at the far end of the park when she was out walking with Harry.

That evening she found it difficult to concentrate on her writing. All sorts of conflicting emotions beset her. She wanted to go. Yet even the thought of walking in full view along the street and entering his close was an agony. *Someone might see her*! She struggled to assure herself that it would not matter if the whole of Bearsden saw her. Why should it matter? What was the harm? She was being ridiculous. She *knew* she was being ridiculous. What she could not fathom was why, despite all her self-chastisement and self-ridicule, the irrational fear and guilt remained. But she would beat it, she determined. She *would* go. Immediately she made the decision and knew she would carry it out, she felt on the point of collapse.

What if he *did* want to make love to her in a loving way? She quailed inside with terror at the thought of facing the look in his eyes before he turned away from her. That kind of rejection she could not cope with. She felt physically ill. Her legs could hardly carry her about. Some strange stubborn spirit kept masochistically forcing her on. The same spirit perhaps that fired her writing.

The next evening, she put Harry down to sleep earlier than usual, and then began to get ready. She had a bath and scrubbed herself all over until her skin tingled and flushed a bright pink. She polished her shoes. She put on clean underwear, stockings, skirt and blouse. She put a clean hanky in her pocket. She cleaned and polished her handbag. She cleaned her teeth. Then she set out in such a state of distraction she forgot to give her usual reminder to Mrs Robertson to be sure and listen for Harry.

The cul-de-sac was quiet and ultra-respectable-looking, like all the streets in Bearsden. She felt that there was a huge placard hanging in front of her telling everyone all about her sordid life history, her character and her present intentions. Up the close now with legs in danger of folding like a concertina. The door with the 'Summers' nameplate. As if some sadistic demon had hypnotized her to do so, she knocked loudly on the wood panel. There was a silence. She knocked again. The silence lengthened. Andrew Summers was not in. She allowed herself a brief taste of relief, but knew she could not abandon herself to the enjoyment of it until she was safely far away from Park View. She hurried breathlessly through the streets back to the Robertsons' house.

Only once she was shut upstairs in the attic did she breathe easily and give thanks to God for her safe deliverance. Then suddenly, she was possessed with such energy she was able to sit up half the night and, working with the speed of a tornado, finish one of the best chapters she had ever written.

40

Rory was leaning back against the cushions of the fireside chair enjoying a whisky and a cigarette when the phone rang. She waited, still pleasurably relaxing for a few seconds, before stretching over and picking it up.

'Is this Mrs Donovan of "Rory's" department store?' a man's voice asked. It had a broad Glasgow accent and she had not heard it before.

'Yes.'

'I wondered if I could come and see you tonight? It's a business matter.'

'You know my shop,' Rory said. 'Come there.'

'Well, eh . . ., this is kind of confidential, like.'

She began to catch his drift. He probably had some black market nylons for sale. 'Oh?'

'Confidential business.'

'I see.' She thought for a moment then said, 'where are you just now?'

'In a phone box not ten minutes from your house.'

'No harm in coming and having a word,' she said, 'but I'm not promising anything.'

'You won't regret it,' he said. 'I'll be at your door in about five minutes.'

She replaced the phone and took another drag at her cigarette. It was lucky that Winnie was out at the pictures and she was in the house by herself. Black market deals were better done in complete secrecy. She was just stubbing out her cigarette when the door bell rang. The man introduced himself as Pat Connelly. He had a typical Glasgow swagger, a cross between a fighter's hitching of the shoulders and a sailor's roll. A brown paper parcel was clutched under one arm. She led him into the lounge and indicated a seat.

'What can I do for you, Mr Connelly?'

'It's what I can do for you, Mrs Donovan.'

'Really?'

'Rumour has it that you're not averse to buying extra coupons when you get the chance and I've got ten thousand of them.'

Rory tried not to show the slightest glimmer of emotion. Although a haul of coupons of this magnitude would be a Godsend to her. 'Clothing coupons?'

'Every one of them.'

She pursed her lips and tapped them with her cigarette holder to indicate uncertainty and a general lack of enthusiasm. 'Too risky,' she said.

'Who's to know? This is a private and confidential business deal between you and me.' Connelly sat the parcel on the table at the side of her chair. 'I give you the coupons. You give me four hundred quid. We're both happy. What's wrong with that?'

'Open it,' Rory told him.

With deft enthusiasm he opened the parcel. She stared thoughtfully at its contents. She knew exactly how she could make a huge profit with the help of those coupons. She had racks and drawers of expensive clothing that she could not sell because even her wealthy customers did not have enough coupons. Now she could offer the clothes secretly without coupons and at three times the price to people desperate for new outfits. The coupons would be there to send in as the law required.

'I'll give you two hundred pounds cash. Now!' she said. 'Take it or leave it.'

'That's bloody daylight robbery,' Connelly shouted.

'Robbery shocks you, does it?' Rory said. 'Santa Claus gave you these, did he?'

'You think you're smart, eh?' Connelly's mouth twisted. 'Just because you're bloody rich?'

'I didn't get bloody rich,' Rory said, 'by throwing good money away to greedy sods like you.'

For a moment he looked as if he was going to lunge at her but her steely stare proved enough to deter him.

'Do you want the money or not?' she repeated. 'I haven't any more time to waste.'

He glared hatred at her. 'You're a bigger bloody crook than me.'

'You're right,' she said. 'Much bigger.' She crossed the room to a cabinet, took her cash box out of one of the drawers, opened it and counted out two hundred pounds. She gave Connelly the bundle of notes, then lit up a cigarette. 'Now we forget we ever saw one another,' she said.

He pocketed the money. 'I'm not daft!'

After he had gone and she was alone again, she lovingly fondled the coupons. She could hardly believe her luck. Next day in the shop, she took the opportunity of telling one or two of her wealthiest customers that they could purchase some garments without coupons, providing that they kept this transaction strictly to themselves, of course. The delighted customers swore eternal secrecy. Later in the day, Sir Alexander Forbes-Cunningham and the Drummonds arrived in the shop. Rory groaned. The elderly Alexander Forbes-Cunningham expecting personal service was one thing. He was one of her oldest and most valued customers. But Jamie Drummond and worse, Fiona, his little upstart of a wife, she had no time for. Sir Alexander obviously doted on them both, however, and he was too big a spender to risk offending. Especially nowadays when he was more likely to be buying for his grandson and wife than himself. She supposed if he was happy, and he certainly looked a much happier man since Fiona and Jamie had got their claws in him, why should she care? Sir Alexander could spend all he liked today, thanks to her new acquisition of coupons.

In the salon she was charming as usual to the old man, but she could not help retaining only a thin veneer of politeness when addressing the Drummonds. She regarded these two as being of the same mould as Amelia Drummond. Leeches, all of them. Useless on their own, only good for latching onto someone else, living off them, sucking them as dry as they could. Victoria was the same. She was a useless dreamer. Living off Matthew, holding him back, draining him. At least Douglas had got rid of Amelia. Poor Matthew seemed stuck with Victoria. It was a wonder he had not throttled the woman years ago. Victoria would never forgive her for trying to stop the marriage between Douglas and Amelia.

'You think my daughter isn't good enough for your son!' Victoria had accused and, losing her temper and patience, she had replied with a definite 'That's right. She isn't!'

Victoria had taken it as a personal insult. It was not that she had ever had any time for Amelia herself. Jamie had always been her favourite.

'Dear gramps,' the obnoxious Fiona was simpering, 'insists on spending all his precious clothing coupons on me. Just because I happened to mention I was needing a new coat.'

'Damned coupons!' Sir Alexander growled. 'If it wasn't for them I'd buy the pair of you a decent wardrobe.'

'Ah yes,' Fiona sighed. 'I often dream about shoes and lots of lovely dresses and skirts and undies. And of course all the things that poor Jamie needs. But as I keep assuring Jamie, I don't mind making do and mending if that's how it has to be. Be thankful for what we've got. Count our blessings. That's what I'm always telling him.'

'Liar,' Rory thought. And her eyes must have registered the word because she detected in Fiona's wide baby-blue eyes a glimmer of hatred. For a brief moment Rory was tempted to miss the chance of a fat profit in order to spite Fiona. But Sir Alexander was her wealthiest customer and the one, in his present circumstances, who could be tempted to spend the most. She decided, not for the first time, that there was no place for sentiment in business. Profit was profit. She lowered her voice.

'Strictly in confidence, strictly between ourselves, and only because you are my oldest and most valued customer, Sir Alexander, I can arrange something about the coupons. Today you can buy whatever and as much as you please.'

'Oh!' Fiona clapped her hands in what looked like childish delight and flung herself around Sir Alexander's neck. 'Oh gramps, isn't it wonderful? This is the happiest day of my life. This is the day all my dreams are coming true!'

Rory winced with embarrassment and distaste, but Sir Alexander laughed delightedly. 'Kit the both of them out!' he ordered Rory. 'From top to toe. Everything they need.'

'I must warn you,' Rory said, 'before they go any further, Sir Alexander. There will have to be an adjustment of price on everything.' She smiled at him. 'I am sure you'll appreciate that to offer garments without coupons is not only a risky business but it also involves a small miracle, and in this day and age miracles cost money.'

'I'm no fool,' Sir Alexander laughed and, although Rory kept the smile on her face, her mind was registering the words, 'That's what you think, mate!'

'I know how these things work,' he went on. 'But what use is money in the bank to me at my age?'

Rory was going to say, 'As long as you don't get a heart attack when I send you my bill.' But she thought better of it. Instead she turned with smiling mouth and unsmiling eyes to Fiona and said, 'What would madam like to see first?' Little blonde tart, she was thinking. For all her big innocent stares and childish simpers, she was a madam all right.

41

Drummond made a determined effort to concentrate on the stream of constituents that kept trickling into the rooms he used for his surgery in Springburn. Long-suffering men and women dressed in their Sunday-best clothes to come and see him, their faces stamped with a mixture of anxiety and hope. Most of the problems involved tackling the Housing Department or the Sanitary Department, but he had first of all patiently to question each constituent to make sure they were giving him not only all the facts but the correct ones. There were also old couples worried about their pensions and others who were having difficulty in filling up forms. All these he could cope with and do something about. What he had always dreaded, and never more than now, were people who came with marital problems. How was he supposed to help and advise them, he kept asking himself, when he was so unable to do anything about his own intimate relationships. On the whole, of course, people felt satisfied enough with a sympathetic listener and a shoulder to cry on.

He kept wondering where he would go after late surgery was over. The mere idea of trudging back up the hill to Balornock to suffer Victoria's never-ending bitterness, exhausted him. To avoid it he usually retreated to his old corner in the Boundary Bar and stayed there until closing time. Two or three times he had caught a tramcar over to the Southside and visited Rory. She had made him welcome and it was a relief to relax in comfortable, civilized surroundings and enjoy a dram and a cigar. He could not even enjoy a cigar in peace at Hilltop Road. To Victoria, smoking a cigar was yet another proof of how he was sliding into despicable depths of Toryism, how he was a traitor and a turncoat, how he was just putting on airs.

'You can't possibly be enjoying such a filthy evil-smelling thing,' she insisted.

It was exactly the same with any mention of the opera or a classical concert. If he played a classical record on the gramophone she told him it was just another of his snobberies.

'Nobody likes that stuff,' she had insisted. 'They just kid on they do because they think it's the done thing.' It reminded her, she said, of the story about the Emperor's clothes.

He wondered if he should go to Rory's this evening. The awkward thing about visiting Rory was that first of all he had to be careful not to mention to Victoria where he had been. Apparently she and Rory were now sworn and bitter enemies. Fiona and Jamie patronized Rory's shop. That was bad enough. Fiona seemed a compulsive mischief-maker despite her angelic appearance. She and Jamie hardly ever came to Hilltop Road, but when they did Fiona invariably managed to upset Victoria. The last time Fiona's talk was all about the special attention she had been given by Rory and how Rory was a very dear friend of hers, and how Rory would do absolutely anything for her, give her any amount of clothes she fancied without coupons, for instance. He made a mental note to warn Rory again about her illegal trading. The other disadvantage of seeking refuge at 'Rory's' was the fact that she never could resist needling him about leaving Victoria.

'You've wasted your life on that woman,' she would say. 'I've never understood what you saw in her in the first place, or why you stuck with her in the second place.'

In desperation he had tried to explain about the career situation rather than go into the intricate personal side of his relationship with Victoria, or Caroline for that matter.

'To hell with the scandalmongers, I'd say!' Rory flung back at him. 'Plenty of people have tried to dig up dirt about me in the past. I've helped them. I've said, "There you are! So bloody what!" '

'Rory, that might work in business but not in politics. If Victoria divorced me and cited Caroline as correspondent, that is the end of my political career.'

'Why should you worry?' Rory insisted. 'Her old man's a

265

landed aristocrat. You've got it made, Matty. Don't be such a miserable old martyr.'

It was all very well for Rory to talk but she would know all about it if her illegal activities came to light. She had always been pretty ruthless in business and had certainly been accused of a few dirty tricks. But she had never actually broken the law, until the war, that is, and the shortages caused by it tempted her into the black market. Her attitude to this never ceased both to worry and anger him.

'Everybody does it,' she would say. Or 'If I didn't do it, someone else would.'

He decided he had better just go to the pub. The way he felt tonight, he could not bear Rory's usual jibe of 'How's the eternal triangle, Matty? Still going strong, is it?' The only time he had any semblance of peace was with Caroline in London and the few times they could snatch alone together in her flat. Caroline understood the situation with Victoria. At least, he hoped she did. He had tried to explain.

'One can't just abandon someone like Victoria,' he had said after confiding in Caroline some of the difficulties.

Caroline had just sighed and said, 'She doesn't deserve you, darling.' At other times she would stare at him worriedly and say, 'Oh Matthew, for your own sake, darling, I wish you could make the break. You look so strained and unhappy.'

This was true. He *was* strained and unhappy and he too wished he could make the break. Part of him knew he had to, no matter what it did to Victoria and how it distressed her. He simply could not go on like this. He had a responsibility to Caroline too. Every time he thought of the trap he was in, because that was how he felt his situation to be, a headache and a tightness in his chest began to build up. He was glad to reach his quiet corner table at the pub eventually. The whisky helped to relax him and stop the sickening roundabout of his thoughts.

He had only been back once to Innerleithen House since that dreadful day when he had returned from a visit to the National Gallery in Edinburgh with Caroline and had been told that his wife had been at the house. He had been so shocked he still had nightmares about it. Lord and Lady Ridgeway had been kind and understanding. Indeed, rather too kind. They obviously felt keenly sorry for him and their pity rankled. It made him in turn feel not only acutely sorry for his wife but a kind of defensive loyalty on her behalf. He remembered he kept thinking over and over again, 'Poor Victoria, poor proud Victoria!' He could not get to Glasgow quick enough to speak to her, to try to make her understand.

Of course, once Lord and Lady Ridgeway realized that he had decided not to leave Victoria and at the same time was going to continue his secret liaison with their daughter, they had put their foot down. Caroline had told him they said, 'There's clearly more to this than meets the eye and we don't want to know about it. What you do is your own affair but not under our roof.' It was a perfectly natural reaction to the situation and he did not blame them.

Tonight the whisky failed to help. He took out his diary and made his daily entry. He never had any peace or privacy to write in it at Hilltop Road and it was still the one most private and personal area of his life that he ferociously guarded. Once when he had found Victoria reading it he had rushed at her and grabbed it from her, nearly knocking her over in the process. She had called him a madman and 'Why shouldn't I read it?' she wanted to know. 'What's in there?'

What was 'in there' was his self. Not Victoria's husband, or Caroline's lover, or Rory's friend, or Amelia and Jamie's father. But Matthew Drummond. Matthew Drummond, the wee boy who had loved his strange, withdrawn and unloving mother. Matthew Drummond, the teenager alone in digs worrying about spots and being too thin. Matthew Drummond, the over-earnest young man who kept spouting politics and who could not understand why he was always being stood up by girls. Matthew Drummond, falling in love and blissfully starting married life in a home of his own. Oh, what a joy that had been. Matthew Drummond, full of loving hopes and plans and dreams.

He did not know whether or not it was the whisky that was having a strange effect on him or whether it was sentimental thoughts of the past, stimulated by his diary, but he began to feel so sad. No, more than sad. He had a terrible longing for closeness with Victoria again, the young woman he had once known, and with the young man he had once been. He wanted them back. He had only had a couple of drinks and it was long before closing-time, but he left and made his way with a vague feeling of urgency along Springburn Road and up the Wellfield Hill.

Victoria was sitting by the fire reading a book when he arrived. He remembered often seeing her sitting like that back in the old days in their room and kitchen in Springburn Road. How proud they had both been of that house. Victoria was a rapid reader, her eyes skimming across one page after another, her face set in a tense dramatic expression that reflected the Ethel M. Dell or the Annie S. Swan romance that she was enjoying. She looked up when he entered the shabby comfortless living room with its threadbare linoleum and matted rag rugs and one of the hinges hanging off the sideboard door. Why had it all come to this, he wondered? What had happened to Victoria and him? He smiled at her tentatively, hopefully, in the same way that he used to smile at his mother.

'You've been drinking,' Victoria accused in disgust.

'Victoria,' he said helplessly.

She tossed aside her book and got up. 'I'll go and make you a cup of tea and something to eat.'

He nodded, not trusting himself to speak, not daring to put out a hand to her. Yet needing a closeness. He took off his coat and went to hang it in the coat-stand in the lobby. Victoria was clattering about in the kitchenette. He was going to take off his jacket, too, and hang it neatly on the coat-hanger he kept there for the purpose. But first he had to take his diary from his inside jacket pocket and lock it safely away in his briefcase. He was horror-stricken to find it was not there. In heart-thudding panic he searched in every pocket of his jacket. Then he rocked the coat-stand in his desperate haste to tug his coat about to search through it.

'What on earth are you carrying on about?' Victoria asked from the kitchenette doorway.

'My diary!' he shouted at her. 'Where is it?'

'Don't you raise your voice to me. How should I know where your diary is. You've probably dropped it in the pub. You'd be too stupid with drink to know what you were doing.'

'My God!' he said. 'I'll have to go back down.' He struggled into his coat and with two or three long strides he was at the front door. He jerked it open but, just before leaving, the strange feeling came over him again. He turned and gazed uncertainly at Victoria.

'Well?' she said. 'What are you standing there for?'

He went out and away down the stairs. The panic had returned and the horror. It was the worst kind of nakedness. He ran all the way down the hill and reached the Boundary Bar with heart bursting, fighting for breath. The pub was crowded with railwaymen but all standing at the bar. His faraway corner was shadowy and empty. And there, on the floor beside the table, was his diary. He could have wept with relief. Then suddenly his cheek lay beside it. He could see a red river pouring from his mouth and making a red island of the diary. He was marooned.

42

Donovan, like many an incautious foreigner, left off his heavy clothing too soon and became ill with bronchitis. He had to be admitted to hospital. Helena had faith enough that his toughness would soon pull him through. What she panicked about was in case Burgeyev would consider this development as the end of his assignment with them.

'Don't leave me,' she burst out, after she had returned from seeing her father settled in his hospital bed. She thought she detected tenderness in Burgeyev's eyes.

'No, Helena,' he said, thrilling her with the intimate way he used her first name. 'I will not leave you.'

Her physical feelings were no longer lustful. They were still passionate, but the physical passion was infused with an aching need that was almost a sadness. She did not know where the sadness came from. Unless it was the unconscious realization of the difficulties and differences outside and beyond physical passion that could come between them. Her physical passion had another new element. Before, any time she had any sexual need she had assuaged it. There had never been any complications, any worries, any guilt. Now, she felt nudged this way and that and confused by nuances of feeling that were disturbingly strange to her. Instead of, as she once might have thought, love making her even more confident, more direct, more uninhibited, she had become insecure and vulnerable.

Spring and summer came with the flowering of her love. The change in seasons had not come gradually as in Britain, preparing you with signs of buds and gambolling lambs. In Russia everything came in a rush and all together: catkin, coltsfoot, anemones, violets, celandine, apple blossom. There were no primroses, daffodils or bluebells, but peasants gathered armfuls of lily-of-the-valley in the forests and dripping masses of other wild flowers, like lilac and sweet-smelling creamy orchids and golden globe flower, and offered them for sale in the centre of Moscow.

Helena had never witnessed anything more dramatic than this leap from muffled winter into summer. Double doors and windows were flung open and fastened open. Light as well as air streamed in. Gone was the cold that slowed everyone down like premature old age and dragged them resignedly into sealed life indoors. Out in the sunshine there was a swarm of activity around building sites and damaged roofs and roads, and a hurling away of rusty ironwork.

Donovan was out of hospital and amazed at how well her Russian lessons were progressing. 'You're a miracle worker!' he complimented Burgeyev. 'All this and your writing, too?'

For Burgeyev had never lost touch with his creative work. It had been one of the conditions of his employment that he should have some private time each day to devote to his writing.

'That is one of the advantages of being a writer,' he told them. 'One can work anywhere and at any time. It does not matter, no?'

Helena felt like crying out, 'Yes, it does. It does.' It mattered a great deal to her but he shut himself away on his own at every opportunity. How could he sit alone in his room knowing that she was alone in hers? Surely he must know that she longed to be with him. Her growing expertise at the fiendishly difficult Russian language was a hard-fought battle in order to please him. She went to the extra trouble of learning words he had not taught her, like the Russian for 'I love you'. She had tried to pluck up courage many times to say them to him but knew she could not bear the anguish of finding out for certain that he did not love her in return. Yet surely there had been signs? Surely her acutely sensitized instinct and intuition could not be wrong? He was so tender and kind. But now that she could speak the language, now that she had suffered the trials of winter along with the Russians, now that she had got to know them better, all her Russian friends were overwhelmingly kind.

Burgeyev had referred to her as *nash*. It was a complimentary word of great potency. It was applied with pride to the Russian landscape, to Lenin, to vodka, to a good friend, to the Soviet army, to Chekhov, to the Russian steppe. But, in this good-natured community, if any ordinary Russian took a liking to you, he would take you to his bosom and delightedly declare you were *nash*. (Especially if you had taken the trouble to learn his language.)

When she and Burgeyev danced, however, surely there was a special magnetism between them that he must be aware of. She longed to cling round his neck, to merge into his lean graceful body. In a society in which it was considered grossly indecent for a man and woman to be seen kissing in public, however, she became afraid that any physical indulgence, at least in public, might make him lose respect for her. It was no use ignoring the society in which he lived and had been brought up. It stood to reason that he would be as affected by his background as she had been by hers. It was not that the Russians were cold. They were not as demonstrative as other people of the Soviet Union, like the flamboyant Georgians and Armenians, that was all.

After Donovan came out of hospital, Burgeyev went home to Leningrad on a week's visit to his family. Helena had pleaded with Donovan for them to go too but he preferred to stay in Moscow to catch up with his work. She tried to help him by sorting out his notes and taking a turn at his typewriter but her mind refused to concentrate on the job.

'What the hell's up with you?' Donovan burst out in exasperation. 'You're away in a dream half the time.'

Miserably she shrugged. Donovan eyed her sharply for a minute. Then he said, 'You're missing Burgeyev! You haven't fallen for him, have you?' After another minute's silence, he answered himself, 'Christ, you have!'

'So?' she said, trying to recall some of her impudent manner.

'So I hope you know what you're doing,' her father said.

'I'm not doing anything.'

'You know what I mean. He's not the type to play

around. It's my guess it'll be all or nothing at all with him.'

She recognized the truth in this and groaned. 'Oh God, what am I going to do?'

'I think he's fond of you, Helena. What you'll have to make up your mind about right now is, if it came to it, could you settle here, make Russia your permanent place of residence? It's very different and a long way from home. You don't need me to tell you that. Settling here for good would also be different from bumming around as we've been doing these past few months and as I've done most of my life. I spent a few years in the States. I got to like the Yanks and got used to their way of life. But I wouldn't want to settle there. I'm a Glaswegian. That's where my roots are and so are yours.'

She saw his point. The Russian people had had centuries to acquire their detachment, their composure, their truth to feeling, and most of all their strong, largely unconscious sense of community. Could she ever grasp what those things really meant? Because they meant something different here than in the West.

'I love him,' she said. 'Where he is, that's where I want to be.'

'Christ, now you're sounding like a Russian. They're so bloody romantic; worse, sentimental!'

'They are not!' she said, angry now.

'Of course they are. Even when they play jazz they romanticize it. All their popular music, painting and fiction is sentimental.'

'What are you talking about? Their most popular writer is Pushkin and most popular composer is Tchaikovsky.'

Donovan rolled his eyes. Then he said, 'Look, honey, I'm only trying to make you think about whether or not you'll be able to fit in. Being in love doesn't last. There's a lot more than that to living happily with someone for the rest of your life.'

'I don't even know if he's in love with me,' she said.

When Burgeyev returned, he at least gave her a clue about how his mind was working. Strangely enough it seemed to be working along the same lines as Donovan, because one day his dark eyes held hers and he said, 'I want you to think about this, Helena. Do not reply to my question immediately. Would you live permanently in the Soviet Union?'

She nearly laughed. If this was a proposal of marriage, how unromantic could you get? She did not care. She could have danced with joy. 'Ivan Mikhailovitch,' she said, 'I love you!'

43

The first book had been written slowly, laboriously. The second had the speed of lightning and was more painful but in a different way. She wanted to follow Wordsworth's dictum 'Emotion recollected in tranquillity'. Andrew Summers had advised her of this. She had tried, but her emotions were anything but tranquil. They were a seething furnace, the flames of which had either to be let loose to shoot out as reckless claws of fire, or kept locked in.

'You can't have written it in such a short time,' Summers insisted. 'Not a properly revised work. You must regard it as no more than your first draft. Go over it again and again. Re-write the whole thing again and again before you send it away.'

She was ashamed to tell him she had already rushed to the post office and sent it away. That was where she was returning from when she had met him. He did not say anything this time about visiting him, as she was afraid he might. He just stood talking for their usual five minutes or so until Harry got restless and began tugging impatiently at her coat.

Her third book, she determined, would be written with more self-discipline. At least she would control the urge to send it winging on its way to London before she had revised it and polished it and written several drafts. She still believed, however, that the first draft was the one in which the creative flow and the imagination must be given free rein. Writing a first draft was flying like a bird, creating new worlds, peopling them with whoever she liked. She passionately loved writing and, when she confided this to Andrew Summers, he had smiled down at her and told her what Robert Louis Stevenson once said: 'If any man love the labour of any trade . . . the gods have called him.' It was as if he had fed her with a spoonful of tonic that she knew was going to do her a great deal of good, once she had time to digest it thoroughly. She left him absentmindedly, allowing the words to sink in and soothe all her secret troubled places.

She started her third novel as soon as Harry fell asleep that night. She had stopped writing short stories now, despite her desperate need for money. Novel-writing had grown to obsessive proportions. Each time her first book came back now, she did not allow the rejection to wound her, telling herself that if the first book did not make it, the second would. Nor did the disappointment at its history of being turned down cut too deeply. At least it did not hurt for too long. In some strange way it seemed to harden her steely persistence. There were times when she was exhausted and her spirits sank, and she would think what a fool she was, and how she had no talent and how she could never succeed. Even that thought became the spur that immediately roused her mentally to clench her fists and grit her teeth and repeat to herself, 'Damn it, I will succeed. I will! I will! I will!'

Sometimes she would go to sleep during a difficult part not knowing what the answer was to a problem in her novel. Then she would waken in the morning with the answer leaping unbidden to her mind. Sometimes she would waken in the night and have hastily to switch on the bed-side lamp and scramble for her notebook so that she could scribble the answer down. She developed secret antennae for picking up tiny clues about people. The flash of fear in her mother's eyes, the momentary droop in Mrs Robertson's mouth, her father's sad glances, the flicker of wounded vanity that turned Andrew Summer's gaze away for a second when she criticized something in his book. Her biggest struggle and the thing that caused her most pain was trying to be honest. 'Here I am,' her books tried to say, 'warts and all.' 'Right or wrong, this is what I think about life and people.' 'What I am seeking is not what *actually* happened but what is emotionally true.' '*This is how I feel!*'

'Remember,' Andrew Summers said, 'writing from your own experience means using everything within your orbit of experience. That could be anything and everything, from a snatch of overheard conversation between strangers on a bus, to a tragedy that happens to a close friend.'

She learned in her third book how to make an amalgam of different character traits from real people and fuse them together to create something new. She began to see fictional characters in her mind. They moved about and spoke and had opinions and feelings of their own. They became more real to her than real people. It was a great joy each night to meet them again. She looked forward all day to the reunion.

Winter had returned with early darkness. She welcomed it because it cut down on the work she was able to do in the house. This gave her more time to think about her book during the day and take furtive notes.

It had been evening when the phone rang and Mr Robertson went out to the hall to answer it. They had finished their meal and Amelia had brought her tray down to the kitchen from upstairs so that she could wash her dirty dishes and stack them neatly away in the cupboard. Harry was sleeping. She knew, as soon as Mr Robertson returned to the kitchen, that something terrible was wrong and it concerned her. She tightened every muscle and squeezed up her shoulders ready to ward off whatever blow was to come. Mr Robertson came forward, his flabby face and eyes drooping, melting down with sympathy.

'I'm afraid I've bad news, hen. It's your father.'

She flicked her hands at him trying to make him keep away. 'Don't touch me.'

'He's dead.'

'No!' She put her clenched fists up to her mouth, elbows crushed tightly together against her chest, hugging herself. 'No, daddy, no.'

'You've to go to your mother's right away. I'll drive you over.'

'Daddy.' She rocked herself backwards and forwards. 'Daddy.'

'That was a friend of your mother on the phone, a Mrs McDade. She's phoning your brother as well. Your mother's in an awful state, she said.'

Amelia could see Mrs Robertson's chair hovering in the background. She looked like a ghost, with a face that had gone the same grey colour as her hair.

'You poor wee soul,' she said. 'Let Roller help you, dear.'

Somehow Amelia grabbed a cloak of calmness around her. 'I'll manage. Please listen for Harry. Mr Robertson needs to be here to go up the stairs if he cries.' She ignored their repeated offers of help. She passed them as if they no longer existed, collected her coat and purse and left the house.

She had to take a bus into town and then another bus from there up to Balornock, and it was not until she was on the bus on the way to the city that she realized fog was coming down. The bus slowed to a crawl. The lights inside were brown-hazed and growing dim. Outside all was still and dark. She had to grope her way out when the bus driver eventually announced he could go no further. It reminded her of the black-out during the war, when you could lose your way in the most familiar of places and go round and round in circles and ever-increasing panic. But the blackout did not have the sooty taste of fog, or the insidious choking menace. She did not know which way to turn. For a time she groped along the tenement walls, until at long last she heard the muffled clang of a tramcar. It appeared wraith-like a few feet from her. She called out to the conductor, 'Are you going Springburn way?'

'You're in luck, hen,' the man shouted back. 'Hop in.'

It meant she'd have to walk up from Springburn to Balornock, but it was better than nothing. She shivered with thankfulness, with the cold that was seeping through her coat, and with mindless agitation. All she could keep telling herself was that she must be all right for Harry. Harry would waken up in the morning and she had to be there as usual, and laugh and talk and play with him as usual. Life had to go on. She kept thinking about Harry in the tramcar and while she was shuffling blindly across Springburn, hands outstretched in an effort to protect herself, and while she was feeling her way along the tenement walls that led up the hill to Balornock.

She paused outside her mother's door, bracing herself, trying to draw strength from somewhere. But her hand trembled as she raised it to knock on the door. Mrs McDade opened it a crack to peep nervously out.

'It's me, Mrs McDade.'

'Oh, Amelia. Come in. You're the first. Your poor mother. What a shock. Oh dear, oh dear!'

Her mother was sitting on the settee, her head, her shoulders, her usually straight proud back all sagging forward. She looked boneless, as if at any moment she would disintegrate into a heap on the floor. She looked up when Amelia entered, her face swollen and mottled with weeping.

'Oh, the pity of it!' she said. 'Oh, the pity of it!'

Amelia went over and put her arms around her. 'Daddy wouldn't want you to be so upset.'

Mrs McDade said, 'I'll go and make a cup of tea.'

Victoria gazed up at Amelia with tragic eyes. 'He went out. Then for some reason he came back. He stood in the doorway and just looked at me.'

'Mummy, please, try not to get in a state.'

'He stood there looking at me. And I said, "Well, what are you standing there for?" ' The tears were already streaming down her face. Now she began to sob and moan.

Amelia said, 'Jamie'll be here soon. That'll be him,' she added, hearing a loud knocking. Lowered voices in the lobby, now, as Mrs McDade spoke to Jamie. Then both Jamie and Fiona entered. Amelia felt a rush of anger that Fiona should add to her mother's distress by her presence, but her mother was beyond petty dislikes and jealousies.

'Oh Jamie, oh Fiona!' She sobbed and gazed with wide wet eyes at them.

They both hurried over to embrace her and, as Fiona stroked and patted her mother-in-law's head, she said to Amelia, 'I phoned Rory and Sir Alexander, of course.'

44

'Mother, what's wrong?' Douglas said. 'It's not dad or Helena, is it?'

Rory shook her head and allowed herself to be helped into a chair. Tears were streaming down her face. Douglas poured her a glass of brandy and held it up to her lips. 'Come on, drink this.'

She did as she was told, her eyes wide with tears.

'Tell me, for God's sake,' Douglas insisted. 'What's wrong?'

'My friend,' she said. 'My dear friend . . .'

'Who?'

'Matty.'

'Matty?'

'The Right Honourable Matthew Drummond.'

'Amelia's old man?'

'He died tonight.'

'I've often wondered what he meant to you. Maybe it's just as well dad isn't here.'

She shook her head at him. 'What do you know about friendship, Douglas? What do you know about love?' She gave a shuddering sigh. 'I'd better go and try to help Victoria. It's what he would want me to do.'

'You can't go anywhere tonight. I'm not going back to the flat. There's a right pea-souper out there.'

'I won't be able to sleep a wink. I might as well try to get there. At least I'll feel I'm doing something.'

'You're crazy. Why should you do anything?'

She stared at him for a minute through the mist of her tears. Then she shook her head again. 'Go to bed, Douglas.'

The journey to Balornock was a nightmare and not only because of the fog. She had plunged back in time to her first meeting with Matty at the Railway Dance at the Co-op Hall in Angus Street. What a strange young man he had been.

280

She had never met anyone like him before or since. Oh, how earnest, how full of fire at the world's injustices, how loyal, how conscientious in his efforts to help working people, how intelligent. More, much more than that, he had been a kindly loving human being.

The thought of how Victoria had made him suffer intensified her grief a thousand times. 'Cow!' she thought. 'Ignorant, frigid bitch. How could you. How could you!'

She did not know how she would even be able to be polite to Victoria once she arrived at Hilltop Road. She wanted to say, 'You've managed it at last, you stupid cow. You've destroyed him. I hope you get paid back in the same coin. I hope somebody gets the knife in you.' *She wanted to be the one.*

She arrived at Victoria's close with its dark painted walls and plaster flaking off the ceiling. A mouse of a woman in a brown felt hat opened the door, then fussed her through the cold carpetless lobby and then into the shabby living room. Victoria was surrounded by her family. They separated back at the sight of Rory who looked like a being from another planet in her glossy mink coat and matching pill-box hat.

'Oh Rory.' Victoria stretched out her arms to her like a helpless child. Suddenly a thousand memories came tumbling back to Rory. She remembered the terrifying night of the abortion when she had held out her arms to Victoria. She thought, 'Aw shit!' and crossed the room. Victoria clung tightly round her neck just as she had once clung gratefully to Victoria. Eventually she disentangled herself and gave Victoria a shake. 'Come on, you've got more courage than this, Victoria. We've come through a few things together and we can come through this. I'll stay with you until after the funeral.'

'Thank you, you're very kind.' Victoria wiped her eyes. 'There's tea in the pot and some home-baked jam sponge.' She struggled to her feet. 'I'll get you a cup.' The others made to stop her but Rory gave them a warning shake of her head. Victoria had always liked to busy herself being hospitable.

281

'Nobody can get back tonight in that fog,' Victoria said quite calmly when she returned with a tray of dishes and a plate of sponge cake. 'I'll see what I can do about make-up beds.'

'It'll get light soon, dear,' Fiona said, 'and Jamie has his work to go to.'

Jamie was now a collar-and-tie man in one of Sir Alexander's offices. The thought had occurred to Rory on more than one occasion that the elevation from his railway fireman's job could not be agreeing with Jamie. He had lost all his old swagger. There was an air of dejection about him.

Amelia said worriedly. 'I can stay until it's light, but I must catch an early bus and get back for Harry.'

'I'll be all right,' Victoria assured them. 'As long as Rory's here. It's very kind of you to come,' she repeated to Rory. Then turning to the others, 'We knew him since we were all youngsters together.' Her voice sounded perfectly normal, almost cheerful. But tears welled up and spilled down her face again. She hastily mopped them up and blew her nose. 'Have a piece of sponge, Rory.'

It seemed like the distortion of a dream sitting drinking tea and chatting with Victoria and Mrs McDade and Jamie and Fiona without Matty being there, and yet the Matty she remembered never belonged here. She sighed to herself, her gaze turning inwards. Where had he belonged?

They drank tea and talked until the dawn's light filtered through the skimpy ill-hung curtains. The fog had lifted and Fiona and Jamie said they had better go. Jamie offered Amelia a lift and she gladly accepted. Jamie now drove a blue Ford Anglia (blue was Fiona's favourite colour.) Fiona and Amelia both kissed Victoria and Victoria insisted on seeing them to the door and waving them off. It was something she always did when she had visitors. Then she strode to the front room window to wave to them from there. She had also, Rory noticed, called after them from the doorway exactly as her mother, Mrs Buchanan, used to do. 'Haste ye back!' the old lady used always to say.

Thinking of Victoria's mother brought back another jumble of incidents from the past. Mrs Buchanan knitting her her first pair of stockings. Mrs Buchanan managing to get her a pair of shoes. Up till then she had run about barefoot like a wild thing. Mrs Buchanan shaming her own mother into discarding the hated parish clothes and fitting her out with some decent second-hand garments she had begged from people on her rag-collecting round. Victoria and her parading to church and Sunday-school believing they were such grand ladies.

'That's them away,' Victoria announced, returning to the living room. 'Jamie's going to do all the arranging about the funeral. Both he and Fiona insisted. Everybody's been terribly kind. Mrs McDade, just leave the dishes. Sit yourself down. You must be dead beat.'

Rory said, 'We should all go to bed.'

'Och, right enough,' Victoria agreed. 'Away you go home, Mrs McDade. I've kept you long enough.'

'If you're sure, Mrs Drummond? If you're sure you'll be all right?'

'I'll be fine now that I've got Rory,' Victoria assured her.

Rory took off her hat and coat and hung it on the hall-stand after Mrs McDade went away. Then she helped Victoria with the dishes.

'I'll put clean sheets on Jean's bed. That's my lodger. She's away on a catering job in Perth just now.'

But after the bed was made up in the bedroom, and the bed-settee was put down in the living room and they had said goodnight, Rory turned back into the living room again. It was impossible to leave Victoria standing so helplessly and tragically by herself. Nor had she any desire to lie in bed alone tonight.

'Victoria,' she said, 'do you mind if I sleep with you? Remember how we used to?' Often she had spent the night in the Buchanan house when they had been children, and they had cuddled into one another and whispered secrets in the dark.

'Of course I don't mind,' Victoria said, her face brightening with gratitude and relief. Wearing one of Victoria's bell-tents of a nightgown, Rory climbed into the

283

bed-settee. It was incredibly uncomfortable. An iron bar seemed to stretch along the small of her back.

'All right?' Victoria asked, tucking the blankets around both of them.

'Fine,' Rory assured her.

Victoria had switched off the light before coming to bed. There was not such a luxury in the house as a bed-side lamp. They lay quiet and still in the grey light of dawn, listening to the birds happily chirping and trilling. Suddenly Victoria abandoned all attempts at self control. 'I loved him,' she sobbed.

Rory put her arms around her. 'I know,' she said. 'I loved him too.'

45

'Never mind any work today, dear,' Mrs Robertson said. 'Go back home if you like. Take a few days off.'

'After the funeral, perhaps,' Amelia said dully. 'A friend of my mother's is staying with her until then.'

'Never mind doing any work,' Mrs Robertson repeated. 'I know how you must feel.'

It would have been better to keep herself busy but she found that she was too absentminded, too distracted to concentrate on what she was doing. She could not even write. It was a cold, bleak day but the weather outside was nothing compared with the desolation in her heart and soul. The word 'daddy' kept repeating in her mind like a desperate cry that surely had to be answered. He had never felt closer, more vividly real to her, yet so heartbreakingly inaccessible.

When she was a small child, she would watch for him coming home from work, and then run to the landing and press her face against the railings of the stairway and sing out, 'Daddy! daddy!' He would come running up to her, his long legs taking the stairs two at a time. He would grab her by the waist and hoist her high in the air and say, 'How is daddy's wee girl?' Then he perched her astride his shoulders and carried her into the house. Before her mother hustled her off to bed, she sat on his knee and he read her a story. She cuddled against him, cocooned with him in a magical world of happiness and love and make-believe.

'You do that child no good filling her head with nonsense every night,' her mother accused, making Amelia quail inside in case her few minutes of magic would be taken away from her. 'You'll just get her over-excited and give her bad dreams,' her mother insisted.

Sometimes she did have bad dreams and she would suddenly wake up sweating and afraid. She did not believe it was anything to do with her father's stories. She believed it had everything to do with the conflict between her mother and father that forever reverberated around her, even in her dreams. It had everything to do with the insecure shifting sands of her existence. At the time she only knew that she was afraid. Sometimes she lay shivering with fear in the dark, completely bereft of faith that anything or anyone could help her. At other times she got up and went through to the living room to stand in the doorway helplessly staring at her parents.

'I told you!' her mother always accused her father. 'Now look what you've done.'

'Oh, be quiet, woman,' her father said, but he strode over and swept the child into his arms and out of the room. Then he sat beside her and patted her back as he used to do when she was a baby until the rhythm of his hand hypnotized her into sleep.

He had introduced her to the world of books and to intelligent conversation. He had taken her to the Art Gallery, to the theatre, to political meetings. He had enriched her life a thousandfold and now he would never know it. She had never been verbally articulate. She had never told him. Looking back she seemed to have gone through life like a zombie. Everything she had thought or felt, even as a small child, had remained locked inside herself. More often than not it was as if she was in a state of shock, mercifully dazed and numbed to what was happening to her or what was going on around her. Her mind, it seemed, had become programmed to react in this way. It was as if her real self, forever retreating deeper and deeper, searching for a safe place in which to hide, had lost its way and become incapable of surfacing.

She wished it could have been different. If only she could have told her father how much he had meant to her. She longed to thank him for enriching her life. But she also wished she could express her bewilderment at how he had betrayed her. She wanted to say out loud, 'Daddy, why did you do this to me?' Sitting in her attic room, her mind kept repeating the question, 'Why did you do this to me?'

286

Again and again she relived the incident when she was twelve and he had come into bed with her. She was totally innocent about sex and yet she instinctively knew that what was happening was terribly wrong. She instinctively knew that she was being used, and her love and trust were being betrayed. She remembered the sickening wave of disbelief, of silent pleading that it should not be true. 'Oh no, daddy,' she kept thinking. 'Oh no.'

It was as if the last person in the world, the very last person in the world she could trust was gone. There was only another enemy, another stranger after all. She was alone. She was totally bereft of self-esteem. She felt dirtied and weighed down by a guilt that had never stopped crushing her. She had not been able to stop physically shrinking from him. She no longer believed that he loved her. Yet she still loved him. If only she had been able to explain to him. If only he had been able to explain to her. She wanted to understand. But more than anything, she longed for him to know that she had never stopped loving him. Her greatest grief was the knowledge that it was too late.

Through her anguish she became aware of Harry tugging at her.

'Mummy, I'm hungry.'

'Oh, is it lunch-time already?'

Harry had been playing with his plasticine and his colouring book, two pastimes that could keep him quietly absorbed for hours. She made an effort to rouse herself. 'Come on downstairs to the kitchen with mummy, then.'

It was snowing outside. White flakes danced against the kitchen window delighting Harry. Indeed he was so keen to get out to experience the white wonderland, he forgot to make a scene after lunch when he was made ready to go to the nursery. He skipped along quite happily in his welly boots, stopping every now and again to form a snowball between his gloved hands. In the playground of the nursery the other children had already begun, with the help of the nursery nurses, to make a snowman and Harry eagerly joined in the fun.

Amelia stood absently watching him for a few minutes before wandering away. She was halfway back to the house when she saw, through the white haze of snow, Andrew Summers approaching from the opposite direction. Panic immediately jerked her out of her apathy. She was in no state for writing talk, or any kind of talk. Before he had even stopped in front of her she was babbling out, 'I won't keep you on a day like this, Andy.'

It was then she noticed his eyes were full of compassion. He said, 'It's all right, Amelia.' And bent down and gently kissed her on the lips. 'I read in this morning's *Herald* about your father. I'm so sorry.'

She could not say anything. She was still trying to register the fact that he had kissed her.

'I'm leaving tomorrow for Yorkshire,' he said. 'I've given up teaching in order to write full-time. I've been awarded a Writing Fellowship at York University. I'll be away for a few months. Would you mind if I kept in touch with you by letter?'

She shook her head. He was intent now on searching in his pockets for a notebook and pen, oblivious of the snow whitening his hair and the shoulders of his fawn-coloured anorak.

'Write your address in this,' he said.

Still not trusting herself to speak, she penned her address on the paper he held out for her. While she was doing so, his hand touched hers for a few seconds before she began moving away. She felt the warmth of his lips and his fingers all the way back to the house. Yet they only warmed the edges of her despair. Nothing could reach or soothe the pain of her grief. She seemed to disintegrate and swirl about with the blizzard in random, aimless confusion.

'Oh, daddy,' she kept thinking. 'Oh, daddy.'

46

Victoria had always said that Matty had no friends. He shunned friendships, she insisted. How strange then, Rory thought, that his funeral had been the largest anyone had ever witnessed. The whole of Springburn turned out, as well as innumerable Glaswegians from other districts who had known Matty through his council work. There were also colleagues from London. The black tenements of Springburn were colour-dotted with people at open windows. A silent crowd lined both sides of Springburn Road between the Co-op Funeral Parlour and Sighthill Cemetery. Men removed their caps as the *cortège* passed. An enormous line of cars followed the slow-moving hearse, including Sir Alexander Forbes-Cunningham's black Rolls Royce in which he sat alone. Fiona, Jamie and Amelia were with Victoria in the first car.

'That's how it should be,' Victoria insisted. 'Family closest to him.'

'But Sir Alex is family,' Fiona reminded her. 'He's the father of the deceased.'

'Matthew never recognized him as his father. My poor man would turn in his coffin if I gave Sir Alexander his father's place. No, I'll not do that to him.'

Rory followed silently in her Rolls with a noisily sobbing Bridget and Jessie, and a quiet Mr and Mrs McDade all dressed in black. Rory had promised Victoria she would give them a lift.

The crowd of Springburn folk lining the streets had spilled over into the cemetery and stood waiting for the hearse and the cars full of mourners to glide past them towards the open grave.

An icy wind attacked the black clothes of the people as they alighted from the cars, flapping trouser legs and flurrying coats. Then, a gust of rain added to the misery of shoulders already hunched against grief. Rory had meant to be a help and support to Victoria but, as it turned out, she was the one who broke down and wept at the graveside. She was the one who had to be supported by a stiff-faced, dry-eyed Victoria.

As the cars moved away from the cemetery after the burial, Rory had given a last look back. It was then she noticed a solitary figure laying a posy of wild flowers on Matty's grave. She was a studious-looking young woman in a black coat and horn-rimmed glasses. The last glimpse Rory had of her before the car swept through the gates of Sighthill Cemetery was of the girl kneeling beside the grave.

Later at the funeral tea in the Co-op Hall, Victoria sailed about smiling and serene among the long tables, making sure that everybody was all right and having enough to eat. It was exactly what she did at home. She had always been an excellent hostess, keeping an eye on everyone, seeing that no one was neglected and everyone was enjoying themselves. She laughed and talked and chatted as if the funeral was any ordinary gathering of friends. Rory admired her courage. Since the night of Matty's death Victoria had not shed one tear. She had kept herself too busy. Relatives had come to stay overnight. People, including neighbours, were milling about the small tenement flat from morning to night. Apart from a grey tinge to her skin and a deadness about her eyes, she was as bright and chirpy as a large robin redbreast in her scarlet blouse and navy skirt. The proud lift to her head and quirk at her mouth were more noticeable than usual.

'Wasn't that a wonderful turn-out?' she said to Rory. 'He was terribly well thought of, you know. There wasn't another man in the whole of Glasgow better thought of than my man!'

Everyone whispered to each other about how marvellous she was and how well she was coping. Rory dreaded to think what she would be like once all the buzz of visitors was over. She slept with Victoria on the night of the funeral and, as they cuddled into one another, Victoria

290

talked again about what a magnificent turnout it had been and how highly regarded her Matthew was.

'He was a wonderful man, you know, Rory. He educated himself and he could hold his own with university-educated people in London.'

'I know.'

'Like everybody else, we had our troubles and hard times but we stuck together, Rory, through thick and thin. We stuck together.'

'I know.'

'He was a good man. He wouldn't hurt a fly. I remember one time we were bothered with mice and I set a trap in the bathroom. He was at home at the time. It was one of his surgery week-ends. I heard the trap go off, and I told him to go and empty it. You should have seen his face.' She made a feeble attempt at a laugh. 'Honestly, it was a picture! He did it, though. Not just that once, but the dashed thing went off, I'm sure it must have been seven or eight times, during the week-end. I kept having to set it again. He said to me in the end that it had been a big mouse and slightly smaller one and then several tiny things. "It must have been a family," he said, with as sad and serious a face as if he was talking about a real family.' She gave another bewildered kind of laugh. 'He took everything so serious.'

'I know.'

'Not that he didn't have a sense of humour. Many a good laugh we had. Especially in the early days.'

'Remember that time . . .' Rory said. And they remembered, and spoke until exhaustion overcame them and they drifted into a dream-disturbed sleep.

Next day, Rory said she would have to go. She was persuaded to stay until after lunch but eventually she had to insist on leaving.

'I've got the shop to supervise. When the cat's away . . . as they say. I'll go straight from here and at least put in a few hours before I go home.'

'But your brother's manager there, isn't he? He'll be officially in charge when you're not there.' Victoria's eyes were anxious and pleading.

'I know, Victoria, but there're things that I must do.'

'You'll come back soon?'

'Of course!'

'When will you come?'

'This is – what? Wednesday? I'll pop over on Friday straight from the shop, OK?'

'I'll have a nice tea ready for you.'

'I'll look forward to it.'

They kissed warmly at the front door. Then once down the stairs and outside Rory looked up at the top floor window to smile and wave. Victoria was standing pressed close to the glass and waving, but not smiling back. Poor Victoria, she thought. She had always looked the strongest of the two of them. She would make two of Rory in bulk for a start. She had never been as tough inside, though. Right from their first meeting Rory had proved she was the tough one.

It had been at primary school and Victoria had been sailing along like a lady in her starched white pinafore over her red velvet dress. She had lovely long black hair and a couple of boys had suddenly grabbed her hair, knocked her down and tried to steal her satchel. Rory had sped up and set upon both boys, punching, scratching, spitting and screaming foul language at them until they had dropped the satchel and run for their lives. Victoria had dried her eyes and allowed herself to be helped up. Then she had informed Rory that it was not nice to use bad words. Rory had been so keen to better herself that she had gratefully accepted this information. Victoria, on her part, had been so glad of the protection she had received that, after sharing her bar of Nestlé's milk chocolate with Rory, she had taken her not only to her heart but also to her home. Rory sighed. Why, oh why, had Victoria not sought medical or some sort of advice? It might have made all the difference in the world to her relationship with Matty.

She had arrived at the department store which bore her name and which was now one of the biggest in Glasgow, and was on her way to her office when she began to sense that something was wrong. The assistants that she passed and said, 'Good afternoon' to, answered her but in a different tone of voice from usual. She tried to put her finger on exactly what she found disturbing. It was as if they were murmuring 'Sorry, Mrs Donovan,' at the same time as 'Good afternoon.' There was an undercurrent of pity and regret in their voices, as well as deference. Miss Bartholomew caught her just before she entered the office.

'Oh, Mrs Donovan, something awful has happened. Your brother has been searching all over the place for you. You must have just missed him. He went away again just a few minutes ago.'

'Out with it then,' Rory said. 'Don't just stand there wringing your hands.'

'The police are here. CID. This is the second time. They were here earlier and, oh, oh dear . . .'

'Where are they?'

'In your office. They're waiting for you.'

'I'd better go and see what they want.' Rory interrupted briskly.

Two large men rose to greet her. 'Mrs Rory Donovan?'

'Yes.' She walked towards her desk, tugging off her gloves. 'What can I do for you? My secretary tells me you are police officers.'

'I wouldn't bother removing your coat, Mrs Donovan,' one of the men said. 'You will have to accompany us to the police station.'

Rory raised a cool brow. 'Oh? Why?'

'We were here earlier with a search warrant and took away a large number of unused clothing coupons. We also took your sales book showing the names and addresses of regular customers and recent sales transactions.'

Rory's face hardened and she lit a cigarette with a perfectly steady hand. 'So?'

'You are not obliged to say anything in answer to the charge I am about to prefer but, if you choose to say something, this will be taken down in writing and may be used in evidence at your trial.' He cleared his throat before proceeding. 'You are charged with resetting ten thousand clothing coupons which have been stolen from the Ministry of Defence premises in Glasgow. Or, alternatively, trafficking in stolen clothing coupons.'

'This is ridiculous,' Rory said, lifting the internal phone. 'Miss Bartholomew, get my solicitor at once.'

She was forced to go with the police officers before Laurence Dowdall arrived, however. She walked in front of the detectives through the store, nonchalantly smoking her cigarette, glad that she could flaunt her mink coat and hat. 'To hell with it!' she kept thinking. 'To hell with everything!' She had always been one for getting any kind of publicity she could and turning everything to her advantage. 'Any publicity is better than none,' had always been her motto. 'The papers will really go to town on this and why not?' she thought, as she slid elegantly into the police car. 'The best of British luck to them!'

She was taken to the Central Police Office in Turnball Street where she was detained overnight. Next day her solicitor, Laurence Dowdall, had her freed on five hundred pounds' bail.

She wasted no time in warning Douglas about what happened but told him there was nothing to worry about. The trial would be a nuisance but she would get off. Laurence Dowdall was not Scotland's best-known lawyer for nothing. 'Send for Dowdall' had become a catch-phrase if anyone was in trouble. Douglas did not share her opinion about the value of publicity. How would it look for *him*? How it would affect *his* reputation was all that he was worried about. Rory just laughed at him.

'You're getting like an old spinster, Douglas, and a self-obsessed one at that. Why should you worry about what anyone else thinks?'

It turned out it was what his girl-friend Patricia would think that was worrying him. She was very straight-laced and good-living apparently.

Victoria had been shocked and terribly distressed when she had told her.

'Oh, you poor thing.' She had hugged her dramatically to her bosom. 'Oh, this is awful! Have you sent for Donovan and Helena?'

'No, and I'm not going to.'

'Not going to?' Victoria echoed. 'But you must!'

'Why bother them and upset them, specially when they're so far away? Anyway they're due home at the end of the year. I'll see them then. Donovan's doing a good job. Have you been reading his articles?'

'Yes, but, Rory, you should have your family around you for support at the trial. I'll stand by you, of course, but surely your husband . . .'

'To be quite honest, Victoria, I can't bear the thought of him saying "I told you so," and he would. I'll get no sympathy from him, I can assure you.'

'Och, you were only doing your job selling clothes. We're all sick of these stupid coupons. It's high time they were done away with.'

'I know. Don't worry, I can explain about the coupons. I'll get off and there will be no harm done. On the contrary it'll get "Rory's" plenty of free publicity.'

Victoria shook her head, her eyes bewildered. 'It would be the death of me. The shame and everything. I don't know how you can keep so perky.'

'It's being so cheerful that keeps me going, as they say.' Rory laughed.

'I still think you should send word to Donovan.'

'No. Definitely not. I'm telling you, Victoria, I know him. He can be a cruel bastard. I'll be better off with you.'

47

The courtroom was packed but there was a hush of expectancy as Rory was identified by the Clerk of Court. She stood in the dock flanked by two policewomen, who wore white gloves and each carried a baton. Rory's slim figure was shown to best advantage in an emerald green Bianca Mosca suit, topped by a little straw hat tipped cheekily forward over her brow. She looked elegant, attractive and totally out of place in the stark, unimpressive dock. She was asked to sit down, after which her lawyer, Laurence Dowdall, addressed the bench and stated that his client pleaded 'Not guilty' to the charge.

The charge was in alternative form, the principal one being the reset of ten thousand clothing coupons, the alternative was illegal and unauthorized possession of the coupons under the appropriate rationing order of 1945 and the defence regulation of 1939.

Dowdall had already explained to Rory that in Scotland, unlike England, there were no opening speeches and proceedings started with the evidence. 'It is considered,' he said, 'that opening speeches can often prove to be prejudicial to the accused. This is because the Crown often pitch their speech at an inordinately high level when, as often occurs, the evidence that the speech leads to does not measure up to the standard animadverted on. Indeed, in England, one sometimes wonders why the accused has had the temerity to plead "Not guilty" in the first place, so convincing does the Crown speech appear to be. And, of course, first impressions can be difficult to budge. Therein can lie prejudice. . . .'

The Procurator Fiscal, Leslie McLeod, exclaimed, 'Call down witness number one, Patrick Connelly.'

Connelly entered the courtroom, ushered by the resplendent Court Officer, a retired Sergeant Major, with the pitch of voice associated with his prior occupation. Connelly was much as Rory remembered him, average height, burly, his ruddy complexion indicating that he enjoyed a good refreshment. It became clear in the evidence that followed that he was fairly intelligent and had a surprisingly retentive memory. He could even recall the colour of her lounge carpet and the painting that hung over the fireplace. Although he was patently dishonest (as his criminal record of nineteen previous convictions for house-breaking, theft and reset clearly established), he detested the use of violence in any shape or form. He had a self-righteous look about him consistent with giving evidence for the Crown for the very first time.

Dowdall had told her that Connelly had been caught 'Bank O' Rights' breaking into licensed premises.

' "Bank O' Rights?" ' Rory had echoed.

'That's what they say in Glasgow for *in delecto flagrante*, caught red-handed, caught in the act.'

'I see.'

'His substantial criminal record meant a lengthy prison sentence, so he did a deal. He told them about you,' Dowdall shrugged. 'You are one of the best-known people in Glasgow, a much bigger fish than Connelly. If they could nail you . . .'

Rory knew Dowdall's reputation in Court. Who in Glasgow did not? Yet, it surprised her to see how he could change from the pleasant good-humoured, comparatively mild man in private to the tenacious, belligerent and most formidable fighter in the Court. He brought out the full criminal record of Connelly, and his defence for Rory was that Connelly had never met her, and that Connelly had only introduced her name to the police to be allowed to give 'King's evidence'. That way he thought he could curry favour with the police after he was caught *in delecto flagrante* at the licensed premises. Rory tried to explain that the clothing coupons found in her office had been acquired over the previous months but, due to pressure of business, she had not returned them to the authorities. The prosecutor in the middle of his rigorous cross-examination of her reintroduced Connelly to the courtroom. 'Look at him,' he shouted. 'Have you ever seen him before?'

'Never,' she repeated.

She was asked why she did not give the same (or indeed any) explanation of the coupons when she had been charged.

'I was shattered,' she said, 'and confused. I had just come from the funeral of a life-long friend.'

Customers were called, including Fiona. She stood like an angel in the dock, dressed in a white dress and a blue hat the exact shade of her eyes. She lied softly and sweetly and with absolute conviction. *Of course* she and her husband had given the proper amount of coupons for the clothes they had bought. They had been saving them up for absolutely *ages*!

Another customer, unfortunately, was not made of such strong stuff. She broke down in the box under persistent questioning and admitted that she had made purchases without the necessary coupons. 'Rory said not to worry about coupons,' the woman sobbed. 'She said she had plenty of them.'

But at the end of the day, the issue very much depended on the demeanour of Connelly who had stuck to his guns despite the most rigorous cross-examination by Dowdall. The Sheriff made the point that 'A man with convictions for dishonesty need not necessarily be a liar.' Nevertheless Dowdall emphasized the background of Connelly: '. . . and this is the man who is the *lynch-pin* and *sheet-anchor* of the Crown case!' he roared in disgust, adding, 'Unless he is believed beyond reasonable doubt, you cannot, in all conscience, consider convicting my client.'

The jury retired to the jury room where they remained for over two hours.

Rory felt seriously worried for the first time. Before the trial she had not allowed herself any negative thoughts. She had mentally thumbed her nose at everything and everybody. She had spurned all offers of sympathy and returned pity with impatience. Only Victoria had been allowed any closeness, or to show any concern. She had kept reassuring

Victoria, who had from the start been far more upset than her, that there was nothing to worry about. Who would take a hardened criminal's word against hers? Occasionally she would wake up sweating in the middle of the night and have to sit up and smoke a cigarette to calm herself. Mostly, however, she really believed that there *was* nothing to worry about. She kept seeing Victoria's strained white face in the Court and thinking, 'Poor Victoria, she's more concerned about me than I am about myself.'

When she had been young, she had always felt Victoria to be more of a sister than her own sisters and she certainly felt that now. Once when they were young, she and Victoria had seen a cowboy-and-indian serial in the Wellfield Picture House in which there had been a 'blood-brother ritual'. She and Victoria had decided to become blood-sisters. They had cut their wrists and nearly killed themselves by mistake. Victoria's father had had to tie hankies tightly round their arms and rush them along the road to Doctor Patterson. It had taken Victoria's mother ages to get the bloodstains off her rag rug. And her own mother had nearly murdered her for causing the expense of visiting the doctor. 'Through thick and thin,' they had vowed.

Victoria had kept her word. Knowing Victoria, Rory thought, she must be as shocked and horrified at the scandal of the Court case, as she had been so long ago at her abortion. (Something not even Donovan knew about.) Victoria had loyally stuck by her then, despite her disapproval and distress, and she was loyally sticking by her now.

There was something extra special and precious about the friendship of someone of one's own sex, Rory decided. There was no need to be defensive, no need to try to explain one's deepest fears and feelings. Another woman instinctively *knew*. They had the same potential vulnerability, perhaps that was it. She felt completely at ease and *safe* with Victoria and, as the clock ticked away the long minutes while she waited for the jury's return, she had never more appreciated Victoria's friendship and her unquestioning sympathy and support.

48

She was found guilty and sentenced to twelve months imprisonment. Male police officers had taken her in a police van to Duke Street prison. She sat in silence between them, outwardly cool and superior-looking. Inwardly her thoughts were in disarray. She hardly knew what to think. Fear and apprehension were tugging her this way and that. She could not properly grasp what was happening. The van stopped. She could hear the creak of a gate opening. The van started again, but slowly. A gate shut behind them. Another stop. Another creaking and clanging. Another start and stop. Then the van door was opened and the officers ordered her to get out.

In a daze she allowed herself to be handed over to a couple of wardresses built like Sherman tanks and dressed in navy blue dresses buttoned high at the neck, with stiff collars and cuffs. Each had a navy blue serge toque covering her hair. Rory was led into a reception area, told to have a bath, given a medical examination which she found humiliating, more because of the doctor's disinterested dismissive attitude than the actual examination. But worse, much worse was the prison outfit of coarse grey skirt, unglamorous blue and white blouse, long thick knitted wool stockings and heavy lacing shoes. The clothes reminded her of the parish clothes she had worn during the worst period of her childhood, before she had been saved by the good influence and practical help of Victoria and Victoria's mother.

Next she found herself being led along one of six flights of long stone-flagged corridors bounded by railings and forming a deep well in the centre. Each corridor held a row of cell doors with spy-holes. A cell door was opened and she was ordered inside. The door clanged shut and she was alone.

She stared dazedly around. It was about the size of her

broom cupboard at home and held no furniture except one small stool. A shelf folded up and set into the wall came down on to the floor at night, she had been told. That served as a bed and was only to be used at night. No lying down on it during the day. A rolled-up mattress stood over in a corner. On another shelf sat striped blankets folded one on top of the other, the stripes of each exactly matching. On top of these were two sheets and one pillow. A smaller shelf hinged down from the wall to hold one mug, one spoon, one comb and brush, one piece of soap, one towel and bundle of toilet paper. There was also one white cotton buttoned jacket that was supposed to serve as a nightgown but was barely knee-length. Four books were stacked beside it, a hymn book, a prayer book, a bible and a book of rules. A small round mirror was glued into one of the walls.

Rory sank down on to the stool. She felt claustrophobic. Tiny jets of panic shot up inside her as realization began to dawn. She was still sitting when a wardress opened the door and told her to make up her bed and get undressed.

'Lights out at nine-thirty,' the wardress informed her briskly.

There was no heating in the cell and, when Rory undressed and donned the jacket, she began to shiver uncontrollably. But she longed for a cigarette even more than the comfort of a warm quilt. She would have given any amount of money for a packet of cigarettes and her lighter. She had been a heavy smoker and she suffered agonies of withdrawal symptoms. She hardly slept the whole night, so terrible was her physical discomfort. It was a mixture of desperate need for a smoke, the bone-chilling cold, and the jaggy hardness of the straw mattress. She must have dozed off eventually, because she awoke with a start to the loud clamour of a bell. Not being allowed to keep her wrist-watch, she had lost all idea of time. She soon discovered that everything was done by the bell. A bell was rung at 6.00 a.m. to make everyone get up. The 6.30 bell was when the day shift of wardresses came on duty and the prisoners started work. The quarter to eight bell heralded breakfast-time, which consisted of one plate of porridge and nothing else, not even a mug of tea. At 10.00 a.m. came the clamour of the exercise bell. 11.00 a.m. was the end of the exercise period. Quarter to one meant dinner, which was a bowl of soup and eight ounces of bread and nothing else. Three o'clock and quarter to four were the afternoon exercise bells. 5.00 p.m. was tea-time. Tea consisted of a mug of tea and four ounces of bread. Nothing else. There was no bell for lights out at 9.30 p.m. The day staff went off then and one night duty officer came on to patrol silently about.

Between bells, Duke Street prison was the most silent place imaginable. There was never any talking allowed, either among those who worked, or among those who did not work but had the twice-daily exercise periods instead. During exercise, the prisoners walked round and round the yard in silent single file. There was a rhythmic swish of scrubbing brushes during working hours as prisoners scrubbed the wooden stairs until they were pristine white. There was the splash of water if you worked in the laundry or the whirr of sewing machines if, like Rory, you were put to work in the sewing room.

But never the sound of a human voice.

'You two are making me feel a right gooseberry,' Donovan said.

'Gooseberry?' Burgeyev delighted Helena with one of his heart-warming smiles. Sometimes, as it did now, it lit up his eyes with a kind of innocence.

'It's a saying we have,' Donovan tossed away his cigarette and Helena winced. People here did not throw litter on to the street. 'Meaning the odd one out, the unwanted one, with a pair of love-birds like you.'

Helena rolled her eyes, 'You're breaking my heart!'

'Donovan, you are not unwanted,' Burgeyev was serious again. 'You are of the greatest importance to me. Without you neither Helena nor I would be here. Helena would still be in the art school in far-away Glasgow and I would be alone in Leningrad.'

Donovan grinned at Helena, 'What did I tell you about being sentimental? Anyway, that was the last writers' shrine you two are going to drag me to. The next one you go to, you go on your own.'

'You'll get a story out of our visits,' Helena said.

'One sentence maybe: "The moment a writer dies, his house and everything in it is preserved exactly as it was and guarded by formidable eagle-eyed old ladies who watch your every move in case you violate Chekhov's desk or Pushkin's necktie." '

'You'll get a lot more than that! You can't kid me.'

'Maybe so, but I've had enough. I'm sick to death of writers. Present company excepted, of course,' he added with a grin. 'Now, I don't care a tinker's cuss what the pair of you are planning to do now, but I'm off to the boozer!'

After Donovan had gone and she and Burgeyev were strolling along arm-in-arm, he said, 'The severity of the old ladies is a mask. Behind it is much reverence and affection.'

'I know. And so does dad. He was only teasing.' She laughed, 'If I didn't believe before about the reverence and affection all of you have for writers, I certainly do now. Especially after seeing Dostoevsky's room.'

The room had affected her deeply. The clock was stopped at the minute of Dostoevsky's death and there was a little note still lying on his desk where his daughter had put it. 'It said, 'Daddy, I love you. Signed, Lyuba.' Not a thing had been disturbed. Not only that, one of the stern guardians who was there to make sure nothing was desecrated, came in every day to put a fresh glass of steaming tea on the desk for Dostoevsky and to take away the cold one from yesterday.

Taganrog, on the Sea of Azov, was Chekhov's shrine. The whole town was a living celebration to his memory. There was even his suit, his hat, his bow-tie, his walking-stick hanging as if ready for him to walk out the door at any minute.

'I hope,' Burgeyev said, 'I have not bored you with my obsession with writers.'

She hugged his arm, 'Of course not. I've been fascinated. Anyway, I could never be bored as long as I'm with you.'

He looked down at her, his eyes darkening with love, and

she experienced, as she often did now, what was almost a physical pain at the sight of him. She would watch him coming across the hotel lounge towards her with his cat-like dancer's grace and marvel at how beautiful he was. The artist in her appreciated him as much as the woman. Indeed never before had she felt so seriously about art. With the first flowering of her love had come the first flowering of her talent. She longed to paint him. So far she had not been able to persuade him to sit for her. Although she *had* managed to take a couple of photographs of him and from these she had made sketches. One was of him standing proudly in Red Square in front of the Kremlin, but she detected behind the aura of composure, the stiffness of unease. His tall figure was dressed in an army-type greatcoat with the high collar turned up and framing his face. His eyes stared straight at the camera, revealing nothing. Yet in the dark seriousness that had become so familiar and so dear to her, she believed she saw the real man. Despite his handsome appearance and proud tilt to his head, he was not egotistical or conceited. His pride only manifested itself about his country and its achievements. On this subject he would only grudgingly admit faults and failings.

He did not like Donovan's article about centralization. Even in Georgia, Donovan pointed out, where there was everything in abundance in open markets, the state, with its long bureaucratic lines of centralized distribution process managed to tie everything in knots. In private homes in Georgia the food was delicious: salads, cold and hot meals, fruit of all kinds, and served in style in rooms perfumed with flowers. In the state hotels, the cuisine was poor and limited. To Donovan it was inexcusable. But Burgeyev insisted, 'Distribution and supply of food is a great problem throughout Russian cities. You do not appreciate the vastness of our land and the difficulties caused by the weather and the terrain.'

Donovan did not see (nor did she) how this difficulty could, or should, be applied to the city they were at in Georgia where food in great variety, in abundance, was in a market just around the corner from their hotel. One day they could not get any eggs in the hotel or anywhere. Yet, a mere two miles from the city gates, sitting on the platform of the country station, was an old lady with hundreds of eggs she could not get rid of.

Donovan had written: '. . . Nobody here seems to have the slightest sense of diffusion, no idea how to make elementary commerce spread evenly throughout the people at large. Restaurants run out of beer or wine while at the same time a stall on the road outside is selling these drinks . . .'

'Come back to my room,' Helena said to Burgeyev.

The look of love darkened to passion in his eyes and she had to avert her gaze, so strong was the effect it had on her.

The hotel in which they were staying was of the older, traditional type. Her room was vast and dimly lit, the tall, elegant windows dusty and half-hidden by too-short net curtains. Too-long, red velvet curtains hung in folds on the floor. The furniture was heavy and bulbous with gilded wood and upholstery that felt as if it was padded with iron. A large, flat-topped desk filled a dark corner and, on the mantelshelf, an ormolu clock monotonously tick-tocked. In the middle of the room stood an ancient grand piano with yellow keys and from some other faraway room drifted sad whispers of Russian folk songs.

Helena trembled so much she could hardly unfasten the buttons of her dress. She had never felt so devastated in her life. She had dreamed so often of this moment. Not only of the sexual act itself but of the closeness, the intimacy, the togetherness she longed for with Burgeyev. They had intimately talked and touched and kissed, yet often his eyes had that mixture of passion and composure that made him different from her. He seemed to typify many of the contradictions in Russia that she kept trying to understand and thought she had succeeded in unravelling, only to be lost in mystery again.

He undressed, and again, through her passion, she saw him with the clear eye of the artist. He was perfection, his blue-black hair and eyes, the firm bone structure of his face, the smooth tanned skin, his body unspoiled by any superfluous flesh. His eyes held her as he drew her down on to the bed. Whispering caressingly in Russian he traced with his fingers every contour of her face, and neck and firm upthrust of breasts. She became breathless at his touch, shivering with need, weeping inside with love. He kissed her very gently but with opening mouth and deeply searching tongue. Her mind swam with opening willing thoughts. She wanted to belong to him and him alone, and it was then that fears she had tried not to face intruded forcibly into her consciousness. He was the only one she had ever loved but he was not the only one she had had sex with. She wondered apprehensively if discovering she was not a virgin would make him feel different towards her. Here in the Soviet Union it seemed nearly every woman was chaste. In Rostov, one of the towns the Germans had overrun, they had, in their loathsome way, produced a statistic that said they had examined all unmarried women and found eighty-five per cent to be virgins.

'What is wrong?' Burgeyev suddenly asked in English.

The physical reflection of her thoughts had been so subtle she had not noticed it herself. His sensitivity had searched it out.

'Nothing's wrong really, darling,' she heard the false lightness in her voice and hated it. 'I do love you, believe me.'

He rolled away from her and took a long, slow breath.

She was in a panic of distress, 'Darling, forgive me.'

'There's nothing to forgive,' he said, without looking round at her.

Oh, but there is, she wanted to say. There are wasted years of stupid, empty promiscuity. I debased myself and gave myself to anybody just for the cheap thrill of the moment. She wanted to tell him but shame prevented her.

Burgeyev sat up and reached for his shirt.

'Oh darling,' she said, 'if only I could explain.'

'We are going to be married, yes?'

'Oh, yes!'

'Then all is as it should be. I respect your natural reticence.' He turned, buttoning his shirt and giving her one of the smiles that so endeared him to her. 'But we will marry very soon . . .'

'Yes?' they said in unison.

'After all the palaver we've got to go through and all the forms we'll have to fill in,' she said, 'we'll have to.'

Laughter brought relief but it was only a temporary surface relief to Helena. Anxiety tormented her. He said he respected her. How could he respect her once he knew the truth, and without respect how could there be love? It was not that she believed for one minute that Burgeyev would take the same arrogant 'I must be first' attitude that her brother Douglas adopted. It was her own shame and regret eating away at her self-confidence. She could not be sure how much the social attitude and conditioning of his background would have affected Burgeyev. Promiscuity was far from being socially acceptable in Britain and she was sure Russia would be years behind Britain in this as they were in so many other things. Often she lapsed into worried abstraction and sometimes she caught Burgeyev watching her. He never asked her again what was wrong. They still walked and talked and touched and kissed. More and more they became isolated from each other by their own sense of detachment.

After they returned to Moscow he announced it was time once more to visit his family in Leningrad. She was unable to bear the thought of being parted from him, especially now that a subtle distance had developed between them. He insisted on going alone, however.

'Before we marry,' he said, 'I want you to be sure. I will be gone just over a week but it may give you time to become more certain.'

He was only gone three days when a telegram arrived from Douglas. It was addressed to both her father and herself and said, 'Come home at once. Something terrible has happened to mother!'

49

Helena could not believe she was on the plane. Everything had happened so quickly. The telegram had shocked her and made her desperately worried about her mother. Donovan had immediately phoned home but got no reply. He had then booked them on the next flight to Glasgow. She felt confused.

'I can't leave without seeing Ivan and explaining.'

'Fling your clothes into a case,' Donovan said. 'I've got the passports, paid the hotel bill and told the porter to collect your cases. To catch that plane we have to be out of here in half an hour.'

'But I can't . . .'

'Shut up and do as you're told,' Donovan snapped. 'Be down in the foyer in twenty minutes. If you're not, I'll come up here and drag you down.'

She had come to suspect that Donovan hid any emotion he might feel behind an increasingly tough exterior. The stronger his emotion, the harder and more unfeeling he seemed. She could not believe he did not sympathize with her, or understand her distress. She wept with confusion and fear. Fears about what could be wrong with her mother mixed with anxieties about how she could contact Burgeyev. There was no phone at his home in Leningrad. The only thing she could do was to send him a telegram. She raced about the room snatching at clothes and shoes and stuffing them into cases, sobbing with increasing abandon. She hastened down to the foyer to be there before her father in case he did not give her enough time to send the telegram. At the reception desk, still sobbing and not caring what anyone thought, she scribbled the words, 'Something terrible has happened to mother. Had to return home. Will be in touch. Love. Helena.' She gave it to the woman behind the desk, along with all the money she had and a plea that it should be sent immediately.

Her father came striding across to her, 'Come on! I've got a taxi waiting outside.'

She could not believe she was leaving, even as she was being hustled outside, even as the taxi sped away, even as she boarded the plane. She felt it must be an ugly nightmare. Then, worse, after the plane made its noisy take-off and Moscow had disappeared beneath the clouds, she had the terrifying feeling that Russia, and Ivan Mikhailovitch Burgeyev, had been no more than a beautiful dream. Donovan sat grim-faced beside her, and barely uttered half-a-dozen words the whole of the journey in the plane and in the taxi after they touched down in Scotland.

How grim Glasgow looked, with its sooty tenements and littered streets. Small boys with dirty faces and holes in their jerseys were yelling abuse at each other and kicking a football about the streets. Pollokshields was a sharp contrast. There, large villas were set back from the road in lofty isolation and the pavements were tree-lined and quiet.

A saucer-eyed Winnie greeted them at the front door. 'Oh, Mr Donovan. Oh, Helena. I'm so glad to see you!'

'What the hell's happened?' Donovan asked as he strode through the lounge. 'Where's Rory?'

Douglas got up when his father entered. 'It's absolutely hellish,' he said. 'Mother wouldn't let me tell you before. But she was arrested and tried and now she's been found guilty of dealing in illegal clothing coupons. She's been sentenced to twelve months.'

'Christ,' Donovan rolled his eyes. 'I knew this would happen. I told her, but she wouldn't listen. Did she have Laurence Dowdall?'

'Yes. But it would have taken more than a clever lawyer to get her off. I'll never live down the scandal of all this. Our name's mud.'

'Is that all you're worried about?' Donovan said.

'I'm sorry about mother, of course . . .'

'I'm glad to hear it.'

'But she did bring it on herself and I don't see why I should be made to suffer. My fiancée has definitely cooled off since this happened. I wouldn't be a bit surprised if she broke the engagement.'

'Stop whining about yourself. Where's your mother being held? Duke Street?'

'Yes.'

Donovan poured himself a whisky, then noticing Helena leaning back ashen-faced in a chair, he passed a glass to her. 'Here, drink this.' Then to Douglas, 'I'll go and see her right away.'

'It's not that easy,' Douglas said. 'She has to get a line or something from the prison office and request a visit from you. You can't just walk in. She's only to be allowed one visitor a month for fifteen minutes.'

'Does that mean I can't come with you, dad?' Helena asked.

'Don't worry, I'll fix it,' Donovan said, striding towards the phone.

As it turned out, nothing Donovan could say or do had any effect. Only one person was allowed in at a time. Donovan made the first visit, Helena the second a month later. Douglas refused even to contemplate going.

'The place depresses me,' he complained. 'Even the thought of it's affecting my work!'

Helena did not argue with him as she used to. She gave him a look of disgust and that was all. The high-walled Duke Street Prison depressed her, too, and she was sick at heart to see her mother incarcerated in such bleak surroundings. Not that her mother complained. She was even more perky and defiant than usual. To all appearances, in fact, she was not in the slightest affected (certainly not in the least contrite) by what had happened, or by her surroundings. Although Helena wondered how much of this was just a brave front.

Helena was deeply distressed, especially by the fact that her mother told her she was going to ask for Victoria to come in the following month, something that Donovan was furious at. Helena could not talk about her mother without tears filling her eyes and it was an ordeal to write about it to Burgeyev. She forced herself to do this, however, because she felt he deserved a proper explanation for her sudden departure. His letter of reply was a very long time in coming, a fault of the postal service between the two countries, not his. It was a long letter which reminded her of his stories. It had the same sombre tone but with an undercurrent of both passion and compassion. He haunted her every waking hour. Even when she was most intensely anxious about her mother, he still hovered, dark-eyed and calmly watchful, on the outskirts of her attention.

Veronica kept insisting, 'You should get back into circulation. It would cheer you up and take your mind off everything. Why don't you come to the dancing with me?'

Eventually, for the sake of peace more than anything else, she succumbed to Veronica's pleadings and went with her to the dancing in town. Greens Playhouse was just as she remembered it. Nothing had changed. Except herself. Ted Heath and his band were playing, 'All of me, Why not take all of me . . .' The rhythm section beat a snappy tiss-ton, tiss-ton and the female crooner, juicy-lipped and glittering with sequins, competed close to the microphone, 'All of me, Why not take all of me . . .'

A sailor asked Helena to dance. His hands were sticky with sweat and when he held her close the smell of it came hot and strong from under his armpits.

'Do you come here often?' he said.

'No.' She felt like adding, 'And I wish I had not come tonight.' She controlled the urge. He was, after all, quite a pleasant, harmless young man and he sang so contentedly as he smooched along, 'All of me, Why not take all of me . . .'

The next dance was a quick-step. Ted Heath, thinly smiling, moustache quivering, conducted his band with a hand weaving around his navel. The brass and rhythm section swelled in volume and then, with one flick of Ted Heath's wrist, they were catapulted into 'In The Mood'. Some couples began to jitterbug and spaces were cleared on the floor for them. Men did a rubber-backed version of the splits and girls kicked their heels over partner's knees and showed their knickers right up to their elastic waists. Desperate now to escape, Helena pushed her way through

311

the crowd of people standing at the side. The whole place was mobbed, a seething mass of flesh. Yet she had never felt so alone or lonely in her life. She reached the cloakroom, struggling not to cry. It was not until she had retrieved her coat and was outside on the street that the tears began to come. She had to stand in a dark doorway and fumble in her handbag for her handkerchief and mop her face.

It was still early and she decided that she would at last comply with her mother's desperate wish that she should visit Victoria Drummond. She had felt reluctant and somewhat resentful about this particular request from her mother and had been putting it off. She had protested to her mother at the time, 'You're in Duke Street Prison and you're worried about your friend? It doesn't make sense.'

'I'm a lot tougher than Victoria, Helena,' Rory insisted. 'And she was depending on me since she lost Matty. Please, for my sake, take an interest in her. Go and see her and, remember, tell her that I'm going to put her name down for the next visit.'

Reluctantly Helena went for a Balornock bus, then walked up to Hilltop Road. Amelia opened the door in answer to her knock. Helena was taken aback at how thin and weary the girl looked.

'How are you, Amelia?' she asked.

Amelia stared at her in bewilderment for a second or two. 'Oh, it's you, Helena. Come in. I'm fine, thanks.'

'How's your mother?'

'She's not so bad as long as there's someone with her. But – you know – the shock of what happened to your mother, so soon after my father . . .'

Victoria appeared at the living room doorway, round-shouldered and looking older.

Amelia said, 'It's Rory's daughter, Helena, mummy.'

'Oh! Come on in, Helena.' Her shoulders lifted and she visibly brightened. 'I'm so pleased to see you. How is your mother? I've been so worried about her. Every night in my prayers I ask God to comfort and help her. She's been a good friend to me. We've known each other for a lifetime, you know.'

312

'Yes, mum's told me. By the way, she also told me to tell you she's organizing for you to visit her.'

'Oh, I'm glad. Maybe I'll be able to cheer her up. Now just you sit there and talk to Amelia, dear. I'll go and make you a nice cup of tea and I've some of my home-baked treacle scones. I know you'll enjoy them.'

'Lovely, thanks.'

After she had bustled away through to the kitchenette, Helena smiled at Amelia, 'Tell me, Amelia, how are you getting on? Are you back living at home now?'

'No. I've a housekeeper's job in Bearsden. This is my night off.'

'Where's your son?'

'Sleeping through in the room. Mummy wants me to come back for good but . . .'

'It's better to be independent.'

A look of gratitude widened Amelia's eyes. 'Yes, and, you see, I need privacy to do my writing.' She flushed with embarrassment. 'I don't know why I blurted that out. I never mention about my writing to anyone.'

'You write?' Helena's attention alerted. 'How fascinating! My fiancé – I'm engaged to a Russian man and I've never mentioned that to anyone either, what with all this happening to mother, et cetera – but Ivan's a writer.'

Amelia was excited now, 'I did short stories at first and got quite a few published, but now I'm trying novels. I'm on my fourth but so far I've had no success. I'm not giving up trying though.'

'Ivan was a short story writer too, and now he's working on a novel!'

'Oh, Helena, I'd love to hear all about him. What kind of stories . . .? What kind of novel . . .?'

Just then her mother returned with a tray. 'My goodness,' Victoria laughed. 'You two seem to be getting on like a house on fire. What's all the excitement?'

Helena caught Amelia's fearful, warning look. 'I was just telling Amelia that I became engaged to be married to a Russian while I was over there.'

'Good gracious!' Victoria gasped. 'How romantic!'

Astonishment was quickly replaced by anxiety. 'But is he all right?'

'How do you mean?'

'Well, he'll be a Communist, won't he? My man could never be doing with Communists. They haven't our freedom in Russia. They're not allowed to worship. There's no churches. And they force women to go down the mines and do heavy work on the roads. Awful jobs like that. That's why all the women are so unfeminine-looking. Great hulking brutes of creatures, they are. I've seen pictures of them.'

Helena would like to have said, 'You're no china doll yourself,' but she controlled herself and the irritation she felt at Victoria's general attitude. It was the kind of prejudice she had expected. Indeed it was exactly what she used to think herself. She realized, in fact, that *this* was the reason she had not mentioned to anyone about her engagement, not because of what had happened to her mother. It was the monumental task of having to contradict and argue all the time. The burden of prejudice was too heavy for her to lift.

'Of course,' Victoria continued, 'if he's coming over here, I suppose he can't be too bad. When are we going to meet him, dear?' she concluded, with more uneasiness than interest.

Helena shrugged, 'I'll let you know what's happening once everything's settled. My mother has to come first just now.'

'Of course, dear. Of course.'

'Amelia,' Helena said, 'would you like to pay me a visit to Pollokshields on your next day off? I'd like to show you some paintings I've been working on since I've come back. There's one of Ivan Mikhailovitch you might be interested in.'

Amelia's eyes filled with fire. 'Oh yes! Thank you. Oh yes, I will!'

Victoria shook her head, 'I know you mean well, Helena, but I don't think that's a good idea.'

'Why not?' Helena asked.

'Douglas might be there and it would be very awkward and upsetting for Amelia.'

'No, it wouldn't,' Amelia said.

'Be quiet, Amelia,' Victoria commanded.

Helena smiled reassuringly, 'Douglas is mostly at his flat, but I'll make absolutely certain he is not visiting Pollok-shields at the same time as Amelia. I promise you.'

'Please, mummy,' Amelia was trembling with anxiety and eagerness.

Helena thought it was both pathetic and ridiculous. She had always known the girl was very odd and she had never much liked her, but still, a writer, and Amelia of all people! She was intrigued.

50

Rory had looked forward to, yet dreaded Donovan's visit. She wanted to talk to him. She needed the comfort of him, yet doubted if he would do anything except make her feel a hundred times worse. Oh, he would try not to say, 'I told you so', but in the end he would. He would be furious that this had happened to her, that she was being made to suffer, that he could not help her. He was a naturally impatient and aggressive man. He could not cope with an over-sensitive, or emotionally charged situation. He was totally incapable of walking on eggs. Then there was the more general male-female situation. The one which dictated that a woman must always be attractive, especially physically, to warrant and to keep a man's love and attention. Donovan, who at the best of times had a roving and appreciative eye, would not, she feared, appreciate her present appearance. No make-up was allowed and no hair-cuts far less hair-dos. Hair had just to grow and somehow be plaited or twisted into a knot or simply left to hang. If you did not have any kirbygrips in your hair when you arrived (and she did not) then you spent your whole sentence without any. Her hair was not yet long enough to do anything with. Never before in her life, she was sure, had it looked such a mess. What with that and no make-up and the dreadfully unflattering prison clothes, she was too miserable and self-conscious to face Donovan. At the same time, she longed for him to take her in his arms.

The day of his visit came and she cringed at the thought of it. All she wanted was to hide away in her cell, to be enfolded in the safety of the prison routine and the silence. But somehow her legs had managed to take her to the reception area where the wardress stood on guard beside the wire mesh that separated prisoners and visitors. This was to prevent them from touching, or from passing anything to each other. Nothing was allowed to be brought in for any prisoner.

'Darling,' Donovan said. 'You look awful. Are you all right?'

'Sure,' she said, in her usual cocky tone. 'It would take more than bloody prison to get me down. Don't be fooled by the ghastly face and hair. That's nothing but lack of the old war paint and the young hairdresser.'

'Christ,' he groaned. 'I can't bear the thought of you in here.'

'I won't have to do the whole stretch. They knock one third off for good behaviour. That means eight months, not twelve.'

'Damn you, Rory. Why didn't you listen to me? I warned you over and over again.'

'Go on,' she said. 'Say it. I know you're dying to.'

His eyes narrowed with anger, 'All right. I told you so!'

'That must make you feel great.'

'You think so? You really believe I feel great?'

'Why are we quarrelling?' Rory said.

'Because you've been so bloody pig-headed and stupid. You worked hard all your life to get what you had and you've flung it all away. I don't care about the business or the money. I have enough to keep us both. But I know *you* care.'

'I'll soon build it up again after I get out.'

'Not in the same way, you won't. Not using the same methods. I'll see to that.'

'What am I supposed to do now? Thank you for your proposed interference? You're so perfect, of course.' Her mouth twisted with bitterness. 'You've hardly ever been with me to do anything.'

'The war wasn't my fault. I was called up.'

'You were hardly back home when you took this Russian assignment.'

'It's my job, Rory. I'm the most experienced man on that paper. The editor knew I was the only man who could do that assignment.'

'Oh, sure, sure.'

317

'Look, we've gone over all this before. I didn't come here to argue with you about my job.'

'No, you came to argue about my job.'

'Not that either,' His voice dropped. 'Darling, I'm crazy with worry about you. I love you. All I want is to take you in my arms.'

Somehow his tender talk was more of an ordeal than his anger. Her heart was breaking with it. She was relieved yet anguished when visiting time was over.

In a month's time when the next visit was due, her hair was an even worse mess, her skin was getting dry for the want of her usual face cream and her hands were red and rough with hard physical work. She persuaded herself that it was only fair to allow Helena to have a visit and that was what she requested on the form. It was also painful to see the horror and pity in Helena's eyes. But at least the visit was calmer and more relaxed. She did not need to be afraid that Helena was making value judgements about her person because of her appearance. Helena would understand what it was like to be without make-up and a good hair-do and nice clothes. She would sympathize and empathize as indeed any woman would. She would know what this kind of female vulnerability meant in a man's world. Helena was still young, though, and had a lot to learn. She had her own worries and problems, her own life to get on with.

Victoria was the one she could be most relaxed with and with whom she had the most in common. She worried about Victoria. God knows how the poor soul was managing. She missed her. Impulsively she said to Helena, 'Tell Victoria I'm going to put a form in for her to come and see me next time.'

Helena had looked nonplussed, then slightly hurt. But she had promised to tell Victoria and to keep visiting her to make sure that she was all right.

'I know she has her friend, Mrs McDade, and Amelia,' Rory said, 'but Mrs McDade has a husband to take up most of her time and Amelia just gets the occasional night off work.'

'All right, mother, but honestly, I can't help feeling it's a bit ridiculous you being in this awful place and worrying about someone like Victoria. I mean, she's not even one of your own family.'

'Please, Helena . . .' she had pleaded.

She realized that Donovan would not only be angry but hurt. But he was tough and he had his job and his drinking buddies and she dared not think what else. He would survive. Would Victoria? She was not altogether sure if she could survive herself if Donovan kept coming in. She was skating on the knife-edge of endurance, just suffering prison life – if life it could be called. Victoria would understand.

Her visit came and they talked and talked about old times and even laughed about one shared memory. The fifteen minutes flew all too quickly.

'Oh Victoria,' she managed, before having to tear herself away. 'Your visit has done me so much good. Will you come again?'

'Of course, dear. But. . . ,' Victoria hesitated worriedly, 'what about your husband?'

'Oh,' Rory said impatiently, dismissively, 'men!' She went back to her cell smiling ruefully to herself. She had sounded just like Victoria.

51

Helena had not paid much attention when Victoria had asked when Burgeyev was coming over to Scotland. She had only experienced mild surprise at the idea. The idea, however, had since taken root. She realized that it would not be easy, but why should not Burgeyev at least make an effort to come to Scotland to be married, and to live? In her next letter she began to persuade him and to tell him how wonderful it would be.

She told him he could work in freedom in Scotland. He replied that no one had ever interfered with his freedom to work in the Soviet Union. She wrote pointing out that there were many other things people had to suffer in the Soviet Union that did not have to be suffered in Britain. He replied (missing, she felt, the point of what she meant) that he heard that in Britain they still had meat rationing whereas meat was no longer rationed in Russia.

She went into more detail in her next letter, mentioning corruption among other things. She had forgotten, when writing, about her mother's black market dealings, and she loved Burgeyev all the more for not scoring a point by reminding her of them. Instead, he replied that, all right, there had been the odd official in Russia perhaps cornering the market in nylons. All right, there had been the occasional person shot for making huge profits on the side. He suggested that they did not bear comparison with the far more numerous exploits of the share pushers and entrepreneurs on the open markets of the West. There were, he contended, almost daily reports of businessmen laundering funds, and diverting them into their own pockets. 'You equate freedom,' he wrote, 'with indiscriminate opportunity.' They argued about freedom and about politics in many letters. Burgeyev was not a member of the Communist Party but he defended the communist state.

'Communism,' he told her, 'is a religion for intellectuals and it is obsessed with morality. But the basic difference between eastern and western constitutions,' he claimed, 'is that in the Soviet Union constitution, the fundamental right of the individual is related to a duty towards the state and not as a protection against it. In the US constitution, the state is, by implication, a necessary evil; in the Soviet constitution, it is a necessary good. Both are fine documents. Both are good examples of different ways of looking at the world.'

She insisted that all was not as perfect in the Soviet Union as he was trying to make out and he would be much better off and happier in the West. He replied, 'Even if I agreed – which I do not – what kind of man is it, I would have to ask myself, who, because there are some things he does not like about his mother, changes her for someone else?'

All along she sensed the undercurrent of caution and suspicion she found so typical of Russian people. Because they had a history of being invaded time and again by western powers, they seemed to nurse an obsession for safety against such powers who had, in the Russian view, shown enmity and double-dealing.

In desperation, she wrote of the horrors of the Russian winter, and he wrote back reminding her of the beauties of the many churches and cathedrals they had seen clothed in snow, or with their golden domes and spires gleaming against the bright winter sky. And the sparkle of the new dry snow in Moscow that cushioned the traffic noises and softened echoes. And the white mist, the crystalline veil of air-suspended ice shimmering in the near distance of the countryside. And ski excursions with Russian friends, all singing together. He wrote with love about his Mother Russia and Helena's heart became heavy. Her love of Scotland, she discovered, was equally deep and strong.

She confided her worries to Amelia when she came to visit, and Amelia listened with rapt interest but offered no opinions or solutions. She showed none of the usual prejudice either, only curiosity. She was thirsty for knowledge about the place, the people and Burgeyev in particular.

Helena warmed towards her. She had such a refreshing enthusiasm and ingenuousness. She could not help comparing Amelia to Douglas and the selfish, unfeeling attitude he had recently shown towards his mother. 'God knows what it must have been like to have been married to him,' she thought.

'What do you think I should do?' she asked Amelia eventually.

'Do you love Burgeyev?' Amelia asked.

She answered without hesitation. 'Oh yes. I've no doubts about that.'

'Well, then . . .?'

'It's not him, it's his country. But don't get me wrong,' she hastened to add. 'It's a wonderful, beautiful, fascinating place and the people, once you get to know them individually, are charming. You can't help taking them to your heart. There's quite a contrast between the impression one gets of the mass in Russia and one's impression of individuals. The difficulty is bridging that contrast in order to understand Russia. It's no easy task to cross.'

'You sound as if you've crossed it, though.'

'I seem to have developed something of an empathy with the Russian people. I feel like them, for instance, that there're so many awful things going on in other countries. . . . Dad's been around the world more than most and he's told me. There're black people suffering in South Africa. There're children struggling to survive alone in the streets of Bogota and Rio. There're people being tortured and disappearing off the face of the earth all over the place, but how often do we hear about them? In papers, books, films, et cetera, it's always Russia and Russians who are the evil ones. Why should that be? It doesn't seem fair.'

'I don't understand your problem,' Amelia said. 'You say you love Burgeyev and you sound as if you love his country . . .'

Helena sighed, 'I'd probably love Bermuda or California or the Seychelles. I'd find those places fascinating but that wouldn't necessarily mean I'd be able cheerfully to tear up my roots and leave dear old Scotland without a qualm.'

'It's just a fear of homesickness, then?'

'Not only that. It's so different, you see. The whole set-up. There're lots of people there who still remember what it was like before the revolution and they have that comparison, that yard-stick to measure against what they've got now. And what they've got now is better by a long chalk. But it's not nearly as good, in my opinion, as what *we've* got.'

'Well, I don't know how to advise you,' Amelia admitted. 'In the end, it's up to you. You'll have to make up your own mind.'

'True,' Helena sighed, then smiled. 'Come, I'll show you my paintings.' She had a make-shift studio in one of the upstairs rooms and her paintings were stacked face inwards against one of the walls. One by one, she turned them around and showed how she had captured not only the different moods but something of the vastness and the sense of infinite variety of the Soviet Union.

Amelia was enraptured, 'Oh Helena, I admit I'm no expert on art, but surely these must be not just good, but brilliant!'

Helena laughed, 'Well, I hope you're right. I'm thinking of having an exhibition soon. Here is the last one, but, in my opinion, certainly not the least in importance. Amelia, meet my Ivan Mikhailovitch Burgeyev!'

Amelia stared at the painting in hypnotic silence. Helena gazed at it in silence, too. The other paintings she was not sure about, but this, she knew, was good. It was the best thing she had ever done. It was life-size and the dark, mysterious background was reflected in Burgeyev's eyes. There he stood, proud and erect in his military-type coat, high collar framing his calm, handsome face.

'Oh Helena,' Amelia, said eventually. 'How wonderful!'

'You like it?'

'Like it? It will haunt me forever.'

Helena laughed again. Amelia was such an extreme kind of person. Yet, now that she came to think of it, there was a haunting quality about the picture. 'I do love him,' she said.

'I can understand that,' Amelia said. 'I could love him too.'

Helena glanced round at her but refrained from making

any comment. It was only once they had returned down-stairs that she asked, 'Have you met anyone else, Amelia?'

'Not really.'

'What does that mean? You don't sound very sure.'

'There is someone I quite admire. He's a writer too. But there's nothing between us.'

'Yet?'

'No, I don't believe there ever will be.' She flushed and averted her eyes, 'You see, I prefer men in my books.'

'You must be joking!' Helena grinned.

The eyes widened with earnestness round at her, 'Oh no, I'm perfectly serious. I enjoy writing so much.'

'But just because you're mad keen on writing books, doesn't mean you can't have boy-friends. That's crazy!'

Amelia shrugged and glanced at the clock, 'It's time I got back to Balornock. I don't like leaving Harry with mummy.'

'Why not?'

'It's been a lovely afternoon,' Amelia said, ignoring the question. 'Thank you so much for inviting me, Helena. I wish you luck with your exhibition. You're not going to sell that painting of your fiancé, I hope, though.'

'No, I'll never part with that. You must come and visit me again, Amelia.'

'Your mother will be out soon. I don't think she would like it if I came.'

'We'll see. After all she has made it up with your mother. All is forgiven and forgotten, I think.'

After Amelia had gone, however, Helena began to wonder if her father would ever forgive Rory for not requesting that he should have any more prison visits. Victoria had been the one asked for each time. It was really a dreadfully hurtful thing for her mother to do. Neither Donovan nor Helena could understand it. She believed her mother's behaviour in this respect had affected Donovan more than he would admit. He had acquired a hard, haggard look that frightened her. He was drinking pretty heavily too. To have denied him one visit so that she could have her friend in could have been understandable. To have her friend in every month for the precious fifteen minutes was unforgivable.

Helena wondered if this was her mother's revenge against her father for taking the Russian assignment and leaving her alone for so long. Even so, it would still be an incredibly wounding thing to do. It pained her to see how miserable her father looked but she did not dare show any pity or sympathy. He was a man who would have no truck with weakness of any kind, particularly in himself.

Then, when the day drew near for her mother's release, word came via Victoria that Rory did not want anyone to come to the prison for her. She would see Donovan at home that afternoon. Helena decided it would be diplomatic to leave them alone and so she arranged with Amelia to meet her in town and spend the afternoon with her. She also told Winnie to take the afternoon and evening off. She had no idea what kind of reunion her mother and father would have, but feared, after her mother's cruel injustice to her father, it would be an explosive one.

52

Freedom! And on such a glorious spring day! Rory took a deep luxurious breath, then, wrapping her mink coat around her, hugging herself, she walked away from Duke Street Prison. The first place she made for was the best hairdresser and beauty parlour in town. There she enjoyed the whole works, from a hair cut and set and a facial to a manicure and pedicure. At the end of her session she wriggled her brightly painted fingernails and toenails and admired her well-groomed hair and made-up face in the mirror at the salon.

'That's better,' she sighed with satisfaction. 'I feel human again.' She also felt more able to tackle the world. A brave face was not enough. It needed to be the best-looking face she could muster. The first person she would have to tackle, of course, would be Donovan. After nearly a year in a silent, submissive and uncomplicated world of women, she viewed the prospect of Donovan with mixed feelings. In a way she was looking forward to seeing him but had no desire to renew the minefield of differences between them. They still niggled her, though. Why should he be allowed to indulge in his wanderlust? Why should he think he had a right to bum about the world most of the time? Would he allow her to do the same? Not on your life! There was so much unfairness between men and women – she had had plenty of time these past few months to think of it all and to allow resentment to build up. Why should she spend her life pandering to any man's ego? Why should she have her life hedged in and inhibited? Donovan was a hard-drinking, hard-hitting, selfish, unsettled, unsettling bastard. Women were far better companions, so much easier to get on with, so different.

She took a taxi home and, when she arrived in the lounge, Donovan rose to greet her. As soon as she saw him, she thought, 'Aw shit!' and went straight into his arms. She had forgotten how strong they felt, like a band of iron around her.

'What the hell did you think you were playing at?' he growled against her ear, 'keeping me away like that.'

'I looked awful,' she said. 'You told me so yourself.'

'So what?'

'I wanted to get my hair done and some make-up on first.'

'You're crazy!' he said. 'An absolute nutter.'

'Is that all you're going to do,' she asked, 'call me names?'

He grinned down at her. Then suddenly he swung her up into his arms. She squealed with laughter as he took the stairs two at a time on the way to their bedroom. There, they undressed each other and made love quickly, urgently at first. Then, slowly and with long-drawn out enjoyment of each other.

'Vive la difference,' she kept thinking. 'Vive la difference!'

At last Donovan rolled from her with a sigh of satisfaction. Then, after a minute, he propped himself on one elbow and grinned down at her. 'You can't fool me,' he said. 'I knew all the time that's what you were missing!'

'Not any more than a good fag,' she said, jamming one in her holder and lighting up. 'Or a good belt of whisky.'

But best of all was the sound of Donovan's laughter.

Before going to meet Amelia, Helena went to the Kelvingrove Art Gallery and sat staring at the paintings. It was a quiet and dignified place and there were some wonderful works of art in the various rooms. A few people wandered in and out peering at each painting in turn. Helena thought about her own work. It was strange how the creative urge had grown and matured in her since her stay in the Soviet Union. Was it Burgeyev who had inspired her? Or his country? Did painters have the same kind of curiosity as writers, the same obsession with what went on behind the mask, with what motivated different kinds of people? Did the artist, like the writer, have the need to understand as well as to communicate?

She was far from understanding either Burgeyev or his country. But having lived among his people, even for a comparatively short time, she had gathered a few clues, some small keys to understanding. The important thing was, as she and Amelia had agreed at their last meeting, to *want* to understand. There were two ways of looking at everyone and everything. If you wanted to see bad, you would see bad. It was all too easy to put a bad interpretation on anything and everything. It was much more difficult to try to cross the bridge of understanding, to try to see things from the stranger's point of view, to learn to love and trust so that you could merit love and trust in return. It was Einstein, however, a scientist, not a writer or artist, who had said, 'Peace cannot be kept by force. It can only be achieved by understanding.'

She loved Ivan Mikhailovitch Burgeyev and wanted to live in peace with him. Their countries were worlds apart. Not even a terrible war in which they fought on the same side had brought them closer together. Burgeyev had said his people would never forget that conflagration and never wanted to suffer such a tragedy again. The constant stream of citizens, many crippled by the results of the war, who made regular pilgrimages to the harrowing mass graves scattered all over Russia testified to this. Children guarded eternal flames, and brides, on the way to their honeymoon, reverently laid their wedding bouquets on the graves or at the foot of the tombs of unknown soldiers. Beside them old women wept at the memory of whole families and whole towns that had been wiped out. Of one thing Helena was totally convinced, the people of the Soviet Union wanted peace. There was no talk or theory there of the possibilities of a 'limited nuclear war', or of surviving one, or winning one. Indeed, there was a law banning such 'war propaganda' and a severe punishment for breaking it.

'Only people who have not had their country overrun and their people massacred can talk in such terms,' Burgeyev said. 'Only people who have been largely spared the sickening realities of war can glamorize it. The people of the Soviet Union fear and abhor any idea of another war.'

328

This she could understand, but this she knew was the thing most people could not. She felt a huge wave of sadness sweep over her and with it a great pity for the people of Russia.

As she sat alone in the Kelvingrove Art Gallery, the sadness encompassed Ivan Mikhailovitch Burgeyev. And suddenly she knew, beyond all doubt, that she had to return to Russia, that she had to be by his side, come what may, sharing the bad as well as the good, facing whatever the future might bring, and facing it together. For he was her life, her art, her inspiration and everything was meaningless without him.

Amelia had managed to get Harry in to a nursery every afternoon. He did not want to go and screamed and struggled and fought with her all the way to the nursery premises. She tried to convince herself that it was the best place for him. It could not be good for a boy always to be with his mother. At the nursery there were other boys for him to play with, lots of educational toys and trained staff to look after him. She was forcing him to go for his own good. She knew in her heart, however, she was making him go because it would give her more time and peace to write. She could easily organize all the work to be done in the house in the forenoons. Writing had become her life, her total obsession.

This afternoon, though, instead of working on her fifth novel, she had promised to meet Helena. Quickly she washed her face and combed her hair. If she did not stay too long in town with Helena, she could still have time to write a paragraph or two when she returned before having to collect Harry.

She hovered in the hall, hoping to catch the second post of the day before she left. Her days were regulated by the postman. She listened eagerly for his footsteps and always ran hopefully to see if there was anything for her. She hated holidays when the post office was closed and there was no postal delivery. She was just about to give up and go because she did not want to keep Helena waiting, when she heard the familiar tread on the drive and then saw the blurred form of the postman through the glass door. Two or three letters came winging through the letter-box and landed at her feet. She picked them up. One of them was typewritten, had a London postmark, *and was for her*. She stared at it for a long minute. Then she squeezed up her shoulders and stiffened. She braced herself for she knew not what. She tore the envelope open and read the letter inside.

It was from a publisher. He wanted to buy her fourth book. He said it was passionate and steamy and a tear-jerker of the first order. He had found it totally riveting. Could she come down to London to discuss a contract?

She read and re-read the letter several times, then folded it and put it carefully into her purse. She looked furtively around to see if Mrs Robertson was watching and, finding herself completely alone, she did a mad dance around the hall, hands wildly waving in the air. She had done it! She had done it! She would be able to get her flat at last. Surely for a book described as 'totally riveting' she would be paid a big enough sum? If she was not, surely she would be paid enough for the next one?

Freedom! Joy of joys! She would be able to write when she liked, she would be able to do whatever she wanted, she would be able to entertain friends like Helena in the flat. She would have lots of friends one day, and they would talk about life, and writing, and art, and people, and all sorts of fascinating things. Perhaps one day Andrew Summers might be included in this coterie.

Her legs trembled so much they could hardly carry her out of the door and down to the main road for the bus into town. She willed the bus to take wings and fly her straight to her meeting with Helena at Copland & Lye's corner in Sauchiehall Street. Helena was her first girl-friend and she wanted her to be the first to know.

Helena watched in astonishment as Amelia's thin figure came racing along the pavement towards her, cheeks on fire, fair hair streaming out behind her, arms outstretched. Reaching her, Amelia warmly embraced her, and hugged and kissed her until Helena laughed in protest. But before she could ask what the excitement was all about, Amelia enthusiastically linked arms with her and cried out like a hallelujah, 'Oh Helena, what a marvellous, marvellous day. Aren't we lucky to be alive today in this wonderful, wonderful world!'